I'M GOD
YOU'RE NOT

JEWISH LIGHTS BOOKS
BY LAWRENCE KUSHNER

The Book of Letters: A Mystical Hebrew Alphabet

The Book of Words: Talking Spiritual Life, Living Spiritual Talk

Eyes Remade for Wonder: A Lawrence Kushner Reader

Filling Words with Light:
Hasidic & Mystical Reflections on Jewish Prayer
with Nehemia Polen

God Was in This Place & I, i Did Not Know:
Finding Self, Spirituality and Ultimate Meaning

Honey from the Rock: An Introduction to Jewish Mysticism

I'm God; You're Not: Observations on Organized
Religion & Other Disquises of the Ego

Invisible Lines of Connection: Sacred Stories of the Ordinary

Jewish Spirituality: A Brief Introduction for Christians

The River of Light: Jewish Mystical Awareness

The Way Into Jewish Mystical Tradition

FOR CHILDREN

Because Nothing Looks Like God
with Karen Kushner

The Book of Miracles: A Young Person's Guide
to Jewish Spiritual Awareness

How Does God Make Things Happen?
with Karen Kushner
(SkyLight Paths Publishing)

In God's Hands
with Gary Schmidt

What Does God Look Like?
with Karen Kushner
(SkyLight Paths Publishing)

Where Is God?
with Karen Kushner
(SkyLight Paths Publishing)

FICTION

Kabbalah: A Love Story
(Morgan Road Books)

I'M GOD YOU'RE NOT

OBSERVATIONS ON ORGANIZED RELIGION & OTHER DISGUISES OF THE EGO

LAWRENCE KUSHNER

JEWISH LIGHTS Publishing
Woodstock, Vermont

I'm God; You're Not:
Observations on Organized Religion & Other Disguises of the Ego

2010 Hardcover Edition, First Printing
© 2010 by Lawrence Kushner

Library of Congress Cataloging-in-Publication Data
Kushner, Lawrence, 1943–
I'm God, you're not : observations on organized religion & other disguises of the ego / Lawrence Kushner.
p. cm.
Includes bibliographical references.
ISBN 978-1-58023-441-2 (hardcover)
1. Jewish way of life. 2. Spiritual life—Judaism. 3. Cabala. 4. Kushner, Lawrence, 1943—Anecdotes. I. Title.
BM723.K873 2010
296.7—dc22

2010028898

10 9 8 7 6 5 4 3 2 1

Manufactured in the United States of America
Jacket design: Lawrence Kushner
Jacket photo: Lawrence Kushner

Published by Jewish Lights Publishing
A Division of LongHill Partners, Inc.
Sunset Farm Offices, Route 4, P.O. Box 237
Woodstock, VT 05091
Tel: (802) 457-4000   Fax: (802) 457-4004
www.jewishlights.com

For Tricia Gibbs

one of the finest students
I have ever been honored to teach

Contents

4. WORLD

5. MYSTICISM

6. HOLINESS

INTRODUCTION

THE FIRST TIME I SERVED AS A RABBI was in a small town in West Virginia. It was not what I had expected. I'm pretty sure it was 1965 but I am certain it was Yom Kippur, because Jan Peerce, the great operatic tenor, sang *Kol Nidre.*

I found out I was going to be the rabbi there only a few days earlier.

A standard part of rabbinic education involves serving a student pulpit. This is a congregation too small to afford a full-time, ordained rabbi and is served, instead, by a student. Upper-class students, that is, fourth- and fifth-year graduate students, naturally, get their pick of the litter, which, in effect, means larger and biweekly pulpits. Below them are monthlies. And at the bottom, are congregations so small they can only afford inexperienced underclass students and only for Rosh Hashanah and Yom Kippur—the High Holy Days. Since, at the time, I was in my second year of rabbinic school (age twenty-two), I didn't even rate a High Holy Day pulpit. That year there were only a few but I had missed the cutoff in the student-pulpit lottery.

Then, just two days before Yom Kippur, the student who had been assigned to conduct High Holy Day services in Logan, West Virginia, was taken ill and confined to bed. Since I was next on the list, within only a few hours, I found myself standing in the hallway outside a sick classmate's bedroom taking notes:

You take the Norfolk & Western to Huntington. Then you rent a car and drive through the mountains to Logan. There will be a room reserved for you at the hotel. When you get in, phone a mister so-and-so and tell him you're the replacement rabbi. He'll tell you where the synagogue is. Services begin at 7.

He gave me his prayer book, marked with all the cues for the organist and the choir, and explained that, when it came time for the chanting of the *Kol Nidre* prayer, I should reach under the lectern where, hopefully, there would be a phonograph ready to play a recording of Jan Peerce (nee: Jacob Pincus Perelmuth) singing *Kol Nidre*.

"Have you decided what you're preaching on yet?" my classmate asked.

Preaching? It hadn't yet even dawned on me that I was supposed to give a sermon!

Nervous would be an understatement. I was terrified.

Within two days, on the holiest day of the year, I found myself standing up on the bima leading a congregation in prayer. Everything went pretty much according to plan until we got to the *Shema*, the declaration of God's unity. (I am not making this up.)

Before I could invite the congregation to rise—as per the dramaturgical instructions written in my prayer book—I felt a slight rumbling in the floor of the building and heard a distant roaring sound. Then the chandeliers began slowly swinging back and forth. At first, I thought it might be an earthquake. But the rumbling and the roar steadily increased. Soon, the whole building shook. The noise was deafening. Maybe I was having a mystical experience. I can only imagine what the expression on my face must have looked like.

But—and this is the crazy part—*no one else* in the congregation seemed to take any notice at all. Some began casually whispering to one another. Others simply closed their eyes and seemed to be meditating. Excuse me but does anyone else hear this loud roar? Pardon me, but are we concerned that the building is violently shaking? Perhaps I had slipped into an Isaac Bashevis Singer short story and a village whose inhabitants had become inured to the earth shaking and the heavens roaring whenever they pronounced the declaration of God's unity.

My consternation lasted only a few moments. Thankfully, a member of the congregation, recognizing my obvious dismay, came up onto the stage with a whispered explanation: A few feet behind the back wall of the synagogue—he inconspicuously gestured, right behind the five-member choir—was the main line of the Chesapeake & Ohio Railroad's coal division, and as it happened, every now and then, a two-hundred-car-long coal train passed by.

Fifteen minutes later, when the rumbling and the roar faded off into the distance, we continued our worship: "Hear, O Israel, the Lord our God, the Lord is One."

That winter, in my Hebrew Bible class, we read 1 Kings 19:12: *"And after the roar there was the thin, barely audible sound of almost breathing."*

As I review the following essays, stories, and teachings, I am surprised by how many of them share a common theme: The goal of all spiritual life is to get your ego out of the way—outwit the sucker; dissolve it; shoot it; kill it. Silence the incessant planning, organizing, running, manipulating, possessing, and processing that are the ineluctable redoubts of the ego. Not because these activities are bad or wrong or even narcissistic—indeed they are indispensable to living and often potentially, themselves, very spiritual—but because they preclude awareness of the Divine. To paraphrase the Talmud (*Arakhin* 15b), God says, "There ain't room enough in this here world for your ego and Me. You pick."

I now suspect that the real reason for religion is to help you keep your ego under control. And the principal strategy for accomplishing this is to acknowledge the reality of an even more important Ego, the Source of your ego, the Source of everyone's ego, a Source into whom you might safely deposit and, then, dissolve your ego—with the natural but, of course, un-guarantee-able hope that it might be returned to you. What shall we call it? God? *Schmod*? Whatever. In other words, it's not about you; it's about God. This same theme initiates God's theophany at Sinai.

The first two of the ten utterances at Mount Sinai are already in a class by themselves. According to *gematria*, the ancient system of assigning numerical equivalents to each letter of the Hebrew alphabet, the Hebrew word *Torah*—the Five Books of Moses— spelled, *tav vav, resh, hey*, totals 611. This is tantalizingly close to 613—the total of positive and negative commandments in the entire Torah. The discrepancy is resolved in the Talmud (*Makkot* 23a–24b). There it is claimed that Moses gave us a Torah (611). Or, to put it another way: Moses, a human being, gave us 611/613ths of the revelation. But God, God's self, gave us the first two directly: (1) "I am the Lord, your God … "; and (2) "You shall have no other gods before Me...." And these two bring the total up to 613. They initiate and perhaps even contain the revelation yet to come.

On closer examination, these two utterances turn out to be the flip sides of one another. You take one, you get the other. "I'm God." "Have no other gods." If God is God, then there can be no others. If there can be no other gods, then God is God. They are, effectively, two sides of one sheet of paper, inextricably joined. It's as if God gets us all together at the foot of the mountain and says, "I've just got two things to tell you: 'I'm God; you're not.'" Indeed, it seems to me, we might distill the entire Torah down that life- changing but fleeting realization. The Torah is the story of what happens to people when they forget about that and when they remember it again. *I'm God; you're not.*

Obviously, assembling essays, stories, reviews, and speeches writ- ten over a span of almost three decades poses unique literary chal- lenges. Whenever possible, I have left the original texts as they were—deleting only obvious redundancies and changing the most annoying inconsistencies. I have not rewritten anything more than an occasional sentence.

I am grateful to Emily Wichland and the rest of the staff at Jewish Lights Publishing for their attention to detail and frequent willingness to cut me creative slack and, especially, to Stuart Matlins, the publisher, for his continued friendship and support. This book was his idea: "You have too many important pieces of writing, often in obscure places, that have never been assembled into a single volume," he said. "Why don't you rummage through your hard drive and see just what you've got."

I want to thank Bill Novak and Jonathan Cott, who have graciously allowed me to reproduce their interviews with me. I am grateful to be able to call them friends. I want also to acknowledge my gratitude to the clergy, officers, staff, and members of the Congregation Emanu-El of San Francisco—above all, to Stephen Pearce, the senior rabbi—for their continued support and permission to serve as a resident scholar, teacher, and author in their community.

Finally, and of course, I want to thank my wife, Karen, for helping me think through this whole project and then for rereading it so lovingly and carefully. When you look up "helpmeet" in the dictionary, there should be a picture of her.

San Francisco

1

RABBI

WHO AM I?

SEVERAL AUTUMNS AGO, I WAS ABOUT TO BEGIN TEACHING a new class on an old topic and shared my anxiety with a friend. "I've been teaching for fifty years," I lamented, "and I still get nervous before the first session."

"My mother taught first grade her whole life," she replied. "And she was always a basket case at the start of each new semester. When I asked her why, my mother explained that, for her, the anxiety reminded her that she respected her students. 'The day I'm sure this will be a piece of cake is the day I quit.'"

Alas, some professions just seem immune to any amount of prior experience or self-confidence. No matter how well prepared or how good (you think) you are, you always feel inadequate, unworthy—perhaps none of them more than the tightrope act of impersonating a rabbi.

No matter how old you are, it always seems you're never quite old enough to be a rabbi. No matter how much you know, you're never wise enough. No matter how devout, you're never pious enough. Tough job, the rabbi thing.

Rabbi Levi Yitzhak ben Meir of Berditchev (d. 1810), in his *Kedushat Levi*, like many teachers among the early generations of Hasidism, is particularly interested in crafting the job description of a would-be rebbe or *tsaddik* or spiritual master. And this, not surprisingly, leads him to what may be the ultimate ordination scene in the Hebrew Bible, the one at the burning bush where God commissions Moses to lead the Jewish people out of Egyptian slavery. Now that's my idea of an ordination. (God ordained me; who ordained you?)

After a very close reading of the biblical text, however, the Berditchever notices an apparent lacuna in the story. In brief, God says to Moses: I want you to free the Jews from slavery. To which, Moses, not unreasonably, replies: "Who am I to go to Pharaoh?" Then God answers: Don't worry, "I will be with you.... And this shall be for you the sign that I have sent you ... " (Exodus 3:10–12)

It's a powerful scene. There's only one problem: God never tells Moses what the sign is—leaving Moses and us wondering how someone is supposed to know he or she is a fit leader. And that is where we pick up Levi Yitzhak's explanation. It has four parts.

A *tsaddik*, says the Berditchever, must constantly be aware of the spiritual level he has attained even as he must also be aware that there is a still higher level that he has not yet attained. Indeed, no sooner does a *tsaddik* attain one level than he becomes aware of the next. There is always another, higher level yet to attain. And there is no end to it, either. No matter how high one ascends, completion will always elude him. He is perpetually and painfully aware of his deficiencies and inadequacies. He must endure a continuous state of incompleteness.

Levi Yitzhak cites a tradition that even Elijah himself confessed, "I know nothing of You at all!" (*Tikkunei Zohar, Hakdama*, 17a).

But just this, the Berditchever teaches, is the highest form of serving God: One is constantly aware that she is still incomplete. And thus she craves and yearns to ascend to yet a higher level than where she now stands ...

I am reminded of a comment made by Rabbi Jerome Malino, his memory is a blessing. Malino was one of the great ones of the generation. Rabbi of Danbury, Connecticut; faculty of the Hebrew Union College–Jewish Institute of Religion; president of the Central Conference of American Rabbis. A man of extraordinary depth and literacy. Well into his eighties, he was asked at a communal luncheon meeting marking his retirement from teaching rabbinic students, what he intended to do now. He rose to his feet and without hesitation, in all seriousness, replied, "I intend to continue my *preparation* for the rabbinate."

[4]

Levi Yitzhak now invites us to examine the grammar of God's Name as revealed to Moses only a few verses later in our story. Moses says to God, "When the Jews ask me who sent you, what name shall I give them?" God replies, *"Ehyeh asher ehyeh"* (Exodus 3:13–14).

But that Name does not, as it is frequently mistranslated, mean "I am that I am." That is static and present tense. And *ehyeh* is clearly future (or imperfect—that is, the verbal idea is not yet "perfected" or complete). *Ehyeh* means, in effect, "I will be" and alludes to an unfinished future and what might only be attained then. Indeed, a cumbersome but accurate translation of *Ehyeh asher ehyeh* would be "I am not yet who I am not yet." Which means, therefore, that if God is not done yet, then neither are we.

Such is the way of a *tsaddik*, says the Berditchever, someone who is continuously aware of her deficiencies yet trusts that God will help her attain a higher level in the future. Indeed, if the Name of your God is "I am not yet who I am not yet," then you too get to keep on learning and striving and growing.

My own beloved teacher Arnold Jacob Wolf, whose memory is a blessing, used to mischievously complain that his problem was not that God was silent. "My problem," he would insist, "is that God won't shut up. Now what do You want? Leave me alone. I did that *mitzvah* last week. What do You mean, You want it again and better?"

For his third observation, Levi Yitzhak turns to a frequently cited teaching in the name of the Baal Shem Tov. The Besht used to pun on an odd word in Psalm 48:15, *almut*, usually rendered as either "until death" / *al mavet*, or "worlds" or "evermore" / *olamot*. Thus: "He will be our guide until death" or "He guides worlds." The Besht, however, deliberately misreads the phrase as "He guides *almut*/children."

It is like a parent, Levi Yitzhak explains, who wants to teach his child how to walk. No sooner does the little one take a few steps toward his mother or father than the parent intuitively steps back, thereby urging the child to take yet another step. And, once the child takes a few more steps, the parent moves still farther away. And why? All in order that the child might walk even more.

[5]

Our self-dissatisfaction, our stumbling, our failures, our fear that we are inadequate to or unworthy of the holy task, in other words, are nothing more than God's loving ever being one more step just beyond reach. And it never ends.

Rabbi Adin Steinsaltz, arguably the smartest Jew of this generation, echoes this same theme. He reminds us, "Jewish thought pays little attention to inner tranquility and peace of mind…. The very concept of the Divine as infinite implies an activity that is endless, of which one must never grow weary." Indeed, Steinsaltz continues, "The Jewish approach to life considers the man who has stopped going [on]—he who has a feeling of completion, of peace, of a great light from above that has brought him to rest—to be someone who has lost his way" (*The Thirteen Petalled Rose* [New York: Basic Books, 1980], 131–2).

Levi Yitzhak now returns to the textual lacuna where Moses asks his original question, "*Mi anochi*? Who am I to go to Pharaoh?" and God cryptically replies, "This shall be for you the sign," without apparently specifying the sign.

God *does* give Moses a sign, says the Berditchever. And it has been right there in plain sight all along; we just didn't notice it. From his native humility, Moses cannot imagine he is worthy of such a holy task. This is why he says, "Who am I that I should go to Pharaoh and lead the children of Israel out of Egypt?"

But precisely this fear of inadequacy is the source of his true spiritual authority. It is not an expression of unworthiness; it is a necessary qualification and precondition for the job of any would-be Jewish leader. Your fear that you are unworthy makes you worthy.

God, in effect, says to Moses, "[Schmuck!] your asking, 'Who am I?' *is the sign* that I've sent you!"

I conclude with a true story of my first official task as the rabbi of my own congregation. It was over forty years ago and took me to a hospital.

We had just moved into a two-bedroom apartment in Marlborough, Massachusetts. It must have been late July. I dutifully called the president to inform him of our arrival. He welcomed me and, in the course of our conversation, said that he had heard through the grapevine that a member of the congregation was in Mass General Hospital. She was a young mother whom he heard was terminally ill. So I put on my rabbi suit (my only suit), drove into Boston, found MGH, and walked into the room. One of Boston's great physicians was just concluding a counseling session with her. He motioned kindly for me to take a chair and listen in.

The woman said, "But how can I be a mother? I can't even get out of bed anymore."

But, to my astonishment, he only scolded her. "Is that what you have to do to be a mother?" he asked. "Is a mother just cooking and chauffeuring and playing?"

"No, I guess not," she whispered. "A mother is supposed to love and to teach."

"So, *nu*?" he replied. "Be a mother. Maybe you want to teach them about faith and about courage. Maybe you have an opportunity to love and to teach few mothers will ever understand."

She wept. He wept. I wept.

"Oh, thank you, doctor," she said.

He kissed her, nodded to me, and left.

I sat motionless, astonished, dumbfounded in the corner.

Startled, she turned to me and said, "Who the hell are you?"

WE'LL WAIT BACK HERE

I'M PAINTING THE BOTTOM OF MY SAILBOAT, down at Barden's Boat Yard near Cape Cod. End of May, everyone's very busy. There are owners like me who refuse to the pay forty-five dollars an hour for work only a dummy would do so they do it themselves. And, then there are the kids the yard hires for fifteen dollars an hour so they can charge other owners forty-five dollars an hour. People stop by and compare technique and tell jokes they haven't told since the seventh grade. One guy, the carpenter, is called "Space"—that's short for "Space Shot." Then there's "Two Stroke"; he's the guy who services the outboard engines. Other names are, shall I say, more colorful.

So here I am, busy at work, when the young man painting the boat next to me says, "You mind if I ask you a question?"

"Sure," I say. "Go for it."

There's a long pause, and then he says with genuine sincerity, "Are you really a rabbi or is that just some kind of nickname?"

"It's just a nickname."

But it did get me to wondering about what really does make some-one a rabbi anyway.

So, I reviewed all my archived, computerized calendars and, before them, my Palm Pilot calendars and, before them, all those little vest-pocket calendar diaries the Jewish cemeteries used to distribute—you know, the ones that give you the Jewish popula-tion statistics for every major American city. (Twice a week I'd be asked, "By the way, Rabbi, how many Jews live in Akron?" And I'd be the only one at the meeting with the vital information.) I reviewed them all trying to distill the essential *rabbi* part.

What can you remove? Board meetings and committee meetings, right off the top! Fund-raising and most counseling goes, too. Then there are the banquets and the bulletin articles. You can even jettison a lot of the classes. And everyone's glad if you quit giving sermons. Take it from me, at one time or another, I've screwed up all of the above. So what's left? Just the weddings and the funerals, stuff like that. They are close to the heart. But there's something more than merely officiating. Any Jew can officiate.

Like every other rabbi in America, over the years I get asked a bunch of sincere but also predictable questions. If you're under seventy, one is, "Aren't you awfully young to be a rabbi?" Reminds me of how, when I first grew a beard in rabbinic school, my classmate, now Rabbi Les Gutterman of Providence, said, "Kushner, you look just like Abraham Heschel—when he was three!"

Another standard question is, "What ever made you decide to become a rabbi anyway?" which always comes off sounding like, "When did you have your *first* psychotic episode?"

But the most common question is not dumb or funny. It strikes me as profoundly theological. People genuinely want to know, "How can you go from doing a funeral to a wedding in the same day?"

It's easy. You just get in the car and drive there. End of life, beginning of life, space-time warp, piece of cake—as long as you can manage to keep your eyes and ears and heart shut during either the funeral or the wedding. (Actually, going *from* a funeral *to* a wedding has only happened to me twice, but even that was way too much. At least it was going from a funeral to a wedding.)

On the other hand, if you include going from a surgical waiting room to the preschool, or from divorce counseling to consecrating a new home, or any of the other myriad radical disjuncts that are the core experiences of being human, then we're looking at a brick smashed on your forehead sometimes *every* week. You can't prepare yourself for things like that. Putting two events—ones where the players are completely exposed in all their grief, joy, or reverence—side by side, right next to one another, seems to defy the natural order.

It's probably apocryphal and also a little embarrassing, so let me make it anonymous: One of my colleagues tells of how he had to get from the city out to his congregation for a wedding. He left himself plenty of time but not enough for a major accident that turned the Long Island Expressway into a parking lot. This was also before cell phones and there was nothing left to do but sit and sweat and pray. Salvation, he recounts, appeared in the form of a funeral procession moving along the breakdown lane. He decided to pull rabbinic privilege and cut into the long line of cars. Proud of his ingenuity and good fortune, he glided through the traffic, exiting the highway in just enough time for the wedding. Unfortunately, as he pulled into the temple parking lot, he saw in his rearview mirror that the last half of the funeral cortège had also followed him to the wedding!

Rabbis sometimes get them both at the same time.

I once recorded an imaginary conversation between Jacob and his grandfather Abraham. The boy is asking about what it was like to have a vision of God, to be that close:

"Did you ever see the *merkava* / the chariot? I mean, what was it like?"

"Once," replied the old man, "I think I did. I mean once it was clear to me that I was, how do they say it, face-to-face. I took your father, Isaac, up on Mount Moriah. What I saw there was not awesome or thrilling, just frightening."

"Did you see a likeness of God, the way Ezekiel did?"

"No, I saw no image that I remember. I saw something that still seems terrifying."

"What did you see?"

"I saw how our people would endure slavery for four hundred years and how, after all that degradation, God would set us free."

"That sounds pretty good," said the boy.

"I know what you're saying. But I saw it *all at once.*

To see someone a slave, that's painful. To see someone set free, that's a great joy. To see it all at once, that is terrible. The slavery and the freedom are always present *within* one another. The joy contains the sadness; the sadness, the joy. You try to untangle them and set each on its own stage so you can have *one at a time,* but when I saw the chariot, I saw them all at the same time, a stack of transparencies, superimposed, one on top of another. I was unable to cry, because I knew I would also laugh. I could not feel joy, for I knew the price that would be paid."

A member of my former congregation, Dr. Alan Feldman, writing under the name of Nate, wrote a commentary on this. It was published in Sid Schwarz's *Finding a Spiritual Home: How a New Generation of Jews Can Transform the American Synagogue* ([Woodstock, VT: Jewish Lights, 2003], 23). He wrote:

When we see all that God has in store for us, we move beyond tragedy or comedy into pure mirthless, tearless vision. Larry wonders—and Nate wonders—why that didn't just explain everything to everyone, why in fact Nate or Larry or anyone should ever have to write another word. It's probably that those who see this vision don't need to be told and those who can't see it can't be told.

Now, on reflection, I think it's about being a rabbi too.

This seeing past and future, the near and the far, and therefore the joy in the sadness and the sadness in the joy simultaneously is not just some kind of spaced-out, spiritual fantasy. Einstein, who was certainly no cream-puff thinker, demonstrated that space and time are manifestations of the same underlying reality. If space were warped, folded over on itself, then it would be possible to place two distant events side by side—funerals and weddings. That's when time collapses; that's when rabbis do their most important work.

The great American philosopher George Carlin once said, "Time is just God's way of making sure everything doesn't happen all at once." Well, it occurs to me now that sometimes it doesn't work. Sometimes everything just seems to happen all at once. Some people even get paid to remember it.

Reminds me of that incredible scene at the end of the Sally Field, John Malkovich, Danny Glover movie *Places in the Heart*, where virtually the entire cast is singing a hymn in this little Southern church. The camera slowly pans around, letting us have one final look at each of the characters. But then, without any warning, as the camera continues its sweep, we see this guy who got killed at the beginning of the movie sitting right there in song with everyone else, and no one seems to notice. And there are more people, enemies and lovers, murderers and their victims, all sitting there singing hymns as if nothing strange were going on. For a rabbi, the singing and the weeping, the marriage canopy and covering the coffin with earth are, somehow, simultaneous.

Sooner or later, like it or not, everyone winds up being close to God. We bump into what I can only call life-death experiences. You know, when life and death get mashed into one another. Something deep inside tells us that this is the Source of life and all its meaning, just as something also warns us not to get too close. That's why, one way or another, everyone says to the rabbi just before the wedding or the funeral or the bar or bat mitzvah, "Rabbi, make it fast." That's the way it is with what deals life and death at the same time.

Remember that great scene in *The Wizard of Oz*, where the spiritual seekers Lion, Tin Man, Scarecrow (Lion, Eagle, Ox?), and Dorothy finally make it to the highest celestial palace (*heychal*) for an audience with the great and terrible Oz? They find themselves in a great throne room with all those pyrotechnics, only to have the little dog expose the whole thing as a ruse—smoke and mirrors.

My colleague and dear friend Rabbi Les Bronstein says it's the motto of every rabbi: "Pay-no-attention-to-that-man-behind-the-curtain."

God says, "See, there is a place near Me. Station yourself on the rock" (Exodus 33:21).

And just what, you might ask, is this awful presence that passes by? I'll tell you: It is people's lives and souls at the times when they are exposed and uniquely visible: the births and deaths, the weddings and the *b'nai mitzvah*, and yes, sometimes even the meetings and the classes and the worship—when they are superimposed on one another.

Shall we contemplate the bridal party a few minutes before the ceremony? Or bereaved relatives just prior to a funeral? Or the parents before a circumcision? Or (God have mercy upon us) the bar mitzvah family? Jews have figured out that they could not possibly lead *normal* lives in daily proximity to such awesome and awe-*full* power, so they have invented this job called rabbi.

Indeed, this is precisely what the Israelites say to Moses at Sinai: "You speak to us, and we'll listen. But don't let God talk to us, or we'll get fried" (Exodus 20:16). They say, when time collapses, when life and death get mashed into one another, when there is only back-of-the-hand-against-open-mouth hushed silence, "You tell us what it's like. We'll wait for you right *back* here." And then they say, "He did it. Look, our rabbi came out alive again!"

The red carpet in the sanctuary of the synagogue in Sudbury, Massachusetts, where I used to be the rabbi was laid directly over the concrete of the foundation. That's what Michael's head hit when he went down, the concrete. You could hear the crack. He didn't pass out. When people pass out they melt into a pool. They can be caught. Michael just took a half step backward, as if he were trying to give himself some distance from the Torah scroll and his own bar mitzvah. But instead he toppled straight back like a felled tree. When I turned around, I saw blood oozing from his left ear. I was certain he had fractured his skull, maybe worse. His mother screamed, "Oh God, not that, not now!" (Not what? I wondered.) She used his new prayer shawl to try to stop the bleeding. "He has an infantile seizure disorder," she said. "He hasn't had one in over five years. We thought he was cured." Michael lay there, unconscious.

We joke about the danger of holy moments, "the Great and Terrible Oz," *Raiders of the Lost Ark*, "Don't get too close or you might get zapped"—things like that. But we don't really believe them. At least most of us didn't until Michael's bar mitzvah. Now we're a little less cavalier. The congregation came together. People waited patiently in their seats. Physicians who were present came forward. The rescue squad arrived and took Michael to the hospital. Michael's mother, on her way out the door, asked us to please eat the luncheon lest it go to waste.

I told the congregation that the doctors would do their job, Michael's family would do theirs, and that ours—even though none of us felt much like it—was to complete the service. Someone pointed out that we had forgotten to recite the concluding Torah blessing and respectfully suggested that the bar mitzvah might technically still be in progress. I waited around at the luncheon for a few minutes but had no appetite; my heart was at the hospital.

When I arrived in the emergency room, I found Michael all encased in an orange spinal brace and wearing an oxygen mask. But now everyone was smiling. "The X-rays and CAT scan show no serious damage," his mother whispered. "The doctor says he'll be fine." Michael was conscious—maybe more conscious than anyone else in the room.

He looked up at me and proceeded to recite the three rules of checkers as taught by Rabbi Nahum, the son of the Rabbi of Rizhyn, which I tease all my bar mitzvah students they must memorize: "You can't make two moves at once. You can only move forward and not backward. And once you reach the last row, you can move wherever you want." Then he said, "Did I finish? Am I a bar mitzvah?"

"Oh yes," I sighed. "You did the whole thing and more."

And there I was again, hanging by my fingernails to a rock cliff while The Presence passed by. Just another day at the office.

THE CALLING

ME? I DECIDED TO BECOME A RABBI when I was in the ninth grade. My own personal epiphany was ordinary, even banal. There were neither divine voices nor heavenly lights, just an annual community-wide Friday evening service. I was sitting with my family at Temple Emanu-El in Oak Park, Michigan, a suburb of Detroit, where the four area congregations and their leaders had gathered to celebrate Reform Judaism. I looked at the seven or eight rabbis assembled on the bima as if they were in a lineup. Most of them I already knew from my involvement in the temple's youth group, and one I would subsequently know as a professor. It dawned on me that here was a group of men (in those days it was only men) who earned their livings, who were actually paid to help people try to make sense out of the holiest moments of their lives. It struck me then (and it still strikes me now, forty years later) that surely there could be no more gratifying or important way for a person to earn a living. I turned to my parents and said, "I'm going to be a rabbi." They pay you to be a mensch; what a great deal.

In those days there was no notion that graduate rabbinic students should first spend some time "living out in the world" before entering rabbinic school. Indeed, four decades ago, the Hebrew Union College–Jewish Institute of Religion even had a joint undergraduate program with the University of Cincinnati. By taking graduate rabbinic courses over their four undergraduate years, students could earn the equivalent of one year of graduate credit.

[15]

This also meant that you could become a full-fledged rabbinic student at the age of eighteen.

As the calendar turned out, my last day at home in Detroit, before catching the Baltimore & Ohio sleeper down to Cincinnati, was Yom Kippur. For some reason (an educated guess would be terror in the family over my impending departure), we arrived very late at the temple for the concluding service. My father and I dropped off my mother and younger brother (who is now also a rabbi—my mother once called it "her specialty"). Because we were late, there were no parking places in the lot or anywhere for blocks around. So, by the time my dad and I managed to find a parking place and return to the temple, the main floor of the sanctuary was already full. Ushers suggested we try the balcony.

When we climbed the stairs at the back of the hall, the ushers there were not much more encouraging. They told us that there might be one or two seats left in the very last rows. Now the main sanctuary of the old Woodward and Gladstone building of Temple Beth El in Detroit was an ornate cathedral of a hall with ten huge stained glass windows, plush red carpeting, elaborate murals, hundred-bulb chandeliers, and rich mahogany wood paneling. And the balcony was very high. I had never been up there before (nor have I ever been there since).

When my father and I made our way up the steep aisle to the back of the balcony, we saw that only two open seats remained in the entire room. And those were in the far corner of the last row. People had to stand up as we slowly made our way in front of them. I feared for a moment that I might lose my balance and fall. But at least we had seats—even if they were the worst seats in the house.

By the time we sat down, the service was already more than half over. To my surprise, I found myself looking down on the chandeliers and the heads of, literally, thousands of people. The rabbi was half a city block away and, in the light from the ark, looked very, very puny. Indeed, the most vivid memory I have is of how far away he was, how small he looked, and, yes, how trivial he appeared—a tiny thumb of a man, dressed in a funny black costume, walking back and forth between the congregation and an ornate closet full of light. (It struck me even then that this might not have been an accident.) That was the first and perhaps the most important lesson I learned about being a rabbi. But it was not the last.

The learning, it goes on forever.

MY OTHER FATHER DIED

On December 23, 2009, my teacher Rabbi Arnold Jacob Wolf died. He dropped dead in front of his Chicago home at the age of eighty-four. His family invited me to offer one of four eulogies at his funeral; I have reconstructed my eulogy here from notes written on a flight to Chicago.

Wolf's rabbinic school roommate, Professor Eugene Borowitz (who had married Karen and me, and installed me as a rabbi), flew in from New York and also eulogized Wolf. When we met at the funeral, Borowitz kissed me, held me at arms' length, and said, "Now, Larry, you're an old rabbi."

Last year, before the High Holy Days, I phoned my mentor, Arnold, and his wife, Grace, to wish them a happy New Year. They weren't home so I left a message. When I returned a few hours later, there was a message waiting for me. It was from Arnold. He said, "Kushner, whatever you're calling about, I forgive you."

God, I loved that man. He'd probably be insulted if I called him my rebbe, so I'll just say Arnold Wolf was my spiritual father. As I review his teaching, his example, his love, I am astonished by how much there is.

Arnold Jacob Wolf spoke and wrote and taught and, above all, yelled in a wholly unique voice. It was urgent, hortatory, and riddled with freeze-dried, memorable one-liners. It was also supportive, healing, permissive, and encouraging. Probably everyone who spent any significant time with him in one way or another has heard him say, "My love is unconditional. I'm sure whatever you do will be great."

His voice was challenging, combative, destabilizing, annoying, infuriating, and ever-goading us to tell ourselves more of the truth, to be even better than we thought we wanted to be. And, while he was dogmatic and opinionated, he, just as often, confessed that he didn't have a clue.

He never spoke in platitudes or "rabbi" talk and couldn't understand why, when most rabbis got on the bima, they talked funny. Indeed, he believed that religious language is almost always soporific. He countered this by being uproariously funny, unpretentious, self-doubting, and disturbingly modest. You wanted to take care of him. "Religion is a serious business," he said, "but this congregation is a joke."

He loved the White Sox. And he loved playing baseball, especially when we'd let him pitch. He smoked cigars.

Arnold Wolf believed in a sharp division of labor in which laypeople should run their congregations and rabbis should teach them Torah. He renounced all coercive rabbinic power and that, in turn, freed him to say whatever he thought.

He believed that it is the inevitable nature of groups to argue and that a rabbi's job, therefore, is to make sure they argue about *important* things and fight *fair*.

Forty years ago, in an age when so many rabbis confused their titles with their first names, wore black robes, had reserved parking spaces and portraits (and even busts of themselves) festooning the foyers, Arnold Wolf was called "Arnold," had no secretary, and routinely confessed his mistakes from the pulpit.

"Nothing succeeds like Torah! It is the only merchandise we rabbis have," he said. "And to sell it does not require much charisma, salesmanship, or brilliance. It does require consistency, diligence, and a combination of modesty and guts."

Even though he grew increasingly observant, like his uncle and mentor, Rabbi Felix Levy, he remained a Reform Jew his whole life. "There is only one Judaism and it is Orthodoxy," he taught, "but all Jews are Reform."

"You don't look at the Torah, you let it look at you."

And once, in one of those painful moments when a woman had been called to the Torah but was initially unable to find her place, he shouted out, "Oh, just read anything; it's all good!"

Wolf was suspicious of mysticism and much of what passes for contemporary spirituality as wasteful, self-indulgent, and dangerous, reminding us, instead, that "all the old lies are true."

Through spoken word, written word, and deed, Arnold Jacob Wolf believed that serious religion inevitably means politics. And politics means confrontation. He forced us to acknowledge our complicity in the pain and brokenness of our society and our planet. He marched for civil rights in the South. He was the first rabbi to refuse to pay a telephone tax supporting the war in Vietnam. "We should draft dogs," he said. "People would say, 'But I love my dog; I wouldn't send him to Vietnam. He might get killed.'"

Once I was with him in his office when a congregant, who had tried to get him fired for his opposition to the war and whose son had just received a draft notice, had the chutzpah to call and ask if he knew of a doctor who could get his son a medical deferment. "I can't tell you," Arnold said without missing a beat "My phone is tapped!"

Arnold Jacob Wolf heard what I can only call a *Voice from Outside*. I remember how at an evening plenary session of the Central Conference of American Rabbis annual convention in Minneapolis, half the audience got up and walked out in protest while the other stayed to give him a standing ovation. We have a word for someone like that: prophet.

And here's the thing: He was sort of always right. He was bull's-eye about social justice, liberal politics, Israel, and Jewish education.

I am reminded of a story told of Rabbi Shmelke of Nikolsburg, who would always hang his walking stick and knapsack on the wall of the synagogue. When the officers of the congregation asked him why, he would reply: "I will call out the truth as best as I can, even when that makes us all uncomfortable. And if anyone is displeased, I am always prepared to pick up my staff and my knapsack and to live as a wanderer—begging from door to door." In effect Wolf said to all of us: I like you, I love serving as your teacher, I'm honored you want me ... but I don't work *for you*.

Arnold Jacob Wolf, in the words of this week's *parasha*, was an *ish asher ruach Elohim bo*, "a man with the spirit of God in him" (Genesis 41:38).

But there is one very important bit of counsel he gave me that I am confident neither I nor probably any of us will follow. When I left Congregation Solel forty years ago, I asked him for his advice. He said, "Don't take anything with you." I've always understood that to mean, let each new phase of your life be open and without expectation. And, while I imagine he'd say the same thing to all of us this morning, I'm afraid that that love is just too tough. So, Arnold, we refuse to take your good advice. We will take everything you have taught us with us for the rest of our days.

Hebrew has three words for dying: *Mayt*, "to die." It can be said of any living creature—people or animals. The word *niftar* means "to depart"; it is said *only* of human beings. But there is a third word, reserved for the *gedolay ha-dor*, "the great ones of a generation": *nis-ta-laek*, to be summoned to the *Yeshivah shel Ma-aleh*, the Academy on High.

So: *Laykh l'shalom* [Go forth in peace], Arnold, our teacher, our rabbi.

I sure do hope the Academy on High knows what it's got itself in for now.

THE TENT PEG BUSINESS

SOME MISCHIEVOUS, HERETICAL, AND HUMOROUS TRUTHS ABOUT SURVIVING AND HEALING CONGREGATIONAL LIFE

1. If synagogues were businesses, their product would be Jews. The more Jews they could manufacture from otherwise illiterate, assimilated, and un-self-aware members, the more successful they would be. That is (to continue the metaphor) the bottom line. Simply getting together with other Jews may be ancillary and even indispensable to this ultimate goal, but it can just as easily be—as is often the case when Jews get together to watch a movie, eat dinner, or play tennis—a pleasant way to pass time.

2. Jews need one another, and therefore congregations, to do primary religious acts that they should not, and probably cannot, do alone. Doing primary religious acts is the only way we have of growing as Jews. Consequently, it is also the only justification for the existence of a congregation. Everything else congregations do, Jews can always do cheaper, easier, and better somewhere else.

3. There are three ancient kinds of primary Jewish acts: communal prayer, holy study, and good deeds, or in the classical language of *Pirke Avot*: *avodah*, *torah*, and *gemilut hasadim*. This is not a capricious categorization. Prayer (*avodah*) is emotional: song, candles, dance, meditation, and silence—a matter of the heart. Study (*torah*) is intellectual reading, questioning, discussion, rigorous logic, and argument—a matter of the head. And good deeds (*gemilut hasadim*) are public acts: helping, repairing, matching, fighting, and doing—matters of the hand. Only rare individuals are able to do all three with equal fervor and skill. And so our membership in a congregation and association with a broad spectrum of Jews will compensate for our personal deficiencies.

4. In order to maintain their congregations, Jews must do many other things that are not inherently Jewish. These secondary acts include maintaining a building, raising money, and perhaps forming a board of directors. (It should be here noted, however, that in the long history of our people there have been healthy, vibrant, and solvent congregations that had none of the above.)

5. Congregations, unfortunately, often get so caught up in doing secondary acts that they actually begin to think that maintaining the building, raising money, or electing the board of directors is the reason for the existence of the congregation. Their members are busy at work, but because they have forgotten why they are at work, their efforts are hollow and come to naught.

6. People decide, consciously or unconsciously, how many hours each week they will spend at the temple being Jewish. Once there, they assume that whatever they do, whether primary or secondary, is a primary Jewish activity. (There are many Jews today who sincerely believe that running a photocopier, attending committee meetings, and organizing bingo are primary Jewish acts.) It is in everyone's mutual best interest, therefore, to encourage one another to spend at least half of

his or her "Jewish hours" doing primary Jewish acts. Such a system, in addition to guaranteeing individual religious growth, invariably draws upon ever-widening circles of people who will in turn spend no more than half their time doing secondary congregational tasks.

7. Members of a congregation ought to selfishly and routinely demand that the congregation provide them with the instruments (teachers, classes, books, colloquia, services, programs, etc.) they need in order to grow as Jews. In many congregations, unfortunately, this order is reversed. Leaders who have not clarified their own religious goals are supposed to set policies for other members who themselves have not yet even determined that they need to come around at all. Here is the proper sequence: first comes personal religious growing, then comes effective congregational policy.

8. If people selfishly seek their own Jewish growth and do what they do because they want to (*lishma*, "for its own sake"), then there is no longer any need for the ritualized public displays of gratitude that threaten to suffocate virtually every arena of congregational life. Such obeisance at services and banquets, in print and on the walls, invariably degenerates into a system in which people give gifts of time, money, and skill to the congregation not for the joy of giving itself but for the communal recognition. If everyone is thanked, the only noteworthy events are the invariable omissions.

9. If people are tricked into attending something they would not have come to otherwise, they will not know what to do once they are there. They will soon grow bored, bitter, and destructive.

10. There is no evidence whatsoever to support the notion that people who are drawn into the congregation for an innocuous nonreligious event, such as gourmet cooking, move onto activities of more primary religious worth any sooner than if they had been left alone to discover their own inevitable and personal religious agendas and timetables. Indeed, there is

substantial data to suggest that congregations that run many "basement" activities in hopes of getting people from there onto upper floors only wind up adding on to the basement.

11. The quality of interpersonal transactions between the members of the congregation is the single most important factor in determining its health. Do they bear witness to the piety the congregation claims to perpetuate? Where the human relationships are self-righteous, deceitful, and toxic, congregational life is wretched. Where they are tolerant, honest, and nurturing, congregational life can be a transforming joy.

12. The way a congregation gets its money may be finally more important than how much it gets. Consider the religious impact, for instance, for congregations getting, say, half their operating budgets from (a) bingo, (b) a few wealthy members, or (c) dues. There is a widespread misconception that because the congregation is nonprofit and tax-exempt, it is therefore a charity. Actually, even though the analogy makes us uncomfortable, a congregation is (with the possible exception of offering membership to anyone with a financial hardship) precisely like a country club. And as in all such clubs, you get what you pay for.

13. Most forms of fund-raising within a congregation might simply be understood as the establishment of a small business within the congregation that is staffed without charge by its members. This little fund-raising business allows the members to think that since their dues were lowered, they are getting something for nothing. It works as long as the people who run the little business remain convinced that they are really doing primary Jewish acts.

14. Any attempt to get someone other than the members of a congregation to pay for what they want only cheapens the institution. Serious, quality, well-run organizations, with rare exceptions, do not solicit advertisements, sell cupcakes, or run raffles in order to meet their operating budgets. They may, of course, do such things for people other than themselves, that is, for charity.

15. Freud may have been correct in postulating that religion originated on account of some primal crime, the guilt for which continues to motivate and organize religious life to this day. But any attempt to use guilt to motivate religious behavior in a community is certain to generate an equal amount of resentment. People simply must be regarded as if they are wise and decent enough to do religious things and support congregational functions without manipulation.

16. The amount of creativity within a congregation stands in inverse ratio to the number of people, groups, or levels in the institutional hierarchy empowered to prohibit anything. With the exceptions of spending a congregation's money or using its name, the members of a congregation should not need anyone's permission to initiate anything—be it a letter in the bulletin or an alternate religious service.

17. The price of congregational vitality is the frequent appearance of confusion and even anarchy. The communal tolerance for such creative unpredictability is a learned skill. There can never be too many people trying too many things. If it's a good idea, people will keep coming. If it's not so good, no one will come. The committees, the board, and the rabbi ought not get into the business of approving or disapproving anything; they should only help whomever and whenever they can.

18. Since no one can be sure of what someone else must do to serve the Holy One, anyone who thinks he has a new idea or an old idea must be given a chance. (This includes the rabbi.) Unqualified mutual support for one another is indispensable in a would-be community.

19. The amount, quality, and intensity of adult study, perhaps more than other modes of congregational activity, will liberate its members to make wise decisions for themselves.

20. The congregation, like an extended family, is a closed, homeostatic, organic system. Any anger, guilt, or malice, or any nurture, kindness, or encouragement put into the system

eventually (it may take years) returns to those who put it out. Sooner or later, it always comes back to you.

21. Rabbis, as Arnold Jacob Wolf has observed, do not own *their* congregations. Congregations belong to their members. For this reason, congregants have ultimate decision-making power and rabbis are well advised to invest their egos in something less mercurial over which they have more control than *their* congregations.

22. Rabbis should treat Jews more like rabbis. Jews should treat rabbis more like Jews.

23. The chief goal of a rabbi is to teach the members of the congregation how to run their congregation without rabbinic help. The rabbi must tell them what he or she knows and then persuade, cajole, and even trick them into doing what they want to do with their congregation. The congregation belongs to them; but only when they realize that their rabbi will not "do it" for them can they (and it) begin to realize their full creative and religious potential. In the imagery of Lurianic Kabbalah, as liberal Jewish theologian Eugene Borowitz has wisely suggested, this is called *tsimtsum* or voluntary self-contraction, resulting in the creation of a space within which people have room to experiment, fail, learn, and grow.

24. Rabbis ought to treat their congregants as members of an *am kadosh*, a holy people. Neither judging nor scolding, the rabbi ought to give congregants permission, encouragement, and support as they try to discover for themselves what they must do to be Jews.

25. Rabbis and congregants have it in their mutual best interests to encourage the rabbi to develop his or her own spiritual life and to discourage the rabbi from serving as a communal surrogate for religiosity or as a skilled but hollow performer. The leader of the prayers, in other words, must also pray.

26. People must always feel free to establish mechanisms for telling one another the truth about their congregation. Boring

worship, irrelevant classes, or cowardly social action programs can change only if members can share their evaluations. The bulletin ought to have its own independent (of the rabbi and the board of directors) editor and be a forum for real and open debate. Arguments are a necessary part of vitality. The opposite of telling the truth here is not lying but, out of some misguided attempt to protect the congregation, "keeping it a secret." Nothing so paralyzes a social organism as secrets—especially those that are widely known yet never spoken.

27. The reality of a congregation's mood and vitality is a highly volatile, subtle, and even capricious creature. Ultimately our evaluation of the reality of a congregation and indeed the very standard of evaluation we choose may tell us more about ourselves than the congregation. Precisely because they are so amorphous, congregations tend to function as a kind of communal Rorschach for their members.

28. Finally, the members of the congregation must nurture one another because they need one another; they simply cannot do it alone. Hermits and monasteries are noticeably absent from Jewish history; we are hopelessly communal people.

When the wilderness tabernacle is completed, near the end of the Book of Exodus, we are told, "And it came to pass that the tabernacle was 'one'" (Exodus 36:13). Commenting on this curious expression, Rabbi Mordecai Yosef Leiner of Izbica (d. 1854) observes:

> *In the building of the tabernacle, all Israel were joined in their hearts; no one felt superior to his fellow. At first, each skilled individual did his own part of the construction, and it seemed to each one that his work was extraordinary. Afterwards, once they saw how their several contributions to the "service" of the tabernacle were integrated—all the boards, the sockets, the curtains, and the loops fit together as if one person had done it all. Then they realized how each one of them had depended on the other. Then they*

understood how what all they had accomplished was not by virtue of their own skill alone but that the Holy One had guided the hands of everyone who had worked on the tabernacle. They had only later merely joined in completing its master building plan, so that "it came to pass that the tabernacle was one" (Exodus 36:13). Moreover, the one who made the Holy Ark itself was unable to feel superior to the one who had only made the courtyard tent pegs.

(*Itturay Torah*, ed. Aaron Greenberg
[Tel Aviv: Yavneh, 1976], 3:275)

THE HUMAN PYRAMID

MORE MISCHIEVOUS, HERETICAL, AND HUMOROUS TRUTHS ABOUT SURVIVING AND HEALING CONGREGATIONAL LIFE

MARTIN BUBER TELLS THE FOLLOWING STORY in the name of the Baal Shem Tov: Once there was this guy who saw a beautiful bird high in the top of a tree. No one else saw it. And a great longing came over him to reach the bird and take it. But the tree was too high and there was no ladder. So he devised a plan. He persuaded the people who stood there with him to form a pyramid so that he was able to climb to the top and reach the bird. Those who helped knew nothing of the bird; they never even saw it. But the one who did would never have been able to reach the bird without them. Indeed had any of them left his or her place, then everyone would have fallen to the earth.

1. A congregation, you might say, is a kind of human pyramid. The goal is to raise more and more of its members high enough to reach the bird's nest. We never know who will be next. We only know that without one another, no one can make it. So that's the first truth of congregational life: we are only as good as we treat the people whom we believe are beneath us.

[30]

There are several more truths. They are organized under the categories of leadership, rabbis, communal prayer, money, and the congregation. More than a few are deliberately mischievous; nevertheless, I believe they are all still true.

LEADERSHIP

2. The first item on the agenda of any board meeting will be discussed for the longest amount of time.

3. Beware of people who won't tell you whom they heard it from. Whenever someone says things like, "I can't tell you who, but I've heard … " or "There's a perception among many people in the congregation" or "Everyone says" but won't tell you who "everyone" is, watch out! They're screwing with your brain. In a system where identities are kept secret, one person could tell twenty people, all of whom would then tell you, and you'd think that there was a major problem out there instead of just one bigmouthed kvetch.

4. Beware of any meeting run by *Robert's Rules of Order*. These rules do not appear in any Jewish book. Robert was not Jewish.

5. As a matter of fact, there was no *last* meeting, there is only *now*. Be suspicious of *any* gathering at which minutes *must* be kept. This is true for voting also: better to just keep listening to one another until you reach a consensus. And if there is no consensus, you're not yet ready to take it out of the oven.

6. Trying to guess what other people who aren't present might want only makes you say and vote for stupid things. It's hard enough to simply explain to others why you want what you want and then have enough courage to vote for it.

7. The choice invariably comes down to judging others or helping them. Whenever you judge, you stifle spontaneity, enthusiasm, and participation. Whenever you help, you risk novelty and anarchy. (I once went to Dr. Alexander Altmann, his

memory is a blessing, with an idea I feared was religiously dangerous. He thought for a while and then, with a kindly smile, said, "Relax, Kushner, you're not smart enough to be that heretical.")

RABBIS

8. The most valuable *capital* investment a congregation has is its professional staff.

9. If the rabbi and the president both want something, they'll get it. If only one of them wants something and the other doesn't, it'll never happen.

10. What you want and need the rabbi and cantor to do cannot be written in a job description. Even if it could, you couldn't pay someone to do it. What you want from them is their enthusiasm, their heart, their soul, and those, of course, cannot be offered at any price.

COMMUNAL PRAYER

11. The amount of communal participation in prayer is in inverse ratio to the combined vertical and horizontal distance between the leader of the prayers and the first occupied row of seats.

12. Responsive reading is dumb.

13. The function of liturgy is not to ingest new information. You already know everything in the prayer book. Liturgical novelty of any kind only keeps the wrong part of your brain awake. Indeed, the more regularly Jews pray, the more they pray by rote, and the more they pray in Hebrew. The goal is to know the liturgy so well you can go onto autopilot, not as a drone, but in an altered state.

14. A gimmick is a way to get someone to attend services that has nothing to do with the service. It is hardly surprising therefore

that people who have come to watch some officers be installed or someone get honored or birthday blessed or a third grade class perform or whatever will spend most of the rest of the time during the service sleeping or looking like he or she is sucking lemons.

15. The more you rehearse anything, the more deadly it becomes. Besides, people make just as many gaffes anyway.

16. We now have over two generations of data conclusively demonstrating that transliterations do not get people to read Hebrew; they discourage it! If you learned that you'd have to go to, say, Portugal on business for six months, you'd go and buy some Berlitz records and learn Portuguese. Sure, you wouldn't be able to read great Portuguese literature, but you'd be able to get around. Well, guess what? You're going to Hebrew Land for the rest of your life. Cold turkey: start learning Hebrew.

17. Family services are just a euphemism for "puerile." Every service should be an adult service where children of all ages are always welcome. Who are we to say that God would rather hear our mellifluent prayers rather than the prattle of a child? Besides, if you're really praying, who cares that the kids are making noise.

18. Virtually every social expectation once reserved for weddings has now migrated to *b'nai mitzvah*. This would only be a fascinating social phenomenon were it not for the fact that weddings are by invitation only and are not celebrated at Shabbat services. What would happen to a typical service, for instance, were we to schedule a wedding within it? The wedding would last a lot longer, the *oneg Shabbat* or *kiddush* would have much better food, and only people who were invited would attend. Well, that's what we've now got with *b'nai mitzvah*. What match are the Shabbos "regulars" for 150 dressed-to-the-teeth wedding guests? Of all Judaism's life-cycle celebrations, *b'nai mitzvah* require the presence of a congregation. And while a minyan of any ten adult Jews can technically suffice, the public

reading of Torah requires an *ongoing* community. We say to the kid: This service, at which you will be called to the Torah to celebrate your sexual maturity, would go on *whether or not* you and your family were here. We're glad, honored, delighted you are, but we did this thing last week and we'll do it next—with or without you.

MONEY

19. There are only three primary means for *predictably* financing a congregation: Fund-raising, user fees, and dues. Although it strikes many people as a surprise—short of draconian measures such as trying to turn the thermostat down to fifty-five degrees, hiring a cheaper rabbi, or closing the building one day a week—one way or another, we gotta get the same total dollars out of the same number of people. If you don't believe me, try adding up your check stubs at the end of the year.

20. Fund-raising can be vulgar, like bingo or Monte Carlo night. These deliver enormous sums of money but exact even higher prices from the soul of the congregation. Fund-raising can be cute, as when the workers earn less for their time than they are professionally worth — you get a professional worth one hundred dollars an hour selling cupcakes in the parking lot for one dollar apiece! Or finally, fund-raising can be intrinsically worthwhile, as when what you do to make the money is why you have a congregation in the first place; for example, bringing Jewish art to Jews and supporting Jewish artists, producing a Purim-spiel production, publishing a book, or hosting an extraordinary Jewish program to teach Jews—whether or not such fund-raisers make money, they are self-validating because they help Jews grow.

21. In the user-fee model of getting money, people pay only for the services they actually use. If they send kids to school, they pay tuition. If they attend High Holy Day services, they buy tickets. If they want to celebrate a *simcha*, they pay a fee. If

they read from the Torah, they pay the *gabbai*. If they take a class, they pay a fee. And, since it's all voluntary—you don't *have* to send your kids to school, attend services, celebrate *simchas*, read from the Torah, or take classes—such a financial model rarely draws opposition. The problems are that user fees discourage people from taking advantage of what is offered; they abuse many households at precisely the times when they can least afford it; and worst of all, by encouraging an every-man-for-himself mentality, user fees ultimately discourage the formation of community. "You pay for what you want, I'll pay for what I want, and don't bother me with any of your problems or dreams." "My kids have grown up; I quit."

22. In an all-inclusive, graduated dues model, everyone's dues are higher in the short run, but the burden is equally distributed over the widest possible financial base. The long-term, overall, per-person cost in this model is the lowest. If it's good enough for our congregation to do, then we should all share in its cost.

CONGREGATION

23. There are three reasons why you should never conduct a congregational survey about anything: First, the people you're surveying don't know what they want (if they did, you'd already know it, too). Second, if you ask them what they want, you'll only get stuck having to do what they say. And finally, even if you give them what they say they want, they won't come anyway.

24. Heated arguments about the correct way to be religious are almost always driven by something personal and secret.

25. What's all this hogwash about measuring success by numbers? Where'd that come from anyway? I heard of one congregation who hired a clown, like they used to have out in front of car washes, to lure in unsuspecting Jewish motorists. The idea is not to collect more Jewish scalps but to make better Jews out of the ones we already have. Don't worry, the word will get

out. What we are selling is a three-millennia-old tradition for how to make sacred sense out of life. You don't have to advertise that or offer it at bargain-basement prices or coax people to check it out. All you need to do is be welcoming, give them the real thing, and expect the highest of which they are capable in return. In other words: no schlock.

26. Worry about your *own* religious problems. If someone is trying to do something religious you don't like, assume he or she has some secret, holy reason unbeknownst to you. As Philip Roth said in his wonderful short story "The Conversion of the Jews," "Don't hit one another on account of God."

27. Our tolerance for forms of religious expression we disagree with is a precise barometer of our own spiritual security.

28. And now the good news: You cannot wreck the congregation. No one can wreck a congregation. If you fired the staff, torched the building, and sold all its assets, next Rosh Hashanah most of the congregation would show up in the field—and most of them would have a pretty good *Yontif*. Even if there were no rabbi, about half would like his or her sermon and half would think it was drivel, half would love the music and half would wish it were more like what they grew up with.

29. A spiritually mature community is one that helps its members learn how to give and receive love.

I will conclude with a teaching one of my rabbinic students, Daniel Lehrman, called to my attention. It is a comment on Exodus 36:7, which describes the conclusion of the construction of the wilderness tabernacle; you might call it the first building fund campaign; "And the labor was enough for them to accomplish all the work of the tabernacle—and more."

The commentary *Tsihot Tsaddikim* notes a contradiction: The text states that their gifts were "enough"—implying that they were sufficient to accomplish the task. But then the text goes on to add "and more"—implying that their gifts were more than what was required! *Nu?* Which was it: just enough or more than enough?

The commentator answers his own question with a curveball: If the text had said only "enough," then there would not have been enough. For if their gifts for the tabernacle were precisely the measure that was required, then there could also be no doubt that each person's gift was indispensable. And then everyone would be smug and conceited and arrogant, saying, "Without my gift, it would have been impossible to erect the tabernacle."

But then the main idea of the tabernacle—the dwelling of the divine presence—could not happen. As we read in Proverbs 16:5, "Arrogance is an abomination to God." And according to the Talmud (*Arakhin* 15b), "God says, 'Ain't enough room in this here building for your arrogant ego and Me.'"

So, when our text in Exodus adds "and more" than what was required, it means that some gifts were necessarily left over and unused. And that meant that everyone's ego took a big hit. "What if it was my gift that was left outside! What if I wasn't the one who completed building God's tabernacle?" And yet it was this very humility that alone made possible the presence of God. In this way, saying that there was "more" actually qualifies the word "enough." For the "more" was what was needed to make it just "enough" (*Itturay Torah* 3:287–8).

30. And that's the last truth: All the building, all the giving, all the countless hours are only to help us get our egos out of the way. Such selflessness and subsequent spiritual fulfillment can be sought in no institution better than in a congregation—you know, a human pyramid.

THE RABBI BUSINESS

SOME ADVICE FOR RABBINIC STUDENTS

THIS IS NOT A SERMON. This is not even a lecture. It is only a list for rabbinic students—a list of random things I've learned, most of them the hard way, about being the rabbi of a congregation. The items on the list fall into six categories: leadership, separation, service, prayer, learning, and politics.

LEADERSHIP

1. Make up a good lie about the congregation and tell it to anyone who will listen. Tell it in sermons, in classes, at meetings, in the bulletin, at social gatherings, during chance encounters in the post office. I don't mean the kind of fluff that winds up on a mission statement. I mean a noble prevarication: We are a congregation of spiritual anarchists; our members understand that quality costs more money; our congregation caters to intellectual Jews. Of course it's all balderdash and bunkum, but after a few years people will try to live up to it anyway. This is called leadership.

2. You must protect people who have no social clout because the health of a congregation is measured by its ability to tolerate dweebs.

3. You are always on the lookout for and then pumping up good people. I do not mean your friends or your *hasidim*. Indeed, you may not particularly enjoy their company, their politics, or their social styles. But they do have both brains and souls. You promptly return their phone calls, suggest they attend programs, invite them to lunch, send them articles. On the other hand, you do not have much time for toxic, angry, *farbissineh*, lemon-sucking people—no matter how much they love the temple. You do not snub them; that is hostile and just another way of giving them more attention. Of course, you return their calls—but only after a few days have passed. You chat with them—but only briefly. And you do not get into arguments with them about *anything*. This is called leadership development. As George Carlin said: "Never underestimate the power of stupid people in large groups."

4. You cannot assume that otherwise kind, intelligent, and thoughtful people will know what to do *unless you tell them*. If people do something wrong, you do not scold or get annoyed; you lovingly explain how to do it correctly. For example: "Never leave a guest standing alone at the *oneg*." "Don't eat in the sanctuary on Yom Kippur." "A bar mitzvah parent's speech should *not* run more than a half hour."

5. One of our colleagues leads services wearing a big shawl tallis. He wraps himself in the traditional manner by first covering his head. He told me that, over the years, he came up with a kind of personal *kavana* or meditation: he does not remove the tallis from his head until he has convinced himself that it is an honor to lead such a holy congregation in prayer. "Sure," he confessed, "sometimes I have to stand there on the bima for several minutes before I can begin. But when I finally remove the tallis from my head, I am ready to be a rabbi again." This reminds me of the words of Nahman of Breslov: "Know that one who would offer real *niggunim* must be able to gather the good points in every single soul—even the sinners."

SEPARATION

6. The congregation belongs to its members, not its employees. You do not vote; you do not pay dues. Spiritual calling, shmeeritual calling: you work there. If you don't believe me, try not working and see if they keep paying you.

7. It's all about boundaries: knowing where *their* congregation ends and *you* begin; knowing where *their* temple ends and *your* home begins; knowing the difference between cherished congregants and personal friends; knowing when you are at work and when you are at play. "Hello. Is everything all right? It's just that you're calling me at home. Oh, it's only routine temple business? Gosh, I'm sorry but my calendar is at the office. Perhaps you could call back on Monday morning. Sure, thanks. Glad everything is okay."

8. Beware of confusing your ego with something as mercurial, capricious, and bizarre as a nonprofit corporation owned and run by several hundred Jews. If you do fall into thinking that *their* congregation is an extension of *your* ego, then, when they do something stupid—and, read my lips, they *will* do something stupid—you will take it personally. You will lose your ability to dispassionately address their error and then politely leave the meeting, murmuring something like, "Gosh, I fear you are on the verge of doing something colossally foolish with *your* congregation. My partner and I are going to a movie."

9. Invest your ego, instead, in something independent of the congregation and its vagaries and over which you have a modicum of control. Become a maven of something, anything—Salonika Jewry in the fifteenth century, local city government, Hebrew poetry. Stay current with its literature, write articles about it, coax your colleagues to let you give free lectures or workshops on it.

10. New vocabulary word: "*Sycophant*: A servile self-seeker who attempts to win favor by flattery." 10a: Do not gently squeeze people's upper arms or run around the room glad-handing everyone. Gag me with a spoon.

SERVICE

11. Rabbis and cantors work when Jews don't. Your work lives and your play lives will be 180 degrees out-of-synch with those of *normal* people. So, quit waiting for the weekend that will never come and instead learn to sleep late on Tuesdays, go to the art museum on Wednesdays, and make Thursdays movie night.

12. For this reason, rabbis and cantors should never request a day off. The job is simply too demanding, too exciting, and too unpredictable. On the other hand, you *should* take off the equivalent of a weekend during the middle of the week at least twice a month. Any other young conscientious, driven professional gets to leave the office at 6 o'clock on Friday afternoon and show up *three* nights and *two* full days later at 8 a.m. on Monday morning and no one would dare suggest that he or she was not conscientious or hardworking.

13. You will be busy at your desk for as many hours each week as you are at your desk. So decide *in advance* how many hours a week you want to be busy at your desk. Hardly anything you do at your desk in the temple office matters for how well the temple works or how good a job you do. One of my Episcopal colleagues claimed that at the end of every month, he just took every piece of paper on his desk and threw it in the trash. "But what about the important ones?" I asked. "Not to worry," he explained. "If it's important, it'll come back."

14. Rabbis and cantors should try not to do *anything* congregants can do themselves. This includes conducting services at a house of mourning, officiating at an unveiling, orchestrating *b'nai mitzvah*, serving as a *gabbai* to conduct the Torah reading, offering communal blessings, or editing the bulletin. Remember: the measure of your leadership is how well it runs when you're *not* there.

15. The capacity to collect lengthy phone messages will not make you more accessible. Why on earth would any busy clergyperson want an office telephone system enabling callers to leave voice messages? The voice system should say, "If you would like to leave a message for Rabbi So-and-so, please press 3 for her *assistant*." This will dramatically diminish both the number and the length of the messages.

16. When agreeing to any meeting, try to get some idea of the other person's agenda. Just ask it straight out: "What's our topic?" "Anything particular on your mind?" "Is it personal? Congregational? Cosmic?"

17. Resist the temptation and frequent invitations to say just "a few words." And, if you do succumb, please, only say them when you have *something* to say. And then, even more difficult, once you've said them, sit down and shut up.

18. Lose your key to the building. Forget how to turn on the lights, and whatever you do, don't let them know you know anything about computers. I know one of our colleagues who had perfected the art of jamming the photocopier with a mere twist of his wrist. "Oh no, Rabbi, don't go near the Xerox machine again. Please, let me do it for you."

19. Because rabbis get paid to be religious, your motivation for performing *mitzvot* will be inescapably contaminated. If *anyone* finds out that you do a particular *mitzvah*—giving charity, studying Torah, praying daily, offering hospitality to wayfarers, etc.—there will always be a suspicion that you're only doing it to impress the congregation. (Maybe you'll get a raise.) Several months after stepping down from my last pulpit a few years ago, I ran into a former congregant in Starbucks. As I asked her how she was, in my most caring voice, I realized, to my amazement, that I meant it. My God, I really was a caring human being. For this reason, rabbis should cultivate a *secret mitzvah* life. Put on a disguise, go to another city, and visit someone in the hospital.

PRAYER

20. Rehearsing ceremonies only dulls their immediacy and dilutes their power. And guess what, people make just as many gaffes anyway. Of course, you rehearse it all in your own head; you get there early and check out the lighting; rearrange the chairs, test the sound system. That is what it means to be a *misadaer kiddushin*, a master of holy ceremonies. You are a dramaturgist. You envision who stands where and when. You walk into the room wearing a beret and one of those little movie camera eyepieces on a cord around your neck and you stop and imagine the scene, because if you don't, you'd better believe that the function manager at the hotel will turn it all into canned, liturgical spam.

21. Once people sense that someone is in charge, they relax. I used to say to the family just before a bar mitzvah or a wedding something like, "Friends, I will assume that once this balloon goes up most of you will lose control of your higher cognitive faculties and only be able to follow simple, monosyllabic, whispered instructions, like, 'Walk,' 'Speak,' 'Sit down,' 'Stand up,' 'Roll over.' And that's all I and the cantor are going to give you. So, please, just sit back and leave the driving to us."

22. You may not presume to know and tell people what ceremonies marking the passages of their lives mean to them. (You barely know what yours meant to you.) But you may ask people instead to tell *you*, and anyone else in the congregation who happens to be listening, what the event means to *them*. Ask the parents of a child about to be named to tell everyone why they have chosen the name they did; privately ask the bar mitzvah in front of the open ark to tell you what kind of a man he hopes to become; have the bride and groom publicly speak to one another at the *ketuba* table or *hatan's tish* (groom's table) about what they love about one another or what kind of a home they hope to build; and let the members of a family, if they write it out in advance, eulogize their dead. Your job as the rabbi is to cajole the celebrants into putting in their *own* words what would otherwise remain unspoken.

23. And throw away your rabbi's manual. When you bless someone in the presence of others, wing it. Sure, while you're
starting out, it won't be very elegant or polished, but your
words will be alive and everyone will listen. And, for the love
of heaven, don't try to sound rabbinic.

24. I am now convinced that rabbis should *not* lead communal
prayers at all. That's what cantors do. They are *shlikhey tsibur*,
emissaries of the congregation. Rabbis should be sitting deep
in reverent contemplation by the eastern wall. As one of my
classmates, Rabbi Stuart Geller, once titled a speech at a rabbinic convention, "If you've never written a sermon during the
silent meditation, you won't think this is very funny."

25. Virtually all stage directions ("We now rise"; "We pray
together"; "We turn to page ... ") are offered for the sole ben-
efit of occasional and usually non-Jewish guests instead of
routinely attending members. Such directions say, in effect,
"No one knows what's going on." I say, let guests do what they
do everywhere else—discretely observe the regulars and then
mimic them. What would happen if services were designed,
instead, to make the regulars feel at home? And don't worry
about the liturgy being unwelcoming. It's the members of the
congregation who are welcoming or unwelcoming.

LEARNING

26. It is okay *not* to know the answer, the translation, the law, the
date of the event, the author of a book, or the reason for the
custom. Practice saying, "I don't know," or "Beats me!" or
"That's a wonderful question. Give me ten years." And here's
the crazy part: people assume that only a truly wise man or
woman would have the temerity to make such a confession.

27. Vary the length of your sermons and teachings. My first Rosh
Hashanah as a newly ordained rabbi, I sat on the bima while
Arnold Jacob Wolf, one of the great preachers of our gener-
ation, spoke. At the evening service he spoke for fifty-five

minutes. People were used to serious teaching and listened carefully. The next morning Wolf spoke for seven minutes. As he walked back to his seat, he whispered to me, "Never let 'em know how long it's gonna last." (And, if you're reading a list, like this, never tell people how many items it has.)

28. No one will ever tell you that your teachings are too simplistic; the smart ones will just quit coming. So, instead, always talk to people like they're smarter than they are.

29. Make good friends with a local rabbi or academic who knows more than you do (and who preferably didn't go to the Hebrew Union College, because, as you might have noticed, we all have the same books!). Just say it and get it over with: "I am jealous of your background in texts and would love a chance to learn from and with you."

30. During any lecture or sermon: five coughs from the audience and it's time to tell a joke or sing a song or do a little dance.

POLITICS

31. Once a year, tell the board what you do with your time. You have nothing to hide. Indeed *your* enemy is *their* ignorance. Distribute a multipage, detailed summary including a breakdown of the time necessary to prepare a half-hour Rosh Hashanah sermon, a decent bulletin article, a eulogy, an adult education class. Say: "There's no way you could possibly know what I do with my time. When I go back over my own calendar, I am astonished myself. But I work for you and I am glad to tell you what I do with my time. Please feel free to add anything you like, as long as you also tell me what to remove." The only category that is sacrosanct should be reading and study *lishma*, for its own sake. It should constitute at least one-quarter of your billable hours. Otherwise you'll have to draw on the principal and, within a year or two, start repeating yourself. Think of it as R & D, research and development.

32. Ultimately, rabbis and cantors have only one get-out-of-jail-free card: threatening to quit. You may only play this card twice, and those occasions must be at least three years apart. Otherwise someone will call your bluff and then you won't need to quit.

33. Rabbis and cantors need to learn paranoid street smarts, a sixth sense for what's going on behind their backs, what's really cooking, what's probably coming down. Develop a knack for remembering who's friends with whom, since what you say to or hear from one effectively means telling or hearing everyone else in his or her social circle.

34. You can survive almost any disaster, mistake, indiscretion, or stupid move as long as the president hears it from you *first*. "In about five minutes you're going to get a hysterical phone call from Sylvia Gazonowitz...."

35. And finally: never, ever, under any circumstances whatsoever get into a power struggle. Rabbis do not win power struggles. Even if the rabbi wins, the rabbi loses. On the other hand, never back down from a fight over ethics. Rabbis always win fights over the right way to act. Even when the rabbi loses those, the rabbi wins.

According to Masoretic tradition the *aleph* of the title word of *Parashat Vayikra*, is *z'ira*, small, but it is also the first letter of the first word God spoke at Sinai. For spiritual leaders, that's the whole point: hearing the *aleph* but not getting too big on account of it.

BEING SOMEBODY ELSE

The Hasidim have long been fond of pointing out that *Yom ha-Kippurim*, "the Day of Atonements," could also be read as *Yom k'Purim*, "a day like Purim." On Purim you're happy, on Yom Kippur you're sad, but the psycho-spiritual result may be identical. On Purim you dress up like your worst enemy (and remind yourself that he's not as different from you as you'd like to imagine). On the Yom Kippur, you attain a similar liberation from the ego and its tricks through fasting, prayer, and enduring interminable sermons. It's a good teaching, but I didn't realize just how profound it was until a few years ago when the staff of my former congregation was performing its annual Purim play for the preschool.

I don't remember exactly how this custom got started, but it had become de rigueur for all of us then on the senior faculty and whomever from the office staff was unlucky to be around to act out the Purim story. Four-year-olds are not what you'd call a very demanding audience. The principal dramatic challenge was that we never seemed to have enough cast members to play all the parts. These were usually distributed as we walked down the hall from the office to the classroom.

Each of us would bring in a few costume pieces—a wig, crazy hats, an old dress, a mask, a *Star Wars* light saber—you get the idea. This particular year I got to play both one of the palace guards *and* Queen Esther. Like my other fellow thespians, I communicated this change of roles by walking over to the side and switching costumes—in this case, from a baseball cap to a wig.

The little ones sat on the floor in rapt attention. We got to the part of the play where Queen Esther has to make her great decision. Haman has tricked King Ahashuerus into agreeing to hurt all the Jews, and Mordecai has tipped off Esther. But what to do? Should she save her marriage and her life by remaining silent, or should she reveal her Jewish identity, try to save her people, but risk everything else? To try to help the little ones appreciate her quandary, in my Queen Esther wig, I took a step toward them and, as they say, broke the fourth wall and spoke to the audience.

"Oh dear, oh dear!" I said. "Now what shall I do? If don't tell the king I'm a Jew, all the Jews could be hurt, but if I do, the king could hurt me. I just don't know what to do."

But before I could answer my own question, one of the four-year-olds forgot he wasn't in the play and shouted, "Quick, be somebody else!"

THE LAST GIFT

The last thing that happened to me—after twenty-nine years of serving as the rabbi of a congregation.

For a man who hates good-byes, the last year at the congregation was hell. Every week, it seemed, there was another "last." There were dinners and brunches and parties and concerts and speeches and gifts and hoopla. As the calendar turned out, my last day on the job, after twenty-eight years, fell on June 30, a Friday evening. There was a professionally done documentary film shown for the first time. I presented our cantorial soloist with my *shtender,* my prayer desk, and Liza Stern, who was to become the interim rabbi, my keys to the sound system cabinet. The congregation presented me with a handcrafted music stand that, believe it or not, looks like the letter *aleph.* After the service, about six hundred thousand Jews came up to say good-bye. There was a lot of crying.

I figured, well, this is it. I guess this is last thing I will do. And before I realized what was happening, the hall was virtually empty. "C'mon, honey," I said to my wife, "I do not want the last thing I do as rabbi here be to turn off the damn lights." So I picked up my gifts, waved to the few dozen people still lingering back by the food table, and headed for the door. And then I saw him: Jim, the building superintendent. He was setting up the vacuum cleaner.

Now I've always taken some secret pride in the fact that I have enjoyed the respect of the maintenance staff and believe that a reasonable test of a rabbi's true piety is how the rabbi treats people who don't get to vote on his or her salary increases. Jim is big bear of man who tries to act tough. "Don't start, Rabbi," he said. "It's gonna be hard enough around here without you. I'm not gonna start cryin' now." I smiled. "Don't let 'em give you a hard time, Spud." Then we both embraced and wept. I figured that was it. So that's how it ends, I mused.

We walked down the darkened hallway, past the bulletin board, now devoted to news about the new rabbi search, just beside what used to be my office. Then I noticed a man standing in the shadows. As he turned around I recognized him: it was Len Sternberg. (That's what I'll call him, here.) I had done his bar mitzvah, maybe twenty-five years ago. It was a tough one. His parents were in the middle of a messy divorce. And, to make matters worse, he had some serious emotional and learning disabilities. Len had survived on the edges with menial odd jobs. Len is not exactly menacing, but he is not quite a sweetheart either. He makes people uncomfortable.

Standing in the dim light, he looked awkward, even a little frightening. From the way he was standing, it was also clear that he was holding something behind his back. Whatever it was, it was partially concealed in one of those supermarket plastic bags that he had wrapped around his wrist. In that same split second I thought two things: It's a gift. It's a gun. (I could hear Jim running the vacuum cleaner down the hall.) Oh great, he's gonna shoot me! I was tired. It was over. I was done.

"Here, Rabbi," he said—to my relief, producing an old, dog-eared, binding-broken English volume of the Torah. (It had been ready for the *geniza* twenty-five years ago.) "Don't you remember ... ?" (He should have been happy I remembered his name!) "You gave me this in your old office."

Oh my God, the kid remembers this after all these years! And then it dawned on me: he thought I had only loaned him the book. I had neglected to tell him that holy books are, by definition, *hefkayr*, ownerless; they cannot be stolen. And here he was feeling guilty for over two decades that he hadn't returned it. And tonight, tonight was his last chance: he was doing *teshuva*—making atonement!

He held out the book like a child.

"Keep it, Len, it's yours."
"Do you mean it? I can really have it?"
"Yes, Len, the Torah is yours to keep."
"Oh, thanks, Rabbi. I'll take real good care of it."
"I'm sure you will."

Karen and I walked out to the car and drove home.

2

JUDAISM

WHY I'M A JEW

IN THE DAWN OF THE TWENTY-FIRST CENTURY, with people trying on religions like shoppers trying on clothing in a bargain basement, anyone who remains a Jew must be considered a "Jew-by-choice." Unfortunately, choosing one's way over another's risks chauvinism.

Chauvinism is a distorted self-love, achieved through denigrating others, just as self-hate is a distorted love of others achieved through denigrating oneself. They are both variations of the same primary insecurity. Being a Jew may be the right and, indeed, the only viable choice for most Jews, but not because Judaism is better (or worse) than any other religion.

Look at it this way: Imagine a deck of fifty-two religious playing cards. Each one represents a different, primary religious idea such as salvation, love of neighbor, God, afterlife, guilt, charity, revelation, and the like. Any decent religion must—in order to be a religion—play with a full deck. The difference between one religion and another is the order of the cards, the stack of the deck. In one spiritual tradition the first card is "salvation," while "revelation" doesn't show up until card number forty-three. In another religion the order may be reversed. What, we must ask ourselves, would be the top cards in the Jewish deck?

To hazard an answer we must cut through centuries of apologetics. It was once fashionable, for example, to boast that Judaism gave the world ethical monotheism. The rarely challenged implication was that being the first to come up with an idea meant you owned it or excelled at it. Even worse, it implied that non-Jews were culturally or genetically inferior when it came to figuring out that there is a Holy Oneness to All Being or behaving ethically toward one another. Furthermore, if we are to include in our spectrum of Jews such diverse expressions as Ethiopian, Reform, Israeli, and Lubavitch, we cannot honestly speak of a singular or exclusive Jewish culture.

The following seem to me to be some of the "top cards" of the "Jewish deck," the core of the way we Jews have tried to make spiritual sense out of the mystery of life. They transcend geography and society. They have been with us since we bothered recording what was important. They keep appearing among Jews generation after generation. Apart from my birth, they are why I continue to be a Jew.

Not only does the God of the Jews have no image, the God of the Jews has no personal history, and no Name that can be spoken by human vocal cords. Not only is there nothing to see of this God, this is also a God who was not born, who has neither spouse nor children, and whose very name is unpronounceable. Indeed the Name itself is made from the root letters of the verb "to be" and probably means something like "the One who brings into being all that is." An unutterable Name by which we evoke the unity of all being, just this is our Lord. Nothing else. With a God like this, Judaism is not likely to become one of the world's more populous religions in the near future. But there is more.

Somehow this "Source of All Being" can "get through" to human beings or, at least, anyone who is listening. The result of this "getting through" is what we Jews call Torah. It is, you might say, a description from "the Source of All Being" of "the Way of All Being." Trying to understand Torah constitutes the highest activity of the mind, just as living in accordance with it is the highest expression of human conduct. In the words of the proverb, "She is a tree of life to those who hold fast to her" (Proverbs 3:18).

Now the content of the actual "revelation"—the one that legend says happened on Mount Sinai—was only that it is *possible* for the One of Being to "speak" with human beings. To paraphrase the philosopher Franz Rosenzweig, "And the Lord came down on Mount Sinai" happened. "And the Lord spoke," that is already human interpretation.

This same insight is echoed in another legend: Only the first letter of the first word of the first utterance was given. But that letter is *aleph*, the first letter of the alphabet, which is customarily unpronounceable. But it does not have, as many think, no sound. To be precise, it is the sound the larynx makes as it clicks into gear; it is the mother of all articulate speech; it is the softest audible sound there is. Any other noise will drown it out. This was the same sound Elijah the prophet heard when he stood on the place where Moses stood and heard the *kol d'mama daka*, the thin, barely audible sound of almost breathing (1 Kings 19:12).

This quiet sound and the sustained, silent attention that render it audible place demands on behavior. We Jews believe that such "commandments" are woven into the very warp and woof of creation. Each individual and each generation see them through unique lenses. But taken together they describe how we understand our purpose as a people. And to ignore them is more than abdicating an existential responsibility, it is a sin. This routine and unfortunate alienation from the Source of our true selves can only be repaired through the act of *teshuva.*

Teshuva is the ever-present possibility, urge, and gesture of returning to our Source, the Holy One of All Being. Through *teshuva* all life is returned to its source. As Rav Abraham Isaac Kook teaches, it flows unnoticed throughout creation. *Teshuva* is not simply apologizing or making right the damage we have done—though these surely are prerequisites. It is only this: the Return. *Teshuva* is the hardest thing in the world, for to fully make it would bring the Messiah, but it is also the easiest thing, since it has only to occur to you to make *teshuva* and you've already begun.

More than just an individual gesture, *teshuva* is a great world-yearning that flows through and animates all creation. Through attempting to repair and heal what we have done in the past, we set it within a larger context of meaning and effectively rewrite the past. What was once only some thoughtless or even wicked act now—when viewed from the perspective of our present *teshuva*—becomes only the embarrassing commencement of this greater healing now realized.

We stubbornly and despite all the evidence look forward to a time when all creation will join in the Great Return, a unity of all the world reflecting the Unitary Source of all Creation.

FILENE'S BASEMENT

READING THE COMMONLY REPEATED BIBLICAL PHRASE "You shall follow My laws, My statutes, and My ordinances," our commentators conclude that there must be three kinds of *mitzvot*.

One kind God didn't even need to tell you because you would have done it anyway. An example would be "Thou shalt not murder." "Thanks, God," we say, "but candidly I wasn't going to murder anyway." It's a freebie. Just about everyone has fulfilled one commandment: we haven't murdered anyone.

A second group of commandments are ones that we wouldn't have figured out on our own. An example of these would be "Observe Shabbos." We say, "God I'm a workaholic. I sleep so I can work; I eat so I can work. But the minute you tell me to rest every seventh day, I get it. I understand; it makes perfect sense. If I rest, I'll be able to work even better. From now on, God, you can count me in for Shabbos."

Commandments in the third category are the most problematic. They don't make sense, even once God tells us. Tradition offers as an example here what it considers to be the most unintelligible commandment of all the 613: *sha-atnez*—the Levitical prohibition against wearing garments made from a mixture of linen and wool. God says, "*Sha-atnez*," and we say, "Whaaa?"

I actually observed *sha-atnez* once. We lived in Boston for thirty years. They used to have this store there called Filene's Basement. (They sold the name; the current Filene's Basement is only a shadow of its former self.) Filene's was a high-end department store, like

Nordstrom's or Bloomingdale's—quality merchandise. What they couldn't sell upstairs on sale, they would send down to the basement. But then they would date-stamp the price tag. If something remained on the rack in the basement for seven business days, they took a quarter off the marked-down price; fourteen days, one-half off; and in the unlikely event of twenty-one days, they took off three-quarters of the already marked-down price. It was called a "triple markdown." Jews in Boston would utter this phrase with the same reverence they normally reserved for parts of the Yom Kippur liturgy: "Triple Markdown!"

Well, back in those days, I used to wear a man's thirty-seven-short sport coat. Now, if you know anything about men's clothing, you know that every year in the United States, they manufacture maybe twelve size thirty-seven-short sport coats. It's an odd size. But one day, on my monthly ritual swing through the basement, I spotted a thirty-seven short on the rack. Not only that, but it was made from a really handsome fabric. So I tried it on and it fit like it was tailor-made for me. By this point, I'm hyperventilating. Not only that, but, my god, it was a Polo Ralph Lauren that originally sold for seven hundred dollars! Then I looked at the tag and it was a triple markdown! Be still my heart; I was having a religious experience. I ran toward the cashier, but like a fool, I looked at the little statement of contents sewn into the lining and, you guessed it, it said: linen and wool.

So I put it back! [David Eisenberg, a former congregant, heard this story and said, "God looked down and said, "Schmuck! I was only kidding."]

And here's the teaching. Of the three kinds of commandments—God didn't need to tell you (don't murder); God needed to tell you before you understood (Shabbos); and even once God told you, you still don't understand (*sha-atnez*)—which one is the most satisfying to fulfill? The third—not to mix linen and wool. And why? Because you realize that there is only one possible reason you're doing it: because God wants you to.

INTERMARRIAGE

I ONCE MET A MAN AT A COCKTAIL PARTY who said he was from Iran and that he was a Zoroastrian.

"I've never met a Zoroastrian before," I said.

"That is not surprising," he explained. "There aren't many of us left."

"Why so?" I asked.

"Because we don't allow conversion."

We Jews, of course, do. But notwithstanding all our outreach initiatives and public relations braggadocio about Judaism's joys, we remain surprisingly unfocused about what constitutes being "in."

For the past few generations, Jews in the United States have understood that radical, American social freedom will inevitably lead to the wholesale assimilation of European Jewish culture. It is not at all clear, however, that such assimilation (read: intermarriage) necessarily spells the demise of Judaism. I now suspect that for our generation, intermarriage has come to mean only that a Jew and a non-Jew got married. Period. What happens to the Judaism of their progeny, the Judaism of the couple and their home, and Judaism itself on account of that intermarriage remains almost entirely up to the Jewish people.

I knew a woman who once confessed that she had been raised by fiercely antireligious and anti-Jewish Jewish parents.

"There was absolutely nothing Jewish in my home when I was a child," she said.

"But then how did you even know you were a Jew?" I asked.

"When I was growing up, we lived with my maternal grandfather, and every six months or so, when the two of us wound up home alone, he would take me down to the basement where he was sure no one could hear, sit me in a chair, and say to me, 'Don't tell your parents. You are a Jew; never forget!' Then we would come upstairs. And that," she said, "was the sum total of my Jewish education."

"Perhaps you'd like to attend the introduction to Judaism class we offer for prospective Jews?"

"Do you think I need to convert?" she asked.

"No. But you may want to learn a bit more about who you are."

For centuries we Jews have been preoccupied—some would argue, obsessed—with the creation and maintenance of bright lines, definitions, and boundaries. Indeed, some have suggested that this is the primary enterprise of Rabbinic Judaism: kosher or *treif*, Shabbos or weekday, holy or profane, and, of course, Jew or non-Jew. But now, at the dawn of the twenty-first century, such projects often seem inappropriate and even counterproductive. The definitions and the boundaries that have served the Jewish people so well and for so long now threaten to destroy us. Judaism and Jews are simply no longer surrounded by a bright line. Instead we find ourselves encircled by a fluid border. I offer this not as a normative statement but as a descriptive one. It is a fact of our life. That is simply the way things are. And insisting that it is not so, unfortunately, will not change anything.

"Yes, but is she a Jew?" we reflexively want to ask, in the same way that people once asked of an Alexander Calder mobile, "Yes, but is it art?" The answer to both questions may be the same, "Sometimes we just have to wait and see." Some categories are open-ended. Sometimes certainty is not an option. We cannot provide, in advance, all the necessary and sufficient conditions for membership in them. Most of us now are inclined to suspect that someone who was not born a Jew but who has married a Jew and devoted his or her life to making a Jewish home and raising Jewish children but who has refrained from formally converting, say, out of respect to a non-Jewish parent, is not exactly a non-Jew.

It is coincidentally fascinating that there seems to have been little discussion about when someone has stopped being a Jew. Can you, for instance, still be Jew and a Buddhist? Why? Why not? Can you still be a Jew if Jesus is your personal savior? Why? Why not? Many Jews are surprised to learn that renunciation of God has no effect whatsoever on their status as Jews. Is simply being born of a Jewish mother but not being raised or educated in any way as a Jew enough, at the beginning of the twenty-first century, to be a Jew?

I converted a man (who was already married to a Jew) whose last name was Fitzpatrick.

"But Rabbi," he said, "'Fitzpatrick' isn't a Jewish name."

I said, "It will be."

I now suspect that Jews in America, for better or worse, are no longer a people in any meaningful sense of that word. There are no longer any functional public social signifiers for who is a Jew: not family name, facial structure, hair color, ethnic style, taste, profession, incidence of alcoholism, spousal abuse, not even much of a shared politics or value system. Like it or not, Judaism in America seems to have become the religion of a very extended family. This doesn't make me happy either. But just saying it ain't so will not alter current religious and social reality.

On Sunday morning, January 1, 1905, Emogene Vinton Edwards, a twenty-five-year-old Presbyterian woman with long blonde hair, from Kalamazoo, Michigan—almost five years after her elopement with a Jewish traveling salesman, Max Edwards—walked down the main aisle of Temple Beth El in Detroit and, in the presence of the entire congregation, publicly became a Jew. Rabbi Leo M. Franklin explained in the newspaper account that "the ceremony usually takes place in the home of the convert [so] ... the announcement that it would be performed publicly drew a large congregation.... 'Conversions with us are more or less rare because we seek to discourage proselytizing of any kind on the ground that we do not teach that men must belong to Judaism to be saved.'" Emogene Vinton Edwards was my grandmother. Both of her grandsons are rabbis, and so is her great-granddaughter.

Nothing in our cultural repertoire, not the Golden Age in Spain, Islamic tolerance, or nineteenth-century Germany, has offered anything like the radical social and religious freedom of twenty-first-century America. Previous civilizations may have allowed us internal freedom, but we always remained surrounded by invisible walls of distrust, hatred, and potential persecution. Now that there are no ghetto walls, all Jews are Jews-by-choice.

Obviously, any group of people compelled to live in close physical proximity for a few centuries will create an intense and unique culture. But do we really believe that Judaism's salvation can come only from social isolation? Other great world spiritual traditions certainly have survived "among the nations" and continue to flourish without segregation. To be sure, ghettoization remains a viable option to this day, although very few of us have chosen to move to Mea Shearim in Jerusalem or Monsey, New York. The question is not whether to assimilate but how to Judaize what we take in.

I served a congregation for thirty years. And, while I never officiated at an intermarriage, I was often comforted that many of my colleagues had. Their decision had brought us (or kept) some of our very best Jews. Once, for example, I helped a man convert to Judaism because his wife had died. You see, she was a Jew, and together they had agreed to raise their two sons as Jews. A few weeks after the funeral, he showed up in my office and said that, in order to be true to her memory and his promise, he now had to become a Jew.

Some claim that the more emancipated and prosperous the Jews become, the more impoverished and threatened Judaism becomes. We American Jews are more emancipated, prosperous, and successful than we could have ever imagined. We are also less educated about many things Jewish, but we are also more educated about others. But let us not lose sight of one important fact: we are still here—building new rabbinic seminaries, starting congregations, federations, community centers, schools, and publishing houses.

As a congregational rabbi, I used to take groups of families away for a weekend each semester prior to upcoming *b'nai mitzvah*. In each crop, as you might imagine, there were at least one and sometimes several intermarried couples. And, on every weekend, I would make it a point to chat privately with all of the non-Jews and ask them why, since they were raising their children as Jews, they hadn't formally converted to Judaism. And virtually every one, in one way or another, said the same thing: "Because no one ever asked me." So, I would ask. And, in this way, each weekend we would invariably make a few new Jews.

We now have enough data to say categorically that there is simply no way to stop vast numbers of Jews from marrying non-Jews. Fierce rabbinic bans are risibly ineffective. Insulting forms of covert ostracism only make us look xenophobic and weak. And insisting that we are a people but with no publicly identifiable characteristics makes us look either racist or stupid. Spiritual and cultural strength is measured not by rigidity or power, but by the vitality and flexibility of the response. I believe that that is what we, whom Simon Radowicz once called "the ever-dying people," must consider when we survey the past century and contemplate the next.

We seem so terrified that a Jew might fall in love with someone who is not a Jew that we often forget that, each year, hundreds of thousands of non-Jews also fall in love with, marry, and have children with Jews. They may not (yet) be willing (or able) to become Jews, but they have, with their very lives, thrown in their lot with us. They are, whether we like it or not, members of our extended family. This is simply "a fact on the ground." And truth be told, if we want, we can probably have most of them as Jews.

I say: Bring 'em in. Conversions, especially for those who have already thrown in their lot with the Jewish people, should be an easy and routine process. Living with and loving a Jew should certainly be worth, at least, a semester of Introduction to Judaism credits (and probably also ensure a seat at the table in the *olam haba*—the world to come).

A few years ago I was invited to serve on a *beit din* (rabbinical court) for a conversion. The young woman hadn't intended to convert before her wedding because the groom's rabbi had said it was a long and serious process, and the groom himself, wanting to respect her religious integrity, didn't want to exert any undue pressure. I had run into them at a party six months earlier, where I got to ask my question: "Why don't you join us?" She looked at me and said, "Do you really mean it?"

Now she was on the other side of the closed door standing in the waters of the *mikveh*. As her sponsoring rabbi had urged, she had memorized the blessings and the *Shema* so she could recite them as part of the ceremony. Together with the other rabbinic witnesses, I stood in the hall as her sponsor asked her to recite the declaration of God's unity. But to my surprise, she didn't recite it; she sang it—from there, in the waters, she sang about how our God is One.

GETTING MORE JEWS

FOR TWO THOUSAND YEARS A JEW HAS BEEN DEFINED as anyone born of a Jewish mother or who became a Jew-by-choice. Reform Judaism extended this definition to include someone born of a Jewish father. But it has not worked and neither have our redoubled efforts at outreach. We Jews remain only a tiny fraction of the world's population. Entire neighborhoods in San Francisco are still predominantly Christian.

It is time to take the next logical step. If conversion is too strenuous and having only one Jewish parent still insufficient to boost Jewish population, then we have no choice. We must consider admitting people into Judaism who neither have any Jewish parents nor have undergone conversion. Whereas, in the past, there were either Jews-by-birth or Jews-by-choice, now it is time for: Jews-by-surprise.

We might begin by simply taking names at random from the white pages of the phone book. Just imagine their surprise upon receiving a registered letter informing them of their new religious status:

> *Shalom!*
> *We the board of directors of the Congregation Emanu-El at our last meeting unanimously selected you (and your entire nuclear family) to become Jews-by-surprise.*

Housewife, opening the morning's mail, drops everything and gasps.

"What's the matter, Chastity?" her husband dotingly asks.

"Skylar, we're Jews!"

"Oh God, not the children, too?"

"Yes, all of us."

"*Oy vey!*"

"See what I mean … "

The letter continues:

No matter how ridiculous you consider this decision, there are already tens of thousands of born Jews who know and do less than you do. Even if you are an avowed anti-Semite, relax, there are already many Jews like you, too.

This decision is irrevocable. Once a Jew, always a Jew. Neither changing your name, fixing your nose, nonpayment of any temple dues or charges will release you from your guilt nor exempt you from being solicited by the United Jewish Appeal for the rest of your life.

In order to maintain the traditional denominational spread, you will notice that the lower right-hand corner of your letter has been marked with either an "R," a "C," or a "U." Memorize your movement and then eat the lower right-hand corner of your letter—except in the case where your letter has "U," in which case, please wait three hours before eating it. If your "U" is enclosed in a little circle, wait six hours. And if you only have a lowercase "r," you may eat the whole letter without even reciting a blessing.

Please do not be alarmed by certain changes in mannerism or temperament such as talking with your hands, craving Chinese food, feelings of conflict toward Israeli politicians, heightened anxiety in the presence of your mother, yearning to purchase clothing at discount stores, and if you are a man, the gradual disappearance of your foreskin.

In conclusion, let us say, Mazel tov! *It will be an honor to collect your money even if we never see you again—except, of course, on Purim.*

CUSTOMS AS SACRED TEXT

LIKE ALL REVEALED RELIGIONS, Judaism is classically taught by expounding sacred text. But the weekly Torah portion is more than merely the next chapter in an unfolding saga or the touchstone for homiletics; its literary, legal, theological, and mythic rhythms serve as menu and master outline for every conceivable moral and religious topic. There is, however, another, less well-known, yet equally potent didactic tradition.

In addition to scripture, over the centuries, Jews have also come to "read" the customs surrounding the fasts and festivals of their religious calendar as a kind of second sacred text. Rabbinic study Bibles, collections of Hasidic teachings, and contemporary "sermonica" all routinely intersperse holiday teachings *within* the cycle of the weekly lectionary. In this way, *minhagim*, or customs, are effectively transformed into what we could reasonably call another mode of revelation. Indeed, as Scott-Martin Kosofsky once suggested to me, these inseparable, twin strands of scripture and custom create a double helix of Jewish life-learning. And the "other" Torah of the holiday cycle is also to be plumbed, expounded, and comprehended. But this second sacred text of liturgy and custom differs from its scriptural twin in one deliciously interactive way: it is not fixed.

There are myriad legends about arguments among the sages over the correct interpretation of the scriptural law. One genre is especially instructive here. According to one legend, the dispute was about when the actual appearance of the first sliver of the new moon of the month of Tishri (and therefore the onset of Rosh Hashanah and, with it, the commencement of the entire yearlong sacred calendar) was visible. Since it was daytime, however, the moon could not be seen. In desperation the scholars sought divine guidance, but to their astonishment, the heavenly voice only replied, "Why do you ask Me? Go outside and see [in Aramaic: *pok hazi*] what the Jews are doing!" And, sure enough, when they looked outside, they saw the Jews carrying flowers for their celebration of the New Year. And, from this, the sages concluded that the New Year indeed must have begun. In the words of the rabbinic maxim: *Minhag avoteinu Torah hi,* "The custom of our parents is [also] the way."

This legend and others like it transmit a primary principle of Judaism: what the Jews wind up doing as they attempt to negotiate, comprehend, and live by God's laws attains independent and authentic religious status. Somehow, the Jewish people, through trying to lead sacred lives and make ends meet, are mysteriously, despite themselves, inescapably drawn to what God wants them to do. This is certainly not a matter of privilege or superiority but an expression of vocation and obligation. And just this is the reason that the Jews regard their customs and ceremonies as subjects to be studied, expounded, and taught. For not only do they teach us about who we are, they are a window into the sacred! You might say, in this way, that scripture is from the top down (from God to the Jews), while the customs that flower around God's laws are from the bottom up (from the Jews to God). The Torah tells the Jews about God; the *minhagim* (customs) tell God about the Jews.

Consider two examples. For a rabbi to expound the meaning of the custom of breaking of glass at the conclusion of a wedding is as appropriate as expounding a passage from Song of Songs. For a rabbi to draw religious lessons from the fact that Jews customarily have two *hallot* (braided loaves of egg bread) at the Sabbath table is as acceptable as interpreting the laws of Sabbath observance themselves. Such an attitude toward *minhagim* may also effectively serve to balance any overly rigid reading of Jewish legal tradition. (Sure, God says do it this way; but this is how we do it.)

Dr. Lawrence Hoffman of the Hebrew Union College–Jewish Institute of Religion, noting the fixity of scripture and the fluidity of liturgy, once suggested that Torah is our head but the prayer book and, by extension, the festival calendar and the life-cycle ceremonies marking the passages of life of each Jew are our heart. Torah's vitality comes from its lability. Responding to the unanticipatable exigencies of each new generation, the holiday observances and life-cycle customs sway and dance to the melodies of each new generation.

Most Jews know about Joseph Karo's monumental legal code the *Shulchan Arukh* (The Set Table) and that it is the apogee of Jewish law. Far fewer know that, because it was based on Sephardic (Spanish-Portuguese) practice, the *Shulchan Arukh* remained unacceptable to Ashkenazic (German) Jews—half of world Jewry—until Moses Isserles published his extensive commentary the *Mapa* (The Tablecloth), which incorporated their customs into the legal system. In this way, we are reminded that customs are the mechanism through which the divine will can be comprehended and practiced in lived lives. And that mechanism is unequivocally populist.

As many observers have noticed, Judaism is less a religion than it is a people, a folk. And because Judaism is a people, then what the Jewish people does acquires a theological dimension. Ordinary Jews—as far as Judaism is concerned anyway—possess an almost ontic status. They enjoy a mode of being beyond their individual, personal identities; they are *am Yisroael*, the people of Israel; they are an *am kadosh*, a holy people. Somehow, when it comes to intuitively knowing what Judaism truly requires, they seem to have an inside track. And, while it routinely drives Jewish teachers and compilers of *minhagim* to annoyance and distraction, this includes even uninspired, boorish, and illiterate Jews as well. And this sets up another double helix: on one hand we have rabbinic authorities expounding divine law, and on the other, we have ordinary people leading ordinary lives. Neither could survive alone!

In addition to the 613 commandments that symbolically represent the definitive catalogue of what God wants, there are seven more that are found nowhere in the Torah (lighting Sabbath candles, observing Hanukkah, reciting blessings of enjoyment, washing the hands, reading the *Megilla*, singing the psalms of *Hallel*, and setting Sabbath boundaries). These customs, nevertheless, have been elevated to the status of scriptural commandment. In this way, some observers have suggested that *minhagim* that have been in force for five hundred years are raised to the status of law, even as laws in force for five hundred years are themselves raised to the status of divine(!) commandments. The theologian Eugene Borowitz, noting a widespread social custom in the liberal Jewish community, for example, observes that it now seems to have become a religious law that, with the sweet feeling that fills the room upon the conclusion of a Sabbath eve service, you must kiss the person sitting next to you.

You might say that *minhagim* or customs are proto-*mitzvot*, commandments in utero.

TWO JEWISH MOTHERS

When the executive director of the Central Conference of American Rabbis learned that I had officiated at the first commitment ceremony of two Jewish lesbians in the Commonwealth of Massachusetts, he invited me to share with my colleagues how I reached my decision to do so. I went through a lengthy and serious religious process—talking with my colleagues, reading a lot, and more than one meeting with the board of directors of my congregation who (God bless them all) voted to support my decision unanimously.

THERE ARE, OF COURSE, MYRIAD ARGUMENTS that space does not permit me to rehearse. In the final analysis, however, as I reflect back on it, the actual decision for me turned out to be surprisingly simple.

A decade before my decision, I had got myself into an argument with an Orthodox friend. To tell the truth, I have forgotten most of the details. It had something to do with how to treat someone. I explained my position; he explained his. His position struck both of us as, at best, ethically tenuous. "How can you say such a thing?" I asked.

"I have no choice," he replied. "It's the halakha—Jewish law."

Not wishing to be disrespectful, I allowed him to have the last word. But later, alone in the car, I found myself continuing the argument:

"Oh, and because you claim you have no choice, that's the end of it? You're off the hook? I'm supposed to cave in, back away in shame before the tradition? No [I wished I would have said], you *choose* to believe what you want, and you *choose* to do what you do. First comes life, *then* comes law. You are still responsible. You cannot hide behind anything. Since when does religious tradition permit you to short-circuit any morally uncomfortable decision? Since when does serving the Nameless One absolve you of justifying the behavior you have freely chosen?"

And then and there I promised myself that I would forever forswear resorting to such an argument.

The test of my resolve came a few years later when two members of my congregation asked me if I would help them consecrate their—what shall I call it? union? commitment?—gimme a break, it was a *marriage*. What could I say? "I'm not permitted?" "I'm sorry the tradition doesn't allow it?" "My hands are tied?" "Excuse me while I hide in a book?"

Of course the tradition is sacred; of course it has more to do with God than any of us can imagine; but it can never be an excuse for not looking another human being in the eyes or oneself in the mirror. So, I said to that couple (who, by the way, has since brought two Jewish children into the world), "Yes, it will be an honor to help you sanctify [and by that word I meant *kiddushin*, marriage] your lives together."

It felt pretty scary then, but it felt right. Now it just feels right. I guess I believe, in retrospect, that it was commanded of me.

(RE)THINKING SHABBAT

"AND GOD SAW ALL THAT GOD HAD MADE and behold it was very good.... *Va-y'khulu ha-shamayim v'ha-aretz*, the heaven and the earth were finished ... " (Genesis 1:31–2:1).

At last the world-work was done and it was good. It was very good. A beautiful place. But being done and very good are not the same as perfect.

God had decided, you see, as a final creative act to make men and women. And we are not perfect. We are the unstable element, the restless ones. Too hungry for our own good, covetous, oversexed, neurotic, and conflicted. But we are part of creation, so therefore, on account of us, creation is incomplete, unstable, and imperfect.

"And on the seventh day God rested, *va-yinafash*" (Exodus 31:17), which Rabbi Arthur Waskow does not translate as "and was refreshed" but as "and God said, '*Whew!*'" Now if God can do something as imperfect as setting you and me up in business in the world-garden and then rest, surely we can be excused from our six-day-a-week compulsive fantasies of perfection and rest as well. To help, I offer three metaphors that I have found useful in my attempts to reclaim Shabbat. The first begins on Passover.

My grandfather was a German Reform Jew. We would prepare for Passover by taking any leaven (which we defined as bread and cereal) in our home and quarantining it in an off-limits cupboard. We were conscientious, but we were also human and oversights did occur. I remember how, once, a few days into Passover, we discovered a box of Wheaties that my younger brother or I, weeks earlier, must have left in an unlikely place and forgotten.

"Look, Grandpa, some *hometz* we missed. What should we do?"

"What *hometz*?" he said, staring right at the silent, evil box of "the Breakfast of Champions."

"This one here," I said, pointing.

"I don't see it," he replied.

And I understood.

You do the best you can, but when the deadline comes, whether or not you are finished, you are done. Traditional Passover Haggadahs preserve a similar mechanism for freeing oneself from obsessive-compulsive behavior. We conclude our search for leaven, the morning before Seder, with the Aramaic formula, "*Kol hamira*, all leaven in my possession, whether or not I have seen it, disposed of it, or even know about it, *no longer exists*. I declare it to be ownerless, *k'afra d'ara*, like dust of the earth."

Work, you might say, is to Shabbat like *hometz* is to Pesach. Come twilight on Friday afternoon I make a similar announcement. "All my jobs, tasks, and work, whether they are done or not, I hereby declare are done. I reject their claim on me. I deny their existence." On Shabbos, I can look right at a job that needs to be finished and not even see it!

Indeed, we recite the first paragraph of the second chapter of Genesis just before we make *Kiddush* at home. It begins: "*Va-y'khulu*, the heaven and the earth were finished," which the Talmud (*Shabbat* 119b) deliberately mistranslates, not as the passive "*Va-y'khulu*, and they [the heaven and the earth] were finished," but in the active voice: "*Va-y'khulu*, and they [God and humanity] finished." Partners in creation. Partners also in saying, "We finished."

Abraham Joshua Heschel taught us that the Sabbath is a sanctuary in time, and I would suggest that the reason is because ordinary time has come to an end. Life goes on—but without the clocks. For not only have we closed the books on the past week, we don't care about next week either. On Shabbat there can be no future; only an eternal present.

Without a future, everything we do and the reasons for every-thing we do can only be here and now. If the world-work is at last done, then you cannot do anything toward making it better later because *there is no later*. Shabbat is a daylong spiritual fiction by which we are permitted to stop planning, preparing, investing, con-niving, evaluating, fixing, manipulating, arranging, staging, and all the other things we do, not for the sake of doing them, but with an ulterior motive for the sake of some future accomplishment.

Most of us can forget the past and its imperfections with some practice, but to cut ourselves loose from planning and evaluating and fixing things for the future is unimaginable. We rest so we can go back to work. We play so that we can go back to work. We love so that we can go back to work. One ulterior motive after another. Living in the future.

We are either tied through our uncompleted tasks to the past or compulsively drawn, through our need to complete them, into the future. We stubbornly convince ourselves that all we need to find tranquility is to haul a little bit of past into the present or take just a little bit of the present and arrange it for the future. On Shabbat we do not have to go anywhere; we are already there. On Shabbat we do not have to do anything; it is already done.

We need a way to describe liberal Jews who are serious about Shabbat. *Shomer Shabbat*, "keeper of Shabbat," based, as it is, on the language of the actual commandment in Deuteronomy, could be ideal. Unfortunately the phrase has been appropriated and defined, meticulously and oppressively, by someone else. So we return to the text of the fourth commandment and realize that it is said twice, once in Deuteronomy and again in Exodus. In Deuteronomy (5:12) we are told, "*Shamor*, keep the Sabbath." But in Exodus (20:8) the verb is dif-ferent. There, we are told, "*Zakhor*, remember the Sabbath." Perhaps it is for us to create a new standard of Shabbat behavior called *zakhor Shabbat*. One who is *zokhaer Shabbat* would remember throughout the day's duration that it was Shabbat. (Not so easy as it sounds.) We say to one another, "Do anything you like—as long as you remember it is Shabbat," because that will ensure that whatever you do will be *lich-vod-ha-Shabbat*, "for the honor of Shabbat."

KOSHER

IT WAS JULY 11, 1883, AFTER THE GRADUATION CEREMONIES of the Hebrew Union College in Cincinnati. Isaac Mayer Wise, the founder of Reform Judaism, attempting to bridge the deepening rift between the Hoch Deutsch (High German), assimilated American Reform Jews, and the hordes of newly arriving Eastern European traditionalists, arranged a banquet at the Highland House, overlooking the Ohio River, for delegates from all over the country. The repast was supervised by a non-Jewish caterer. He meant to make it special but succeeded so well that he also made it historic. Without charge, the caterer threw in littleneck clams, soft-shell crabs, and shrimp salad. The traditionalists, of course, fled the restaurant in horror. And the ill-fated luncheon came to be known as the "*treife* banquet." Indeed, it served as an impetus for the creation of what has come to be Conservative Judaism.

Wise disdained to offer either explanation or apology. But ever since then, in one way or another, kashrut has been a problem for Reform Jews.

Maybe we should look at it again? Relax. I'm not going to tell you that you have to keep *glatt* kosher, but maybe it is time to reconsider what we put in our mouths. Let's start with *treif*.

The Hebrew root *taraf* (*tet, resh, fey*) means: "to prey upon" (like a raptor animal), to tear into pieces and, hence, that which is left over after an animal has been torn to pieces, carrion or, even better, simply "roadkill." *Treif* comes to mean, therefore, that which is unfit for Jews to eat.

Let me ask it this way: would you eat the most delicious thing in the world, medically certified to be germ-free and nutritious, if it were roadkill? I hope not. And I hope that the reasons that it is disgusting are because what it is (or was) and the conditions under which it died are *relevant* to your decision of whether or not to take it into your mouth, into your body, to make it part of your living substance.

We are not, in other words, here talking about what tastes good or even what may be good for you. We are talking about what you want your body to be made of and how your awareness of what your body is made of affects how you think of yourself and how you behave.

This notion is so important it is reiterated in three separate places in the Torah. You will notice that in each instance eating is accompanied with a second idea.

Exodus 22:30, "And you shall be holy unto Me; therefore you shall not eat any flesh that is torn of beasts in the field; you shall cast it to the dogs."

Deuteronomy 14:21, "You shall not eat any thing that dies by itself … for you are a holy people unto the Lord your God."

And, in *Parashat Shemini*, we get the whole kazoo:

Leviticus 11:44–45, "Sanctify yourselves and be holy, for I am holy; neither shall you defile yourselves with any manner of swarming thing that moves upon the earth."

We are talking, in other words, about sanctifying how we live.

So this old Jew dies and goes to heaven. While he's waiting in the dining room (where else?), he notices a telescope over in the corner that he aims and focuses down on the netherworld. And there he spies all his old friends having what could only be called a *treife* banquet of every imaginable forbidden food. God comes out and sets in front of him a plate of tuna fish. Surprised and disappointed, the Jew says, "What kind of deal is this? Down there they get to eat all kinds of *treif*. But me, I spend my whole life following every detail of the laws of kashrut and my reward is a lousy plate of tuna fish?"

God shrugs and says, "For just you and me, it doesn't pay to cook."

I can identify six classical reasons for keeping kosher. The first one quickly collapses but it still enjoys wide currency.

Kashrut is for health. This one is especially popular among Jews who *don't* keep kosher. They reason that, since trichinosis was once spread by eating tainted pork, Jews of old were forbidden to eat it. But now (and watch the logic here), since we have the FDA to take care of our health, we may eat whatever we like.

Rabbi Isaac Abarbanel, the fifteenth-century Portuguese commentator, demolished the medical argument thus: "God forbid that I should believe that the reason for forbidden foods is medicinal! For were it so, the Torah would be in the same class as any of the minor brief medial books.... Furthermore, our own eyes see that people who eat pork and insects and such ... are well and alive and healthy at this very day.... Moreover, there are more dangerous animals which are not ... prohibited" (Isaac Klein, *A Guide for Jewish Practice* [Jersey City: KTAV, 1979], p. 302).

The second argument is worthy of more serious attention. Kashrut serves to keep us distinct *from* other peoples and therefore in closer proximity *with* other Jews. If the only place you can get your food is from a Jewish kitchen, then you hang around *Jewish* kitchens.

A third consideration I would call: Garbage in, garbage out. You are what you eat. A member of my former congregation once told me that when he went off to the University of Michigan as a young man, he announced to his Orthodox father that he no longer intended to keep kosher while at school. His father was incredulous.

"You mean you'll only eat what tastes good."

"That's right, Dad,"

"But then," replied his father, "what's the difference between you and a horse?"

Rabbi Samuel Dresner offers one of the most elegant arguments. The purpose of kashrut, he suggests, is to instill in Jews a reverence for living creatures. The kosher laws represent a *compromise* between an ideal vegetarianism and our ineluctable carnivorous appetites. They offer rules and regulations that protect humans from being brutalized as well as help us approach all living things with awe and respect.

The fifth argument I would call: The control of desire. The goal here is learning how to make distinctions and exercise discipline. Maimonides says, "These ordinances seek to train us in the mastery of our appetites. They accustom us to restrain both the growth of desire and the disposition to consider the pleasure of eating as the end all of a person's existence" (*Guide for the Perplexed* 3:48). Observing kashrut is a daily proclamation that we are in control of our most primary appetite.

The last insight, my favorite, sees the function of kashrut as the sanctification of the physical.

Eating is *the* primary volitional act of keeping yourself alive. It forcibly reminds us several times a day that we are physical creatures. Judaism, unlike Christianity or Buddhism, sees sanctification of life in *this* world as the primary spiritual task *and* the primary spiritual goal. And thus, in the very act of taking nourishment into our bodies, we are reminded of our task and goal to sanctify this world. Of all life's necessary functions—breathing, sleeping, procreation—eating may just be the one over which we can ritualize our yearning for holiness.

Woody Allen: Man goes to his rabbi and asks, "Rabbi, why are we forbidden to eat pork?"

"We are? Uh-oh!"

Like so much in contemporary Jewish life, serious liberal Judaism demands that we reclaim territory once surrendered to Orthodoxy. The war is over and I have good news: we won. The simple proof is that we are still here. But for too long now our chronic insecurity and, yes, occasional illiteracy have led us to abandon much of our own sacred tradition. Just because some Orthodox Jews do some things in ways we find obsessive, punctilious, or offensive does not mean we are therefore exempt from the whole package. Orthodox Jews are *shomer Shabbos* but that does not mean we cannot or should not try to observe Shabbos too. Orthodoxy may have strict or *glatt* kosher, but that doesn't therefore mean that our only other option is roadkill *treif*.

We need a contemporary and Reform definition of kosher permitting us to revere and sanctify eating without enslaving us to sixteenth-century technology. Many serious Reform Jews commonly refrain from eating pork or shellfish, they do not mix meat and milk, yet they are not strict about dishes when they eat outside their homes. Many of us have furthermore begun to fashion an additional de facto series of prohibitions, including such things as MSG or non-union grapes, that seem to us to desanctify life and must therefore also be defined as *treif*. But we have not yet come up with a way to describe such a widespread liberal mode of observance. I once suggested in *Moment* magazine we call it "kosher America."

In one sense, of course, kosher is unattainable. As the old adage says, "No matter how kosher you are, there's always someone who won't eat in your kitchen." Better instead to think of kosher as a perpetually evolving approach to eating or what I would call "doing business with kosher." I am convinced that you cannot be a serious Reform Jew and simply blow off kosher. It may not be the first or even the second topic on your religious agenda, and your solution may vary dramatically from your neighbor's, but sooner or later, it's going to come up. (And I hope it comes up as a topic tonight at supper.)

To conclude this mischievous invitation to reconsider what you put into your mouths, I offer twelve, ascending levels of kashrut. But since we must make a distinction between home and away, you wouldn't be the first Jew in history to be more observant at home than when you are on the road. So, I suppose, you could say there are twenty-four. (Remember, hypocrisy is when you lie and claim you keep kosher in ways you don't.)

1. Don't eat limbs from a living creature.

2. Don't eat dead animals you find in the woods.

3. Even though it's packed with nutrients, don't eat blood.

4. No matter how good you think it might taste, don't eat roadkill.

5. Don't eat anything that seems disgusting because of how it looks, how it eats, or how it died.

6. Don't eat shellfish.

7. Don't eat pork.

8. Don't eat meat that has not been slaughtered in a kosher way.

9. Don't eat meat and milk in the same dish.

10. Don't eat meat before milk.

11. Or skip numbers 1 through 10 and just quit eating meat altogether.

12. Consider *increasing* your personal list of *treif* foods in light of their impact on society, the environment, and your health.

Look, I don't know if God cares about what I eat, but I know that I feel closer to God when I care about what I eat.

THE LIFE OF TORAH

ONE OF THE HAPPIER PARTS OF MY JOB as the rabbi of a congregation was making guest appearances in the preschool. Being a conscientious teacher, I would initially prepare short lesson plans. But then it dawned on me: I could tell them anything and they had never heard it! "Abraham was the first Jew," and they'd say, "Wow! What's a Jew?" They were, in other words, a fairly easy group to teach.

A few years ago, as Rosh Hashanah and Yom Kippur approached, the preschool teacher asked me, instead of visiting their classroom, to give the children a tour of the prayer hall. I intended to talk to the children about why their parents would all want to be in the same room at the same time. Then, for the pièce de résistance, I planned to open the floor-to-ceiling curtains at the front of the room that covered the ark—the chest containing the handwritten Torah scrolls of the Five Books of Moses. Then I would remove one scroll, open it on the reader's desk, and invite the children up onto the bima, where they could look inside and, if their hands were clean, they could pet the white part of the parchment. (It's what we educators call an "affective lesson.") Initially, things went as planned, but before I realized it, the time must have got away from me. I saw the teacher at the back of the room discreetly signaling that school was almost over. Parents soon would be arriving. My time was up.

Not wanting to rush through removing the Torah scrolls from the ark, I decided, instead, to postpone this for a later session. "Next week, boys and girls, when we meet again, I'll open these curtains and show you something very special inside." They all said, "Shalom, Rabbi," and, like little ducklings, followed their teacher back to their classroom.

The next morning, their teacher showed up in my office with the following story. Apparently, the preceding day's hastily concluded lesson had generated a heated debate among the little people as to what exactly was behind the curtain. No one knew for sure! The teacher swears the following four answers were given. (I now suspect they may exhaust most, if not all, of the available meanings of sacred text.)

One kid, doubtless a budding nihilist, thought it would be empty. Another, with a more traditional bent, guessed that it held a Jewish holy book or something. A third, apparently a devotee of American television consumer culture, opined that "behind that curtain was a brand-new car!" But one child, the teacher recounted, explained to the rest of the class, "You're all wrong. Next week, when that rabbi man opens the curtain, there will be a giant mirror!"

Somehow, the little one already intuited the great mystery of every sacred text: it is holy because, within its words, we meet ourselves. The idea is so elegant and yet elusive that it must be rediscovered anew by each generation.

There is a fascinating passage near the end of Deuteronomy. It occurs as Moses presents the children of Israel with his swan song, his farewell speech: "And not until this day has God given you a heart to understand, eyes to see, or ears to hear. I led you through the wilderness forty years ... " (Deuteronomy 29:3–4). In other words, for the prior four decades, the children of Israel had wandered clueless through the miracles of the wilderness.

Rabbi Aryeh Lieb of Ger, one of the great Hasidic masters, recounts an interpretation he learned from his teacher, Rabbi Simha Bunam of Przysucha. The passage means that the Israelites did not understand what God did during those forty years because *everything* that happened then was unique to that particular time. There had never been anything like it before, and there would never be anything like it again. The wandering Israelites never figured out what was going on because it never dawned on them that their lives were important enough to be part of such a sacred story.

At the end of forty years however, when Moses presented them with the Torah, the Jews suddenly realized that religious history was about to be clothed in *their* deeds, made from whatever they had done. And not only just from the holy moments, but from the mundane, the wayward, even the sinful moments as well. (Indeed, this is what distinguishes the Hebrew scriptures.) As Hanan Brichto, professor of Bible at Hebrew Union College, used to quip, there's no one in the Hebrew Bible you'd want your kid to grow up to be like.

Imagine: ultimate truth, sacred text, clothed in the stories of your life. Now if you demur that the deeds of your life are simply too irreligious to be included in such a holy book, take comfort in the behavior of everyone from Adam through Joshua: murderers, lechers, liars, cheats, thieves. And the wilderness generation, that wild and wacky, zany band of irreligious forty-year wanderers—who, with their own eyes, saw the Red Sea split and Moses ascend Mount Sinai, who ate manna for breakfast and quail for supper—these were the ones who built the golden calf, denied God at every opportunity, begged to go back to Egypt, and committed adultery with every tribe they met. These exemplary spiritual specimens were privileged to have the serial rights to their life story chosen for the script of the most holy document every recorded. (So there's hope for you and me, yet.)

But, for most of us, only at the end of a lifetime of forty years do we begin to understand that even our life stories are sacred and that God has been involved all along. We reread scripture, not to learn about what happened to our ancestors, but to learn about what is happening to us. The stories of the Torah are not true because they happened, but because they happen. We open the sacred text and our hands tremble.

3

FAMILY

VISITING YOUR CHILDREN

YEARS AGO, WE VISITED OUR, THEN, RECENTLY WEDDED CHILDREN for the first time in their new, second-floor, Manhattan apartment. Karen and I were both excited and even a little nervous. We coached one another on what to say: "Remember, this is their home, not ours." "Be sure to say you like it." "Don't offer any advice unless they ask for it." It was a hot August afternoon, the windows were wide open, and the buzzer hadn't been installed yet, so, as instructed, we stood out on the street and, like kids hoping for someone to come out and play, we hollered their names.

We'd already been warned that there were still wedding presents stacked among the mover's boxes, so instead of another housewarming gift, we chose something we hoped would be more practical. We brought them a tool kit and a cordless power drill. Since the tool set included a utility knife—following an old family superstition that warns against giving a loved one a gift that might symbolically sever the relationship—I insisted that my son-in-law give me a penny, thereby purchasing the knife instead.

I suppose there's no escape. The first time the parents visit the children, it's a big deal for *each* generation—certainly for the kids, but also for the parents. Sure the parents have been through it already themselves when they were young. But they've never been through such a visit *as parents*. And, when viewed from the other side, it's a totally different experience.

I'm beginning to realize that no matter how much you've lived or how old you get, you're always just a kid again doing something important and sacred for the first time.

This all reminded me of the first time my wife's parents visited us, over thirty years ago, in Cincinnati, in our first apartment. I realize now that we were too self-preoccupied and too anxious that our parents approve of our home for it to even dawn on us that this must have been a very big event for them, too.

(Only a few months earlier, Karen's mother had confided that her husband, my father-in-law, his memory is a blessing, had been more than a little concerned. Yes, he liked me, but our engagement had been so short. He was worried that his only daughter, his youngest child, might have made a mistake.)

Without ever deliberately planning it, Karen and I just *happened* to take turns waiting at the window for their car to arrive in the parking lot, one floor below. And the minute it did, we were downstairs before they could even open the doors. Within minutes, Karen was off talking to her mother at speeds rivaling contemporary Internet data transmission, and I was left alone with my new father-in-law. As he finished removing the last package, he looked into the eyes of this young man who had carried off his baby and then, reaching deeper into the shadows of the trunk, produced a small package in a plain, brown paper bag.

Never a loquacious man, he just handed it to me and said, "Here … It's for your cold."

"But I don't have a cold, Charles," I replied. "I feel fine."

He only smiled and winked.

Inside the package was bottle of Seagram's Crown Royal blended whiskey. It was what all the Jewish men in Detroit used to drink. As I remember that wink now, it is clear to me that this was his way of saying, "We are men together now, you and I. I hope you will accept me as I accept you."

UNDERSTANDING YOUR PARENTS

WHAT IS IT ABOUT GRADUATION CEREMONIES that seems to attract parents? Like ants around spilled jelly, overnight they begin to swarm. No sooner does society pronounce you a new kind of person than your family (or their memory) shows up. Here you are, finally licensed to break free from earth orbit and they bring out your parents. My God, these are the last people you want around. If you let them, they'll probably put your doctoral dissertation on the refrigerator. What's going on?

Bamidbar—arguably one of the most boring scriptural lections in the entire Pentateuch—alludes to this same situation. (I'm not making this up.) It's from the Book of Numbers and begins with what sounds suspiciously like the half-time marching band instructions for the children of Israel in the wilderness: this is who is supposed to be there; this is where everyone is supposed to stand, etc., etc.

"And the Lord spoke to Moses in the wilderness of Sinai ... after they left the land of Egypt, saying: Take a census of ... the people ... " (Numbers 1:1–2). And then, get this, in verse 52, almost as if the text were describing some kind of early Nabatean, proto-college-graduation ceremony: "And the people ... shall pitch their tents, *ish al ma-kha-neyhu*, each person by his or her own family camp, *v'ish al diglo*, and each person under his or her own flag."

Right there, in that one verse, you get the whole kazoo. There are the two preconditions that *must* obtain for each person: stand with your family and stand under your own flag. Unfortunately, as anyone over the age of seven has begun to suspect, if these conditions are not mutually exclusive, they are routinely in diametric opposition. Frankly, I cannot imagine a more disjunctive situation: either you can be who your parents want you to be or you can be who you want to be, but no one has yet figured out a way to be both. I mean, if you be exactly whom your parents want, then you are heading for a humongo midlife crisis and probably worse. But, if you ignore your parents and their dreams for you, then give it up, you're just Peter Pan, maybe worse. (Although personally, right now, I cannot imagine anything worse.)

This tension has not gone unnoticed by commentators.

Isaac Meir Rothenberg Alter of Ger, a nineteenth-century Hasidic master, in his *Hiddushei ha-Rim*, first notes that these chapters from the Book of Numbers are always read in the synagogue on the Sabbath preceding the festival of Shavuot. Shavuot celebrates the giving of the Torah on Mount Sinai. This receiving of the Torah, or, as some of you might know it, the Five Books of Moses, is easily *the* defining moment for Judaism. [You may substitute here instead your own spiritual tradition's ultimate experience. It can be attaining a state of grace, satori, achieving nirvana. And, if you don't have (or want) a spiritual tradition, then receiving Torah can simply mean a time when life makes sense and you understand why you were created. For our purposes they are all pretty much the same thing.]

The Rabbi of Ger then goes on to explain that you cannot receive the divine voice, you cannot have that ultimate experience, unless you are standing in your given family place (*Itturay Torah* 5:7b). Revelation, enlightenment, satori begins, in other words, with knowing how your parents have shaped you and placed you and launched you. (*Yucch!*)

The Hasidic master Aaron Perlow of Karlin, writing a few generations earlier, on the other hand, in his *Bet Aharon*, focuses instead on the next few words and reads our verse 180 degrees in the opposite direction. For him, revelation, grace, fulfillment are only attainable once you first realize *your* essential uniqueness. "You are obligated," he teaches, "to understand that you are unique in the world. There has never been anyone like you because, if there were, there would be no need for you to exist. You are an utterly new thing in creation. Your life goal is to realize this uniqueness. And, only when everyone figures this out will the world be repaired" (*Itturay Torah* 5:21–22).

So there you have it. One guy reads the first half of the verse and says: Stand with your parents. The other guy reads the second half and says: Be your own person.

Most of us, of course, don't use the language of family encampments and standing under flags. For us today, standing with parents usually gets translated into: Why on earth do I have my parents? Of all the people in the world who might have cohabited to make a child, why did God pick my parents to make me? What in the name of God was God thinking anyway?

And the second half of our verse, standing under your own flag, becomes: What is my flag? Why am I the way I am? Of all the cockamamie combinations of talents and defects, gifts and disabilities, hopes and fears, why did I get issued the combo package I got?

Now that I think about it, maybe it's no accident that both questions are contained in the same verse. Maybe, like so many things that seem to be opposite in our world, they are intimately related, even interdependent.

Hey, it's not just kids who worry about their parents. Your parents have also begun to suspect that you might be from another galaxy and have been delivered to their home as a cosmic prank. Unfortunately, the warranty period is up and it's too late to send you back. They whisper among themselves, "Who is this kid anyway? How could he have come from us?" Don't get me wrong. Of course they love you very much and are very proud of you. It's just that they were sort of expecting somebody else.

(Now, all together: All the parents smile at your kids. Now, all the kids smile at your parents.) Stand with you parents; stand under your own flag. Why does this happen to the generations?

Let me tell you a story about my two-and-half-year-old grand-daughter, Zella. She has an amazing vocabulary and surprises us daily with new words and the inflective patterns she's picked up. (These, you understand, are the unmistakable signs of genius.) A month ago, she was playing on the floor in her room when my daughter stuck her head in the doorway to check up on her. But, before her mother could say anything, Zella only looked up and said, "Oh, good to see you, Mom." Of course it's adorable; she's my granddaughter. But it's also a very simple example of learning. The baby has learned to mimic her mother, down to the subtlest, adult linguistic pattern. Parents don't set out to teach their children how to talk. Kids just pick it up. In this way, parents become a part of their progenies.

Sometimes it's not as adorable. A few weeks ago, Zella was trying to carry four stuffed animals all at the same time and dropped them all over the floor. She surveyed the mess before her, put her hands on her little hips, and said, "Oh, *shick!*"

My point is: kids get it all, the good and the bad. And a lot of the stuff, maybe even most of the stuff, that gets transmitted from one generation to the next seems to happen below the radar of certainly the receiver and maybe even of the sender, too. We are all recipients of life-messages we don't even know we got—personality traits, dreams, social styles, fears, senses of humor, affections, tastes in music, fantasies, you name it.

As far as I can tell, there are three primary modes of generational transmission. The first is by simple explication: mom or dad just says it outright. "That's disgusting; don't ever do that again." Or, "I would be so proud if you became a doctor."

The second is by example: parents act it out. Dad loves watching ball games. "Hey, maybe I'll become an athlete." Mom seems to become more radiant when she's at the art museum. "Someday I'll be a patron."

The third mode, though, is the most powerful and mysterious: we get stuff from our parents by what I can only call unconscious accident. And here's the kicker: because the parents don't even know they've sent it, they're surprised, secretly delighted, but sometimes also horrified when they see it in their children. They say in honest disbelief, "I don't know where on earth she got that from." And then they try to persuade you to change.

A story: A friend of mine worked at a high-tech company on Boston's Route 128. It turns out that there was one particular guy in his work group with whom he constantly sparked. Their mutual dislike, he confessed, became so potent that it was impossible to conceal. His supervisor finally asked him to meet with the company psychologist. "I was scared to death," he said. "When I walked into his office, the shrink set down my file, looked up at me, and asked, 'So tell me, just what is it about this other guy that reminds you of yourself?'" My friend said, "I saw a blazing flash of light, thanked the psychologist, left his office, and never had another problem with the other guy again."

We have the hardest time, in other words, with the parts of people that we fear are also part of ourselves. And, if we are also uncomfortable with those parts in ourselves and try to conceal them, how much the more so when we encounter them in others—especially if that other person is someone who has watched us in our most unguarded moments, learning how to mimic us to perfection—you know, *like your children*. To be sure, it doesn't have to be a part of you that you dislike—indeed, it could just be a part of you that you like—but, for one reason or another, it's a part of you that you have chosen *not* to realize or even tell yourself about.

Usually it's noble. You figure out, for instance, that dad wanted to be an artist but had to go to work because you were born and one thing led to another and now he's a prominent executive instead. So you become an artist. Sometimes it's fraught with tension. Mom wanted to become a Bohemian, but she didn't have the nerve and persuaded herself that being one was socially derelict. So, when you show up in tattered Levis, mom goes off the wall. And, alas, sometimes it is a source of ongoing conflict. Dad had a thing with authority figures; they made him nuts. So he structured his life around being the only authority figure. But now you need some room to spread your own wings, and that inadvertently undermines your father. So you quarrel a lot and wind up doing things you know will get in his face—not because you want to, but because he doesn't want you to. And so it goes. But make no mistake, whether noble, fraught with tension, or filled with shouting, it all comes from love.

This is not, in other words, a pathological situation; *this is the way of the world.*

All this only raises a more disturbing problem. If parents give kids stuff they didn't know they were giving and kids pick it up stuff they didn't know they were getting, then there is a lot more of our parents in us than anyone wants to admit—a whole lot more.

It also means that it's probably a waste of time to bother trying to distill and identify some original, unique "you" apart from your parents. They, and all their *meshuggas* (that's Yiddish for nutsey-cuckoos), are an intrinsic part of your *essential* nature. You were not raised in a Skinner box. Fate or karma or random chance or (here he goes!) God made you to be *their* offspring or to be adopted by *them*. And the "you" inside, yearning to go free from them, is pretty much an illusion. There is only the "you" who you are *because of* and *in spite of* their fantasies, abuse, neglect, trickery, dreams, and, of course, their great love.

That is who we all are. I'm sorry. Deal with it. And, to ask who might you have become without your parents is like saying that if grandma had wheels, she'd be a cocktail table. You is who you is. Period. And your best shot at becoming more of who you'd like to be is by trying to understand them. (This, it occurs to me, may be the real meaning of the commandment to honor one's parents.) And remember, it's not just you and your folks. Your grandparents made your parents just like your parents made you and, someday, God willing, just like you will make your own children. Yes, Virginia, that's correct, it goes way back, all the way back to the first parents. And the part of you that your parents claim they don't understand is probably not as much you as it is them. You and I, all of us, like it or not, know it or not, are busy completing what our parents often did not even know they began.

And that is how it gets resolved. They go to graduation ceremonies to see how the project is turning out and check up on their investment. Something deep, archaic, primal, spiritual led them into making you, something even beyond their love for one another and beyond their love for you. It was not so that you could merely exist but so that they could be further realized through you. In this way, the parents in each generation are instruments of this great yearning to be better, wiser, kinder, gooder. It is eternal: kids trying to figure out what to put on their own flags so they can become who they think they really are; parents trying to get their kids to stand within the family encampment so they can get them to finish the work they didn't realize that they were unable to complete.

Hey, I doubt it ever gets completely resolved. I'm sixty years old, and I still can't sort it all out. Every few years I discover yet another dimension of my parents inside me. Sometimes I like it; sometimes I don't. Sometimes my mother seems to understand; sometimes she doesn't. We're talking here, in other words, about an unending, lifelong project. (Look at George Bush's invasion of Iraq. Is that in any way related to something his father did?) We pick up where they left off. We get the messages explicitly, by example but probably most of the time by accident. But we all get the messages and weave them into ourselves. We embroider them onto our very own flags. Then we wonder, "Why do I have these parents?" and the parents wonder, "Why do we have this kid?"

Let me conclude with one final story. The Hasidic master Yehiel of Alexander comments on an apparent contradiction in Genesis 25:19. There the text reads: "This is the family line of Isaac son of Abraham: Abraham fathered Isaac."

The Rabbi of Alexander wants to know, why the redundancy? If we are told that it is the family line of *Isaac son of Abraham*, why are we then also told that *Abraham fathered Isaac*? He answers his own question.

Isaac never thought of himself as amounting to much at all, other than being the son of Abraham. For him, everything depended only on the merit of his dad. He was "Isaac son of Abraham."

Abraham, for his part, never thought that he had accomplished very much in the service of God either or that he was deserving of any particular merit except for only one thing: he had raised up a worthy son. "Abraham fathered Isaac."

Such a holy way, says Rabbi Yehiel: Neither one saw himself as worthwhile in his own eyes. Instead his merit came through either his parent or his child (*Itturay Torah* 1:204b).

Oh yes, I almost forgot to tell you the most important thing. The intersection of the notion of how to realize your uniqueness and the often unconscious yearning to fulfill your parents' secret dreams—that is the scene of self-realization. In the words of the biblical verse, each person with his own family camp; each person under her own flag.

TELLING KIDS THE TRUTH

SO MANY OF OUR PROBLEMS WITH RELIGION began when we were children: someone lovingly taught us a lie. We asked an innocent but difficult question, and our teacher, mother, or father panicked. Instead of telling us the truth—which was that he or she didn't have a clue—we were given an answer that was "safe" and enough to satisfy our curiosity. But just as our teacher, mother, or father didn't believe it then, we don't believe it now. In this way, religious "duck-speak" enters the world.

Who could possibly know the answer to questions like, "What happens when you die?" "Why do good people suffer?" "Why doesn't God look like anything?" "What does it mean that God is One?" To make matters even worse, we Jews don't even have any institutional mechanism for deciding what all Jews do or should believe.

When it comes to what Jews do or should believe, the real truth is: no one knows for sure. Even our sages, who thought about these questions all the time, rarely hold the same opinion for more than a few weeks running. One of my teachers, Samuel Sandmel, his memory is a blessing, used to warn us in his Southern drawl, "Gentlemen [in those days, it was only gentlemen], if you don't seriously doubt the existence of God every few weeks, you're theologically comatose!" The only thing we know for sure is that no one knows for sure. Indeed, we should beware of anyone who is sure he or she does.

Unique to spiritual education, indeed, perhaps its defining characteristic, is that the great, Jewish, unanswerable questions are simultaneously relevant to adults and children. This is why we must recite the *Shema* every evening and every morning. As the people who ask them change, so do the meanings of the spiritual truths themselves. And sometimes the fresh insight of a child can hold more wisdom than that of a teacher (which may be why all good teachers learn from their students).

If the truths are so fluid, then what can we teach children? The answer is anything—as long as it is what we really believe, then and there. Children will sense that this answer comes from a different place and is of a different order of magnitude. This is why we must never teach a child something, no matter how safe or officially correct, he or she will have to unlearn as an adult.

You might say that teaching children about God is like teaching them about sex. Just because the level of their development precludes giving them some ideas and requires others (which they will hopefully outgrow), we ought not therefore lie to them. We try to teach them as much of the truth as they can and need to understand and then speak ambiguously about the rest. For centuries, wise parents and teachers, in matters of sex and God, have refined equivocation to an art.

Tell them the truth—especially if it is only that you don't know the answer. Because, if you don't know, most likely no one else does either. (Indeed, if they did, you would've probably heard about it by now.) There are only truthful answers and those given out of a well-intentioned desire to give the "right" answer, which are false. You might say, there are no "right" answers, only "truthful" ones. The next time a child asks you a real, spiritual question, try saying, "I don't know the answer. I've been wondering about it ever since I was your age. It's a holy question."

I'm confident the kid can handle it. Maybe you can, too.

BOOMPA

IT'S FUNNY HOW LOVING WORKS IN A FAMILY. Last year, when she was ninety-one, my maiden aunt Betty (or Bess, as some called her) wanted to go for a ride on our sailboat. But by the time we got down to Cape Cod, it was a dead calm and drizzling. So we suited her up in the "Henri-Lloyd Ocean Racer" foul-weather gear and just motored around the harbor instead. After fifteen minutes, Bess decided she would go up onto the foredeck where, secured on either side by my son, Lev, and my daughter's fiancé, Michael, she posed for a few photo ops.

It was over sixty years ago now, back in Detroit, when Bess became one of my mother's best friends. And it was Bess who first introduced my mother to her kid brother, Tom, who was destined to become my father. And it was Bess who sat with my mother when I was born while my dad was in Australia during the war in the Pacific.

Betty has a *Saturday Night Live* sense of humor that continually surprises and entertains us all. She once observed that she felt fine except that she couldn't see or hear very well anymore and that after the auto accident her jaw had never worked right. "You know," she reflected, "I'd be fine if I could just get a replacement head!"

She was especially fond of the nickname our children gave to my father when they were young. It came from an old Jimmy Stewart movie. They called him "Boompa." I'm sure it would make him smile wherever he is now if we'd had enough nerve to put it on his tombstone.

A few months before their wedding, in response to a shower invitation our daughter, Noa, had sent Bess, an envelope arrived in the mail. Noa's eyes were red when she told me to read it for myself. In it was a check for one hundred dollars and a standard greeting card poem about how "I'm sorry I can't be there with you in person." But what had made Noa cry was that, instead of signing it "Aunt Betty," with the frail scrawl of a ninety-two-year-old woman, Aunt Betty instead wrote, "Boompa."

Noa telephoned her at once to thank her and make sure everything was all right. "I hope it was okay," Betty kept asking. "I don't know why I wrote it. I guess I figured that he would have wanted to be at the party and this might help."

My father had died over a decade before, yet, with one single word, Betty became his agent (again) and brought him back to us in an instant. And sure enough, just like my father would have done, I choked up, mumbled something stupid about how sweet it all was, and went outside to shovel snow and run some errands. I just couldn't face Noa, not then.

By the time I returned a half hour later, there was still a lump in my throat. I shoveled some more snow and went into the house. But, sure enough, the minute I saw Noa in the kitchen, all my John Wayne machismo vanished and I found myself in a flood of tears and Noa's open arms. It was as if she were waiting for me. So we just held each other and wept.

But there's more to this story. You see, when we stopped, both of our faces now wet with tears, just on cue, I mean, you couldn't have rehearsed it any better, stepping softly forward from out of the shadow beside the refrigerator, patiently waiting for just the right moment, there was Noa's Michael, holding two paper napkins, one for Noa and one for her father. And when I saw that gentle smile on Michael's face, it was my father's smile, and I knew why Noa had chosen Michael and I knew that Michael was a member of our family.

AND UNTO US A CHILD IS GIVEN

National Public Radio invited me to write a Hanukkah story that would be broadcast prior to the festival. I couldn't resist giving it this title.

I WONDER WHAT THEY TALK ABOUT ON THE PLANE TO CHINA—at night, in the darkened cabin. What goes through their minds? For so long they must have assumed, like other couples, that they would give birth to their baby in the hospital and now, instead, here they are flying across the Pacific Ocean to receive their new daughter. After all the years of fertility drugs and shattered dreams, they are suspicious of hope. And in the darkness now, there is only the mantra-drone of the jet engines and the questions: Would she be healthy? What if she rejects us? What if she's ugly? Will the Jews back home accept her? What are we doing?

"Adopting a child reminds us," Roberta explains, "that no matter how you *physically* receive your baby, the baby is never *yours* to keep." She smiles with a maternal wisdom we all wish our own parents might have figured out sooner. "Our children don't come *from* us, they come to us. It's a total miracle."

That's what Hanukkah is about: trying to survive the darkness on the far-fetched hope there's still some life and light left in the universe. It's more than just a religious story. The days have been growing shorter, imperceptibly but inescapably darker. Just last month, for instance, when I woke up in the morning it was light. Now, I wake up in the night! And when I have dinner, it used to be light outside, but now I have my supper in darkness, too. You want a miracle? Let's get some more light down here! Heading into the night of the winter solstice, every spiritual tradition has some kind of festival of light. We're all just whistling in the dark, hoping against hope that someone up there will see these little Hanukkah candles and get the hint. Maybe if we all buy one another presents, that'll turn this thing around.

And that's probably what the Messiah is too: a symbol, in the shape of a person, who shows up when things get so bad we couldn't survive without him—or her. But a little Chinese girl—whose daddy will teach her Yiddish art songs?

I asked Bob and Roberta to tell me what it was like.

"They call the Chinese adoption connection 'the Red Thread,'" Bob said. "From Beijing we flew to Changsha. There we soon found ourselves, along with a dozen other grateful and terrified about-to-become parents, in a hotel room. From down the hall, we could hear the nannies bringing the babies. Which one was ours? It felt like a cafeteria, an automat of infants. Our child was not being born, we were!"

"One of the nannies," said Roberta, "approached and politely said, 'Here is your baby.'"

"What did you say?" I asked.

"We said, 'Thank you.'"

"And suddenly, all of the nannies, and all of the other babies, and all of the other parents—they just disappeared. Gone. The room was empty, except for the two of us and our little girl—our light and our joy.

"We looked at her and understood the adage at once. Why, of course! 'All parents get the baby they're supposed to get.' It's *bashert*, you know, 'it's meant to be,' that Bob and I should be parents to this little girl born in China. It was a miracle."

Back home, on the Sabbath morning of the naming of their new daughter, Bob and Roberta prepared a festive luncheon for the congregation. There was the regular long table filled with bowls of gefilte fish and pita bread with hummus, but this morning there are also alternating platters of bean curd and plum cakes.

And for her name, they likewise have chosen to combine their daughter's ancestry with a vision for her future.

"We named her 'Ying-tchai,' from the Chinese meaning 'Welcome Treasure.' And we also named her 'Rena,' from Psalm 126, 'Those who sow in tears will reap in joy.' The Hebrew for 'joy' is *rena*."

As miracles go, the menorah burning for eight days was nothing to write home about. It was what you might call a transitional event, occurring just after the extraordinary stories of the Bible but before our modern world. Indeed, seeing such an event as a miracle seems to require some shift in the beholder's perception. Whereas just a moment ago there was only an ordinary event ("That oil should have run out days ago"), now we stand in reverence before the work of the Holy One. ("Oh my God, it wasn't an accident!") Maybe that's the whole point. If only a dramatic interruption of the laws of nature, conveniently coinciding with our latest personal plan, qualifies as a miracle, then we are deprived of all the other explainable, routine, perfectly ordinary miracles. Like the first snowfall. Or, for that matter, the tenth. Or lighting the menorah with someone you love. Or flying to China to pick up your daughter.

"I had this anxiety dream," Roberta confessed. "It must have been about whether Rena Ying-tchai would really be our daughter and whether she'd really be a Jew. I dreamt that one day a delegation of Asian holy men showed up and said, 'Congratulations, our astrologers inform us that your child will be the next Dali Lama!'"

"But you don't understand, she's Jewish. *I* want her to be the Messiah."

"I don't know if she'll be the Messiah," I consoled, "but that fantasy definitely qualifies *you* as a Jewish mother."

And then I reminded her about what had happened at the conclusion of the High Holy Days one September.

Yom Kippur is a day of life and death and hope—the holiest day of the year. The great fast runs from sunset to sunset. By the time we commence the late afternoon service, there is standing room only. People are everywhere—on the stairs, in the doorways, even on the platform up front from where the cantor and I lead the prayers. We are surrounded by a pressing sea of souls. The lights are dimmed; the entire congregation faces the open ark filled with the scrolls of the Torah. It's the only bright light in the room, and everyone, it seems, is trying to get as close to it as possible. Above it are inscribed the words "By Your light do we see light" (Psalm 36:10).

Nevertheless, this particular year, through all this commotion and urgency and fervor, I am suddenly aware that Roberta and Bob are standing just to my side. Roberta is holding Rena Ying-tchai. I don't know what came over me but I turn to this new, young mother and—while the cantor is singing—whisper, "May I hold her?" (Neither one of us knows how exactly I will manage it.) Roberta's eyes are moist with tears as she hands me her daughter. The little girl is much heavier than I anticipated, and she is also wide-awake and *very* active. It is awkward juggling both my prayer book *and* the baby. The cantor and I turn to the open ark, the congregation presses closer and sings louder and louder. The ark's light seems even brighter now, as we lead the congregation in chanting the recitation of God's unity and asking for a year of healing and peace.

Oh my God! There's something wrong with the sound system! It's making strange noises and my own voice is no longer audible. I glance down at the lavaliere microphone clipped onto my necktie and see that the little girl has pulled it loose! She is cooing and waving the microphone at the scrolls of the Torah in the ark. She is radiant.

No one seems to notice.

BABUSHKA

MY MOTHER, HER MEMORY IS A BLESSING, made it to within a few months of ninety-three. She decided to start learning Hebrew when she was eighty. Her Hoch Deutsch (High German) ancestry was precious to her, and she loved the big, downtown German-Jewish, classical Reform temple in Detroit where she was raised and where she raised my brother and me to be rabbis. As a young woman, she played piano on the concert stage and remained an avid reader throughout her life. By her bedside, after she died, we found a five-hundred-page biography of John Quincy Adams. It was underlined. She was also highly opinionated, frequently infuriating, and loved presents. It didn't matter much what it was or how much it cost, just as long as it was a little present. So, besides all the books and magazines, her apartment was filled with hundreds of little presents—scented soaps, handkerchiefs, broaches, chocolates, decorative boxes, scarves—whatever the creative minds of her two sons could come up with.

Mom was very close to her first grandchild, our daughter. I suspect my mother had decided that she should be the one to carry her torch into the next generation. And that explains how, over the decades, many of those little presents wound up in the possession of our daughter. Every now and then, when Karen and I are visiting the kids up in San Anselmo, I'm still startled to find yet another object in their home that I had originally given to my mother. (We don't get to pick what or how something goes from one generation to the next. So it goes.)

This is all a roundabout way of explaining an adorable costume worn by our six-year-old granddaughter, Zella. Recently she and her four-year-old sister, Bluma, slept over at Biba and Django's (that's Karen and me). Their mother informed us that the little girls had had their overnight bags packed and ready to go since early morning. (Now I understand why I travel the way I do!) But this time, when Zella walked through the front door, her head was covered by what had once begun as a woman's silk scarf. It was brown and yellow with a fake Gucci pattern. It took me a few minutes to recognize the design. And then it hit me: I'd given it to my mother when I returned from Europe almost forty years before. And now, here it was, recycled as a six-year-old's babushka.

I don't know if there is life after death, but if there is, my mother is smiling.

Me, I just cried.

"Why are you crying, Django?" Zella asked.

"Someday you'll understand, honey. Someday you'll understand."

TURKEY SHOOT

IT WAS AN HONEST MISTAKE; ANYONE COULD HAVE MADE IT—so near closing time on a holiday weekend. We had just returned from celebrating Thanksgiving dinner in New York with my daughter, where they had cooked their first family banquet. Everyone had a wonderful time.

According to the division of labor in our household, daddy does the photos and daddy was anxious to see how they would turn out. I arrived at the one-hour photo processing store one hour and ten minutes before closing time.

"Can you turn this roll of film into a family before you quit?" I implored.

"You bet I can," the young woman said with a smile.

And sure enough, one hour later, as advertised, I was examining what I hoped would be the next page in the Kushner family album. The first was an excellent shot of the table, festooned with flowers, surrounded by serving dishes, and wine bottles set on a fine tablecloth. And there in the middle was the turkey. (That's odd, I puzzled, I thought we had carved the turkey in the kitchen.) The next picture was even more disturbing. The exposure was perfect. And sure enough, there was everyone smiling around the dinner table—not exactly Norman Rockwell, but one very thankful American family: parents, children, grandparents. Wait a minute! There weren't any grandparents at our dinner. This wasn't our dinner! Who are these people? How did they get in my photographs?

A moment's reflection and I realized the error.

"This isn't my roll of film!" I told the clerk.

She looked at the envelope and bit her lower lip. "Those people who just drove away," she said, "right after you walked in, they must have *your* prints."

(I thought: "And now they have *my* family too!")

She showed me the coupon from their envelope. We did indeed have very similar last names.

Maybe that's all any of us ever get: the same generic Thanksgiving family photo; it doesn't matter who's in it. Everyone is issued one table, a football game, a turkey, and a bunch of relatives. Sometimes you get photos back with people you recognize, sometimes you don't. The holier the event, the more interchangeable the relatives, until ultimately everyone looks like everyone else.

A woman came running into the store waving a handful of photographs. "These aren't my relatives!" she said.

"I know. They're mine; wanna trade?"

GENERATIONS

ONE

OUR DAUGHTER WAS STANDING WITH MY WIFE AT THE CHECKOUT counter in the supermarket. The cashier slid the last item over the bar code reader, looked at her cash register total, and said, "That comes to so many dollars and so many cents."

Our daughter smiled, opened her purse and said, "It's a deal."

She paid the money, picked up her bag of groceries, turned to my wife, and asked, in all seriousness, "Why do I always say, 'It's a deal' to cashiers? That's a funny thing to say."

Karen smiled and said, "That's easy. Because my mother always says, 'It's a deal,' and so I learned it from her, and now it seems that you have learned it from me."

TWO

We were getting ready to leave Los Angeles after visiting our two oldest children a few years ago. They are in their twenties; one was in graduate school, the other had his first real job. They were living on their own. Since we had an early-morning flight back East, we decided to stay at the airport for our last night.

After dinner, our son drove us to the hotel. As he helped me take the luggage out of the trunk of his car (which used to belong to my father), he said—in the most genuine and caring way, "Do you have your plane tickets?" I produced the envelope from my jacket pocket. We hugged and then watched him drive off down Century Boulevard.

"Just who does he think he is, asking *me* if *I* have *my* plane tickets!" I mumbled.

"He's only trying to take care of you the way you took care of him when he was a boy and the way he saw you take care of your father before he died," consoled Karen. "You'd better learn to live with it."

THREE

When my father died over two decades ago, I cried a lot. My children were of enormous comfort. I remember the way my daughter held me and the way my oldest son took a shovel at the graveside and helped my brother and me cover the coffin with earth.

On the morning of the funeral, my then eleven-year-old son came and sat in my lap to console me. We cried and we hugged and sat in silence. And then, in a moment of great insight, the little one burst out crying again and through the tears said, "The hardest part, Daddy, is knowing that someday I'll have to do this for you."

"I only hope you will have such a wonderful son to help you, the way you are helping me!" I said. "Come, it is time to go to the cemetery."

4

WORLD

WHAT ISRAEL MEANS TO ME

LIKE JEWS EVERYWHERE, I AM FURIOUS, livid, that Israel is routinely held by the world press to a higher standard of political ethics. What, for any other nation state, would be just another ho-hum, business-as-usual blunder, misjudgment, or indiscretion, for Israel, is front-page news. But the truth is, like many Jews I suspect, I also secretly love it. In much the same way, I want my kid held to a higher standard and hope to be judged by one myself. I have no desire to be like everyone else. Something in me wants the entry of the Jewish people into world politics to be judged by the highest conceivable measure. Indeed, that may be what is both so inspiring and confounding about the existence of Israel.

I am reminded of a story told by Rabbi Richard Hirsch, one of the *gedolim* (the great ones) of the Reform movement in Israel. He was in a taxicab on his way to Kennedy back in the days when the airport was still called Idlewild. When the cabdriver, whose name was Motke Goldstein, found out that his fare was a rabbi on his way to Israel, he waxed eloquent about how wonderful Israel was and how he would love to live there.

"If it's so good," said Hirsch, "then why don't you make aliyah?"

"Oh, I could never do that," replied the cabbie. "There, they have Jewish thieves, con men, prostitutes, criminals … "

"*Nu?*" said Hirsch. "They don't have Jewish thieves, con men, prostitutes, and criminals in New York City?"

"Here I can stand it," replied the cabbie, "but in Israel, it would kill me."

The great Hasidic master Rabbi Levi Yitzhak of Berditchev, who had certainly never been to the Land of Israel and who died 139 years before the founding of the state, offers a similar teaching. It appears in his *Kedushat Levi* and has been translated by Norman Lamm in his *The Religious Thought of Hasidism*. The teaching, like so many of this genre, is based on a deliberate misreading of a biblical passage, in this case, Numbers 13:2, *Parashat Shelakh Lekha*, where God directs Moses to "send out men who will scout out the land of Canaan which I [God] am giving to the children of Israel.... "

Levi Yitzhak suggests that the verse can also be read as meaning not to send out men, but, even before entering the land, to send away the corporeal part of themselves that is so easily seduced by owning things. Their task was not to spy it out physically (God forbid, says Levi Yitzhak), but "to make a spiritual impression on the land [itself]" by how they would serve God there. And to do this they would have to commit themselves to the highest standard of morality. The goal, says the Berditchever, is that they would make such an impression that "the land itself would long for the children of Abraham, Isaac, and Jacob."

Yes, I do understand that such talk comes from the ethical luxury of two thousand years of political powerlessness. And I am painfully aware that people like myself, who have chosen not to become citizens of Israel, do not have much right to moralize about it to those who are. Nevertheless, for all this inconsistency, that is still what Israel means to me.

MY LUNCH WITH JESUS

WHAT LITTLE I KNOW ABOUT JESUS I LEARNED FROM ONE MAN. R. was the one who first helped me, decades ago, understand about how God might really become a person. He and I were then young clergymen; he was the priest and I was the rabbi in a small New England town. We were cautiously fascinated by each other's faiths.

We visited each other's places of prayer; we visited each other's homes.

At a Sabbath service, I even invited R. to help me with the reading of the Torah scroll.

That Christmas Eve, as our family was about to order out for Chinese food (they were the only place open), the kitchen doorbell rang. Through the window, I could see a car, with its headlights on, idling in the driveway. I opened the door; it was R. He was wearing his collar—a priest ready for the holiest of nights, a rabbi in a sweatshirt about to pick up an order of take-out.

"R., my God, what are *you* doing here? It's Christmas Eve. Aren't you supposed to be in church?"

"Yes," he said, "we're just on our way over there now." (The man is making a social call on Yom Kippur!) He was holding a wrapped gift.

"This was under our tree and it had your name on it. But I figured that since you might not have known to look, I'd drop it off in person."

Our friendship led us to a standing monthly lunch date. We decided to write each other one-page essays on the same topics. We figured it might be a personal way to learn of another religion in greater depth. The topics were predictable: God, Bible, Israel, salvation. The only rule we set for ourselves was that we had to be completely candid and honest. By the sixth or seventh topic, we agreed we were ready to write about Jesus. This is what I wrote to R. many years ago and shared with him over our lunch:

I am wary of Jesus. Not because of anything he taught or even because of anything his disciples taught about him. (Although some of the things John said about me and my people ought to be forever banned from public reading by any person who thinks loving people is important.) Whether they were mistaken or merely premature, the idea that God should at last take the form of a human being, that the yearning God and humanity share for one another should be focused in the mythos of one person is a very compelling vision: word become flesh.

For millennia we Jews had tried to make it work in the other direction, from the bottom up. Raising ourselves to the ideal of Torah's teaching. Judaism seeks to raise ordinary people to the realization of holiness, transforming flesh into word. Then came Christianity teaching that Jesus represented an attempt to understand the yearning from the other direction. Truth be told, neither tradition has yet succeeded.

I am wary of Jesus because of history and what so many of those who said they believed in him have done to my people. Christianity, you could say, has ruined Jesus for me. Somehow through the ages the suffering of Jesus has become confused with the suffering of the Jewish people, my people. That is the key to my problem with him. His death has even become causally linked with some denial on *my* part. And this in turn has been used as a justification for *my* suffering.

In this way Jesus means for me not the one who suffered for the world's sins, but the one on account of whom I must suffer. (Is there anyone who could deny the intimate relationship of Christian Europe and the Holocaust?) Most of my early learning came from Jews who were unable to conceal this hurt-become-anger and who unconsciously portrayed him as enemy.

Nevertheless, I still believe in the coming of an anointed one. A redeemer whose living example will initiate the ultimate humanism and compel even the angriest cynic into confessing that here indeed is a person in whom the eternal yearning for consciousness to behold itself had at last succeeded. The great Sinai teaching at last realized.

That's what I wrote and that's what I handed R. as we sat down to eat.

But then something surprising and transforming happened. R. finished the page, slowly set it down on his plate, and looked up at me. His face was ashen.

I winced, fearing that I had crossed some line, that with my smug bluntness I had injured my new friend. But to my surprise R. only whispered, "Please forgive me, forgive us. It could not have been Jesus *those* Christians served." His eyes were moist with tears.

What was more, this empathy he could not conceal seemed to grow directly from the core of his faith. "Your religion," I said, "it wants you to care about me *that* much?"

"Oh yes," he said. "Don't you see, I must continuously seek to find God in every person. Jesus is only the beginning. You, Larry, are easy, but the ultimate goal is to find my Lord within everyone, even people I like a lot less than you, even people I dislike, even ones I despise."

And then it dawned on me: So that's what it means to say that God can take the form of a human being. That event in the past, for R., imposed an obligation for what might happen in the future. And each human meeting is another potential opportunity toward that ultimate goal. Right here across the table from me was a truly holy man, one in whom the spirit had become flesh.

CARDBOARD SUKKAH

On Fifty-fifth Street, just off Madison, I passed a man who seemed to be living in a cardboard box. It was big, probably originally protected a major appliance that had been delivered to one of the town houses or condos in the neighborhood. Those places go for millions of dollars.

I didn't want to be nosy but as far as I could tell the man kept most of his possessions in a broken shopping cart. At night it starts to get chilly this time of year, so he had carefully erected his home over a grate in the sidewalk to catch the heat. He had to do this because his home had no utilities. He might have been one of the ambulatory schizophrenics who have been put out on the streets with the city's budget cuts. Maybe he was just a failure and had no family to help him out.

But one thing was clear: this was his *home*. Since it could be interpreted as a "permanent dwelling," according to Jewish law it would require that a mezuzah, (a small case with a passage from Deuteronomy) be affixed to the door frame, but obviously it would have been tricky even if we could be sure where the door was.

I was struck by how nonchalant I felt as I looked into the door (or maybe it was the window) of this man's home, as if I were noting an interesting automobile parked at the curb or clever shop window display, without paying full attention. Just another ordinary city street scene: a man living off Madison Avenue in a cardboard box. I was ashamed that I was numb to such a sight.

And Jews wonder why God commands us to leave our half-a-million-dollar condos and apartments and homes for one week and live in a booth, a hut, a sukkah, with no more roof over our heads than what we find laying in the woods. It's not that we should be grateful we don't have to live like this all year, but that we should be aware a whole lot of folks nearby really do.

BILL NOVAK'S QUESTIONS

Bill Novak and I have been friends for close to forty years. He has ghostwritten many very successful and important books and interviews. When asked if he could interview me for Kerem *magazine, I was honored.*

BILL NOVAK: **Since we're meeting just a few days before Rosh Hashanah, when rabbis are busy writing their sermons, I'll begin by asking what you're thinking about these days, and what you're planning to talk about.**

LARRY KUSHNER: What's on my mind is that maybe the only way to salvage religion is to go beyond the old idea of a God who is beyond and above. More and more, I think God is the name we give to our sense that everything is connected to everything else. Now that doesn't guarantee you happiness, but it does give you an inside shot at meaning. I believe that this was the inherent heresy of Hasidism: If God is everything, and everything is God, that turns a lot of classical religious language on its head. It suggests that most of us have been taking the idea of God too literally. I don't think we can talk anymore about God commanding, or rewarding and punishing.

Why do you say "anymore"?

Most of the old religious imagery explaining such things as prayer, creation, or evil is heavily based on a vertical metaphor in which God is "up there" and we are "down here." When we speak of God's being in heaven, some people start to think God really lives up there. Others will tell you that's not true, but when they start doing religious stuff, they act as if it were anyway. So religious teachers get caught in the middle between the idea that God is everything and trying to talk to people who would rather go on taking the old metaphor literally. A lot of them just want somebody to hold their hands and let them hold onto third-grade theology. And if that's all they have, you don't want to smash it. A lady asked me the other day, "Why do bad things happen to good people?"

Sounds like she had the wrong Kushner.

That, too. The simple answer to her question is that God was never really in that business, but by taking the metaphor literally, we thought God was. The same question comes up even more powerfully when you think about the Holocaust. But here, too, the question isn't: Where was God? The real question is: Why do human beings do terrible things? To ask why God allowed these things to happen assumes that God occasionally intervenes in human affairs without human agency. But countless events remind us that God simply doesn't work like that. God didn't die in the Holocaust, only the Deuteronomic idea of an intervening God who rewards and punishes people.

I notice you avoid using a pronoun for God.

I prefer to say "the One." It encourages us to remember that it's all God, that everything else is an illusion. Why is it, for instance, that you and I are not aware, right now, that it's all God? Or to put it another way, what do you do to wake yourself up when you're not aware of the immediacy and power and terror of God? What do you do when things seem to be operating discretely and autonomously and you inhabit a world of separation? How do you attain that higher awareness?

Does that higher awareness occur during prayer?

It depends. There are two kinds of prayer: petitionary prayer, which makes less and less sense to me, and contemplative or meditative prayer—which is an opportunity for heightened awareness of the Divine.

Do you think that awareness is enabled or impeded by our liturgy?

For most of us, it's impeded. But if you get to a level where you've got it all memorized, and you can go on autopilot, the liturgy can function as a kind of verbal, melodic, mantra-like springboard that sets you free.

Which is presumably more difficult during the High Holy Days, when the liturgy is both more complex and less familiar.

The High Holy Day liturgy can be an infantilizing experience. On the negative side, it's loaded with "Our Father, Our King" and images of reward and punishment, which, if taken literally, are rarely helpful. On the other hand, those images can sweep you back to your childhood, when they were healing and important. Understandably, liberal Jews are of two minds about these prayers. It's comforting to remember a time when your parents and God were omnipotent, omniscient, and benevolent. My own congregation rewrote the liturgy in gender-neutral language, but when they got to *Avinu Malkeinu*, they left it alone. The melody is evocative, and people wanted to retain some of that sense of standing before Daddy in heaven.

Does that image have any validity to you?

Sure, if it's part of a larger picture. But the key fact of human life, as the High Holy Days continually remind us, is that the future is unknown. And Judaism is unequivocal in forbidding us to deal with anyone who claims to know what is to come. The Torah is very explicit about this in Deuteronomy, chapter 18. I'm interested in verse 13, which reads, *tamim tih'yeh im Adonai Elohekha*, "You shall be *tamim*—perfect—with the Lord your God." Rashi explains that *tamim* means we should walk with God "wholeheartedly," that we should put our hope in God and not attempt to investigate the future. If we accept whatever comes upon us wholeheartedly, that's what it means to be with God.

When you're facing an unknown future—and the future is always unknown—you have three options. First option: everything is fated, it's all meant to be. In other words, predestination.

The second option is free will. Here the future is allegedly wide-open and is shaped only by our deeds. In order to preserve our free will, God voluntarily steps back, as it were, and refuses to intervene. But this only poses a larger problem. If God never intervenes, then God is effectively irrelevant. Or maybe God intervenes every now and then, although nobody has yet been able to discern a coherent pattern—assuming there is one. Which means we're stuck in a situation where sometimes we're free (when God doesn't intervene) and sometimes we're not (whenever God does). But since there's no way to know when God does or doesn't, our condition is absurd.

The choice between these two options has led many thoughtful people to reject the idea of God altogether. But that would mean life is meaningless, a cosmic crapshoot, and I don't accept that.

I believe there's a third option. Suppose we say that instead of controlling everything, or making an occasional intervention, God is everything.... The entire glorious, horrible, holy, terrifying wondrous mess we call creation is a continuous manifestation of the Divine. Even our sense of independence and autonomy is part of that whole, and therefore "meant to be." In this model, we are neither puppets of fate nor masters of free will. Everything is the way it's supposed to be. We enter each new day wholeheartedly confident that everything is somehow a manifestation of the Divine.

Which leads to a certain acceptance.

Well, it certainly doesn't mean we have to like it or that we shouldn't try to change it. But it does mean that we accept our present situation "as if" it were tailored by God for us personally. We find ourselves saying, "I'm not sure why this has been given to me, or why this has been torn from me, or why this is happening to me, but I acknowledge that somehow it is a manifestation of God."

Not necessarily a comforting thought.

No, there's not much consolation here, which is why I wouldn't say this within ten blocks of any hospital. But I believe it's a theology of hope. It removes our chronic worry that everything is meaningless, because at any given moment things are the way they're supposed to be. This is the old Yiddish notion of *bashert*—it's meant to be, intended.

We also have the popular Talmudic saying *Hakol bi-day shamayim hutz mi-yirat shamayim* [*Berakhot* 33b], "Everything is in the hands of heaven except the fear of heaven." Which isn't free will at all. But if you believe in free will and also in God, how do you know which is which? Whoops! Wait a moment; did God just do that? It's kind of silly. But what if God is All? At any given moment, everything is a manifestation of the Divine. You might not like it, and sometimes you might hate it. Somebody dies, and you'd say, I guess that's the way it's supposed to be.

How is that different from the first option?

In the first option, God is up there puppeteering. In this model, God simply is. God is my parent who just died. God is the sadness. And God is also the hope. In this way, you get to the point where you realize that you yourself are present *within* the Divine. It doesn't make the pain go away, but at least it takes the edge off. There is always the possibility of meaning.

Karen and I were up in the Pacific Northwest not long ago, waiting to catch a ferry in Anacortes, Washington. The guidebook advises you to get there early, so we arrived two hours in advance—just moments after the previous ferry had left. The man in the car in front of us was furious; he had missed his boat by five minutes, so now his vacation was delayed by two hours—until the next boat. Not only did he miss the boat, but he had the misfortune to be standing next to a theologian. "Dammit!" he said. "If I had only left home three minutes earlier, I would have made it."

"No," I said. "I don't think you would've made that boat. You would have been stuck in traffic or had a flat tire. You weren't *supposed* to make that boat. Something else would have delayed you. That boat just didn't have your name on it."

"Oh," he said, startled for a moment. "Thanks, I feel better."

Because things happen for a reason?

Well, it's tempting to lapse into the other kind of theology, that God did this to teach you something. That's not what I mean. But because everything can lead you back to everything else, everything can also be an opportunity to learn. The way one ought to behave is to walk like Yaakov: *ba-tom*, "wholeheartedly."

I don't recognize that word. Are you sure it's in Genesis?

No, it's in Proverbs, 10:9. In Genesis, Yaakov is described as an *ish tam*, "a simple man." By the time you get to Proverbs, the concept takes on an additional meaning—wholehearted and secure: "One who walks wholeheartedly, walks securely." So I'm no longer upset about missing the boat. I got mixed up and thought I was running things, but I've just been reminded again that I'm not.

All of this is part of a teaching I'm working on, and like most of my sermons, it's addressed to me. You know you're on the right track as a preacher when you realize that you're writing the sermon to yourself. I looked at the word *ba-tom* and it occurred to me that my father's nickname was Tom. I was telling myself that I should walk "with Tom." Then I started to remember what it was like to be a little boy with my father, who used to protect me.

Which brings us back to your earlier life. Where do you come from?

I was born in 1943 in Detroit, the older of two boys. During the war, my father was in the Navy, stationed in Australia, and I didn't meet him until I was two. He was a quiet man, uncomfortable with emotions. After his first heart attack I took him away overnight to a little inn. Over dinner I said, "Dad, I've never told you this, but I love you." He said, "You'll hate yourself in the morning." That humor was how we were close. His hero was John Wayne.

Do you remember meeting him for the first time?

I don't know, really. I've been told about it so often that I'm not sure. We all went down to Michigan Central Depot, where my mother, who hadn't seen her husband for two years, was holding this toddler—me—whom he had never met. For him it must have been strange—an instant kid.

What did he do for a living?

All sorts of things. Before joining the Navy he worked for Sears, in downtown Detroit, where he did the window displays. He was also a sign painter. In the 1930s he was the trainer for the Detroit Lions football team. He liked to say that in those days they had twelve men on the team—eleven on the field, and one extra—in case somebody got hurt.

After the war he sold appliances at Sears. Then he became a kind of executive *shammas* at a large Reform temple in Detroit. He had started as a volunteer, but he was so good at taking care of the *shul* that they hired him away from Sears. Years later, his hobby was making museum quality, little wooden models of synagogues from around the world, which are still on display at the temple. When he died, there were seven hundred people at his funeral.

Quite a crowd for a reserved man. What became of your brother?

Also a rabbi. My mother, who's still alive, had surgery on her neck at the age of eighty-five. When she came out of the operation, my brother and I were both there. The nurse said, "Rabbi Kushner?" And we both said "Yes?" "Wait," said the nurse. "You're both rabbis?" Whereupon my mother, who had been unconscious until this moment, rolled over and said, "Yes, that's my specialty." Then she fell back asleep.

What kind of Jewish home did you grow up in?

I use these words deliberately: it was a pious, observant, Reform Jewish home. We did all the things Reform Jews were supposed to do. There was never ham or shellfish in our home, but we had bacon for breakfast.

Bacon but not ham?

It wasn't uncommon in the Midwest for Reform Jews to eat bacon, but not ham. I remember my mother yelling at my father for ordering Canadian bacon in a restaurant, and scolding, "Not in front of the boys." It looked too much like pork. She always lit candles, and we attended Friday night services. But we also had BLT sandwiches for lunch.

Was it a classical Reform temple?

Yes, a big cathedral with stained glass windows, and more lightbulbs in the chandeliers than stars in the sky. There was a gentile choir, and the organist played low notes that you couldn't hear, but could feel in your chest. Everybody dressed up. My aunt called it *fapitzed*, which meant, I think, wearing more expensive clothes than she could afford. I had to wear itchy wool pants, which I hated. I would go with my grandfather, who always sat on the second aisle on the right in the fourth row. "*Shweigenzee*," he would tell me. "Be quiet!" I didn't understand the service, but I liked standing next to somebody big who loved me, and who told me to shut up.

So your grandfather was German?

My mother's father was a German Jew; he was a very important figure. When my father was in the war, my mother and I lived with her parents. My father's family came from Eastern Europe.

When did you decide to come a rabbi?

I still remember the moment. I was in ninth grade, at a community-wide Reform Friday night service. I looked at all those rabbis sitting up on the bima, and I thought: "What a neat deal! Their job is to read and study and be good and help other people make sense of their lives. And they get paid to do this! Why wouldn't everybody want to be a rabbi?" Of course, at the time, I had no idea that I was growing up in one of only eleven homes in America where you never spoke ill of the rabbi.

And before you made that decision, where were you headed?

I was a child prodigy in art. In ninth grade I asked my mother, "What if I gave up my art to become a rabbi?" She smiled, "That would be a higher calling."

But you didn't give it up completely.

No, I still paint. I've always done graphics and artwork. And calligraphy and the jacket designs of my books.

A few years ago I heard you had designed a Hebrew font for computers.

I did several. I got into computers early, but I was frustrated by the fact that I couldn't use Hebrew letters. So I learned enough about computers to program them.

After you finished high school, what then?

In those days, the Hebrew Union College in Cincinnati had a combined program for undergraduates with the University of Cincinnati. By the time you earned your undergraduate degree, you had also picked up a year's credit at HUC. I took the Baltimore & Ohio sleeper from Detroit to Cincinnati, where I moved into a dorm room, opened my first checking account, and registered for classes. I remember sitting at my desk, watching the cars go by on Clifton Avenue, and thinking how nice it would be to be back home. But it was going to be like this for the rest of my life, so I knew I had to get used to it. I cried anyway. I had no idea that at that very moment, my parents were holding each other and weeping. It's funny how people cry when they get everything they have prayed for.

So you were still a teenager when you started your rabbinical training.

It's amazing, but as recently as the 1960s you could be admitted to the rabbinical program without knowing a single letter of

Hebrew. There were Iowa farm boys in our class who learned not only Hebrew, but how to accept food from waiters. All our meals were served by white-coated black waiters. I was there all through the sixties, from 1961 through 1969.

It sounds like you followed a pretty straight path from ninth grade through ordination.

It was easy, because I knew what I wanted to do. In the middle, between undergraduate and graduate school, I spent a year at the New York campus. I wanted to study with Eugene Borowitz; he turned out to be very important for me.

You were interested in contemporary theology?

I was interested in a theology that was human and personal, and therefore spiritual—as opposed to cerebral, logical, and theoretical. I'll never forget the time Borowitz asked a question in class, and the person he had called on faltered. Several other hands shot up, and Borowitz, in the most loving and constructive way, said, "No, give him more time, please." To me, that represented the human face of theology.

Which was exactly what you were looking for.

Yes, and when Karen and I got married, Borowitz performed the ceremony. My first job was as a rabbinic fellow at Congregation Solel in Highland Park, Illinois. Its rabbi, Arnold Jacob Wolf, had been Borowitz's college roommate.

Where did you go after Solel?

When the fellowship was up I came here to Sudbury, Massachusetts. I've been here ever since. I've been offered two jobs in my life, and I've taken them both.

What was in Sudbury when you arrived?

Chaos. A congregation of a hundred households had recently been through some major battles. Should the temple be kosher? Should it be Reform, Conservative, or unaffiliated? They had affiliated with the Reform movement a year before I arrived, but it was an uneasy truce. Of the 66 members who attended the meeting, 5 had voted for Orthodox, 11 for Reconstructionist, 19 for Conservative, 23 for Reform, and 8 for None of the Above.

The impasse was resolved when someone moved that the congregation should affiliate with the Reform movement but would retain a kosher kitchen and observe the second day of Rosh Hashanah. They then hired a twenty-eight-year-old rabbi whom they hoped would be suitable.

Beth El is the most unusual American synagogue I've ever seen. How would you describe it?

First, no plaques. No matter how much you give, your name can't be anywhere.

Because plaques are vulgar?

And, more important, because not having plaques makes us a classless society. Not only no plaques but no public recognition for big givers or for anything. Now, at long last, we need a new building, so we'll be putting this principle to the test.

Why is the principle so important?

If you acknowledge publicly how much money people give, you can't avoid creating a hierarchical social structure. If nobody knows you gave the money, you and the next person are equal. If you asked me today to name our big givers, I couldn't tell you who they were.

Which is amazing.

I think it's even more amazing to walk into a building with no plaques. Plaques bring the Jewish community down. We have no fund-raising at all—no car washes, no ad books, no bingo, no cupcakes in the parking lot. All the money comes from people taking on their fair share of the expenses.

So the dues must be high.

Very high—up to twenty-five hundred dollars, although nobody is turned away for lack of money. If it were up to me there'd be no ceiling on dues, because people at the high end don't really pay their fair share. I'd like to see dues as a percentage of your taxes. Tell us how much you're paying the IRS, and we'll take your word for it.

What is it about this issue that affects you so deeply, even after all these years?

First, it's important for people to confront the true cost of what they want. Didn't Freud say that the payment was part of the cure? Second, we don't want people outside our community to be supporting it. Would you contribute to our ad book? No, this is a spiritual community. if we can't support ourselves, we should give it up. But above all it's about integrity: If you want something, you should pay for it. There's a widespread misconception that because a synagogue is nonprofit and tax-exempt, it is therefore a charity. The harsh truth is that in many respects it's more like a country club.

In so many congregations the fund-raising apparatus creates an entire subculture of people who are not growing as Jews, who are busy instead with bingo or the car wash. I believe the synagogue has failed those people. They feel active in the community, but how are they using their time? If there's no opportunity for fund-raising, it frees up a lot of energy for other tasks.

As I see it, the purpose of a synagogue is for Jews to engage in primary religious acts that they should not, and probably cannot, do alone....

Let's define what you mean by "primary religious acts." I assume you're referring to study and prayer.

I'm referring to the three categories from *Pirke Avot* [Ethics of the Fathers]—*Torah, avodah, gemilut hasadim*. *Torah* represents our intellectual side: reading, study, questioning, learning. *Avodah* is our emotional side: prayer, songs, candles, meditation. And the third category includes acts of help, repair, compassion, attention, and justice. Very few of us can do all three categories well, but by joining a community we can compensate for our personal inadequacies.

And what about people who love to be involved in fund-raising and all that secular busywork?

They're usually not drawn to our community, and fortunately, there's no shortage of synagogues in Greater Boston.

Do you think some forms of fund-raising are worse than others?

I'm an extremist on the issue of legalized gambling. "Come on, Rabbi, it's only a raffle; it's innocuous; what could it hurt? And we'll even use the money to buy something you want!" I feel like the Dutch boy with his thumb in the dike. This is where I draw the line. I realize that bingo or Monte Carlo nights can deliver large sums of money, but I think they exact an even higher price from the soul of the congregation.

You really can have a congregation without fund-raising—without professional men and women (who normally earn one hundred dollars an hour) selling cupcakes in the parking lot for twenty-five cents apiece.... I'd much rather see members of a synagogue demanding that the congregation provide them with facilities—services, programs, lectures, classes, teachers, a library—so they can grow as Jews.

Has this battle been won, or do you have to reinvent this wheel every couple of years?

I do, unfortunately, because new members come in who are accustomed to doing these things in the old ways.

One of the things I hate most in organized Jewish life are the endless, vapid dinners that claim to "honor" somebody. With all the recent changes and improvements in American Jewish life, you would think someone would have come up with a better alternative to the testimonial dinner.

I agree.

Dinners bring the community together, but instead of raising it up, they bring it down. Most people hate these programs and would much rather attend a cultural program or a stimulating lecture. If you're not careful, ritualized public displays of gratitude can suffocate every other area of synagogue life. If everybody is thanked, the only noteworthy moments are the invariable omissions.

How do you encourage members of your congregation to be religiously active?

A rabbi must be willing to relinquish traditional tokens of rabbinic authority. The more you give away, the more secure you become. Most rabbis have it backwards: the more they hoard, the more powerful they think they will be. In fact that makes them weak.

Has your own religious observance changed much over the years you've been here?

In the years after Solel I was on a traditionally observant track, culminating in a couple of years of strict *shomer Shabbos* [Sabbath observant] and strictly kosher. But I came out the other side. I remain very respectful of traditional observance, but I no longer think it's the way for me and, I suspect, it's not going to be the way for many other Jews. Kashrut as it's currently practiced is putting itself out of business.

Because it's so extreme?

Yes, because no matter how kosher you are, there's always someone who won't eat in your kitchen. I'd like to see a reasonable standard of kashrut defined for liberal Jews. There is more than one way to be a serious and observant Jew. We both know a lot of very serious Jews who observe a widely practiced and informally agreed-upon mode of kashrut. It includes not eating anything that could not be made kosher. So these people will consider eating meat out in a restaurant, but they will not consider eating pork or shellfish under any circumstances or eating milk and meat on the same dish. They are not strict about keeping two sets of dishes, nor about waiting between eating meat and milk. They might—perfectly validly—maintain different standards for eating at home and eating away from home. The role of kashrut in their lives is important and seriously religious, and it ought to be taken every bit as seriously as someone who considers him- or herself *glatt* kosher.

We need a vocabulary to describe, not varying levels—that implies better and worse—but different ways of expressing the sacred in our lives. Because there is no name for this mode of kashrut, it exists as a sort of black market. What we ought to do is take ourselves seriously enough to give it a name.

What name would you give it?

Kashrut America, say. If we put this out there and give it a name, I think a lot of people who would like to keep kosher, would. There's an obsessive-compulsive aspect to traditional kashrut that doesn't seem to have anything to do with what God wants; it's just obsessive behavior. How beautiful it would be if someone could say, I observe kashrut America....

But they might say: If you stop doing X or Y, what will be left?

They said that to my grandfather and I'm still here. Yes, some Reform Jews have fallen off the edge, but so have some Orthodox Jews. I have a different attitude toward human behavior; I'm more optimistic about what it means to be a human being. People want to be Jewish and they need help. You can have fences around fences, but that can't be the solution.

A few years ago your congregation produced its own siddur, Vetaher Libenu. How did that come about?

It grew out of an exercise I had given to members of a beginning liturgy class. I wanted them to try writing their own prayers so they could appreciate the prayer book. At the time, the only available prayer books were the Silverman, which was deadly, and the *Union Prayer Book*, which was simply too thin.

So you wrote a new siddur with them?

No. I thought it was important that it be *their* creation. Any rabbinic presence would only skew it. My advice was: "Whatever you decide, tell the truth about what you believe." They came back to me and said, "You know, we don't think God is masculine or feminine, and we really don't think the language should reflect God's gender." Almost nobody was saying this at the time, so they were slightly ahead of the curve.

And when the new prayer book was published, it made the news.

To our surprise, we realized that Beth El had published the first gender-neutral prayer book in Jewish history. The news went out over the AP wire and was picked up by newspapers all over the world.

I was interested in how the editors of the siddur explained their decision in favor of gender neutrality, so I went back to look at the introduction. "Above all," they write, "we questioned why the rich fabric of our psalms and prayers has been woven exclusively on masculine threads recalling monarchs, lords, and fathers, despite the unequivocal statement of the Torah, 'And God created mankind in God's image; male and female God created them.'... We have come to believe that the exclusive use of masculine imagery to describe God invites idolatry, that the imagery too easily becomes the reality."

We weren't really prepared for such a strong reaction on that issue. Some of us thought that translating *Barukh ata Adonai* ... as "Holy One of Blessing, Your Presence fills creation" was actually a more radical step than gender neutrality.

What if you had hated the new siddur?

These were extraordinarily talented and literate people. I knew they weren't going to come up with garbage. They showed me the final manuscript and asked me to look for errors. I found some and missed others.

One thing you don't find in this siddur is any responsive reading.

I hate responsive readings. Do you know anybody who looks forward to them or thinks they're uplifting? But they're all over American Jewish liturgy like some kind of weed. I can understand reading responsively if you have a particular psalm that was intended to be antiphonal, but otherwise I think it's deadly.

But you see it everywhere.

This goes to a deeper problem, the role of the leader of the service. One of the things I have tried to teach the congregation is that I can't pray for them better than they can pray for themselves. Sometimes I joke, "I know more about praying than you do, because I went to rabbinic school. So, if God has time to listen to just one of us, it will be me."

They laugh, and then I say, "If you don't believe that, why do you act that way?"

People must learn to pray for themselves.

Was this something you learned at Solel?

No, Solel did responsive readings too. I thought they were dumb, and finally I said to myself, I'm a rabbi, I don't have to do this. I feel the same way about the sequence of the wedding liturgy.

So what do you do about it?

I do a wedding in two acts. First we all gather around a big table, and the cantor or I will teach everyone a wedding *niggun*. And, as an inducement to get people to join in, we announce that we won't bring in the bride and the groom until everyone is singing. We read and sign the *ketuba*, and then we have the bride and groom speak to one another publicly. It's very powerful and people usually cry. Only then do we erect the *huppa* at the other end of the room. It's intuitive. I don't believe liturgy should require explanation.

Yes, I hate it when everything is explained and the service becomes a simplified lesson instead of a religious experience.

Just because many people are operating on a functional third-grade level of Jewish literacy doesn't mean that we should start with the fourth grade. My approach is, You can run and catch up or you can be left behind. Most people, I find, are thrilled to be treated that way. If you go to a tennis pro, he's not going to play down to your level. He'll try to bring you up to his. You learn something by doing it. A visitor from another planet would probably assume that most synagogue services were designed primarily to make an occasional non-Jewish visitor feel comfortable. What would happen if services were designed instead for the regulars?

In other words, don't keep telling us what we're doing, or why. Just do it. Which means, I guess, no transliterations, right?

None. There are twenty-two letters in the Hebrew alphabet and it really is possible to learn them all. I sometimes tell people: If you were pledging a fraternity, you could learn the Greek alphabet in a week and swallow a goldfish, so you can certainly learn Hebrew. On a scale of difficulty where Hungarian is a 10 and pig Latin is a 1, English is a 7 and Hebrew would be a 3.

Rabbi Moshe Waldoks once said, "There's something terribly wrong with American Jewish worship. Each week in this country there are a couple of thousand *b'nai mitzvah*, and virtually nobody walks out of any of them saying, 'That was great! I want to be here every week.'" We are offering a three-millennia-old tradition on how to make sacred sense out of life. If that's your product, you don't need advertising or bargain-basement prices. All you need is to be welcoming, to give people the real thing, to respect them. In other words: no schlock.

Given the obvious success of services at Beth El, you must have many imitators.

You'd think so, wouldn't you? Visitors to Beth El are always saying, "This is beautiful; we've got to try these things in our shul." My goal was never to change the world, but I thought that if you put some of these principles into play, a lot of other places would try them. But surprisingly few places actually do. It's a mystery to me.

It's also true that religious institutions are especially slow to change. And there has been a dramatic shift over the past two or three decades from the imperial rabbinate to what I would call the empowering rabbinate. When I was ordained, you were expected to wear a robe. There was an aura around the rabbi. When I was a kid, the rabbi actually entered the sanctuary from a hidden door. These days he—or she—is much more willing to be a regular person. So obviously I'm not the only one who's thinking in these terms.

How do you prevent Beth El from becoming too big?

The members have capped our membership at 450 households. And maybe God put us out in the sticks to keep our growth at a more manageable pace.

What do you do about overly fancy b'nai mitzvah, *or the growing tendency of appropriating wedding customs for* b'nai mitzvahs?

The problem, I think, has to do with people getting married later and being afraid that their parents won't be alive for their grandchildren's weddings. Imagine if we held weddings within a typical Shabbat service. Sure, the buffet *kiddush* would have gourmet food, but only people who were invited would attend. Well, that's what we've got now with *b'nai mitzvah*.

What about the growing tendency to hold a bar or bat mitzvah on a Monday or a Thursday, to convene a special minyan just for that occasion?

I don't like it and I won't do it. It has to occur at a time when the congregation is *already* present. In many Reform congregations, *b'nai mitzvah* have closed down Shabbat morning services, which are effectively by invitation only. Technically, of course, any minyan of ten adult Jews can suffice, but the reading of Torah requires an ongoing community. At Beth El we say to the kid: This service, where you will be called to the Torah to celebrate your coming of age, will go on whether or not you and your family are here. We're delighted that you will be part of it, but we did this last thing week and we'll do it again next Shabbos—with or without you.

In effect, the congregation tells the family: We're glad you're here but this isn't really *your* day, and while we love your kid, we don't want a thirteen-year-old leading us in prayer. Parents can speak but we limit the talk to one page in the form of a blessing or a teaching.

As long as I'm listing my pet peeves, here's another: a bar mitzvah speech where one of the parents extols the virtues of the kid—his generosity, his precociousness, even his soccer abilities. I find these speeches vulgar and inappropriate.

We have rules on that, which boil down to this: The kid gives a *d'var Torah* but it can't be used to thank anyone. It can be only one thing: an example of the child's religious erudition.

How can you convey and enforce these expectations, which go so strongly against the grain of most American-Jewish bar and bat mitzvahs?

Anyone who has a bar or bat mitzvah coming up is invited, but not required, to take a class that's taught by the rabbi. And the only way to get into this class, which includes a weekend retreat, is to be accompanied by one or both of your parents. When you have a dozen families taking a class together and going away together for a weekend as a group, you're creating a small, secure community within a larger community. During that weekend retreat we describe the congregation's expectations for their upcoming event. We put a lot of pressure into making the event modest and *haymish*. All of this helps keep a lid on it, and I find that most people are relieved to be given permission to celebrate in a more meaningful way. Sometimes I hear congregants talk about attending bar and bat mitzvahs at other places and how grateful they feel not to be part of that madness.

Your first book was The Book of Letters, ***which I would describe as a combination of calligraphy and midrashim about the alphabet. What led you to write it?***

Twenty-five years ago I was auditing Professor Alexander Altmann's class on Jewish mysticism at Brandeis. One of my classmates was Michael Strassfeld, who had just begun work on *The Jewish Catalog*. He sent me a form letter announcing that they were putting together a compendium of information to guide a new generation of Jews into Jewish practice and that they'd like to list me as a teacher. Could you please tell us what you would teach?

I was thrilled to be asked. I was going to write "philosophy," but then I noticed that they had a real philosopher on their list. I was going to write "social action" until I noticed that Arnold Wolf was mentioned. He had been arrested in Selma. I was going to write that I could tell Hasidic stories, but they already had the Lubavitcher Rebbe! So I wrote back that I could at least teach the letters of the Hebrew alphabet.

I meant it as a joke but the editors of the *Catalog* must've taken it seriously because they listed me as a teacher of the Hebrew alphabet. When the book was published I started getting calls and letters from prospective students around the country wanting to know about the mysteries of the letters. I started reading up on the subject and went deeper and deeper until I had a little book whose subtitle was *A Mystical Hebrew Alphabet*.

I sent it—at your suggestion, by the way—to Harper & Row, where it landed on the desk of Cathy Netter, a young woman who happened to be going through her own Jewish spiritual revival. She took this book on as her personal project. Years later, Stuart Matlins, publisher of Jewish Lights, picked it up and brought it back into print. He's a wonderful and brilliant man to work with. I remember being at a marketing meeting when somebody asked, "How are we going to distinguish Larry from Harold Kushner?" Stuart thought for a moment and said, "Why would we want to do that?"

You two must often get confused, two rabbinical authors and lecturers from the suburbs of Boston.

It happens all the time. Occasionally, after a lecture, somebody will come up to me and say, "Rabbi Kushner, your books have changed my life." Then they produce a copy of *When Bad Things Happen to Good People*. I ask, "Whose name would you like me to sign?" It keeps me humble.

Your second book was Honey from the Rock.

By then I had figured out that mysticism was the repository for core spiritual teaching. I was also trying figure out what a new, American-Jewish mysticism would look like.

The one that really intrigues me is God Was in This Place, and I, i Did Not Know, where you take a single verse from Torah and trace it through centuries of commentators as you try to imagine who they were in real life.

That book was inspired by an interpretation from the commentator Shimshon ben Pesah Ostropler, a kabbalist, who postulated that Jacob at Bet-El saw the *merkava*, Ezekiel's chariot—a well-known mystical symbol. (A similar idea appears in the Zohar.) That teaching inspired the book, which is about the big "I" and the little "i." The "I" of God, and our little "i"—how we understand the divine self, and how it's possible to have a mystical experience without losing your autonomy.

What are some books you often find yourself recommending to students and congregations?

Buber's *Hasidism and Modern Man*, which is challenging on different levels. Scholem's *On the Kabbalah and Its Symbolism*. Heschel's *God in Search of Man* and *The Sabbath*. I also recommend *Your Word Is Fire*, a little book of Hasidic teachings on contemplative prayer edited by Arthur Green and Barry Holtz, which has also been reprinted by Jewish Lights.

Isn't it unusual for a Reform rabbi to be so interested in Hasidism?

I see Hasidism as the last great flowering of the Jewish spiritual imagination. Maybe contemporary Hasidism has given Hasidism a bad name. Originally, Hasidim weren't as halakhic in their approach as they are now. And I don't think halakha is going to be the main organizing principle for Jewish life. Sooner or later, I think we'll see a new metaphor coming out of American Jewry.

In Hasidism I find a lot of support for the idea of God as everything, that God is the ocean and we are the waves. I increasingly believe that the goal of religion is to get beyond the artificial separation between God and everything else. But you can only stay there for a moment.

Is that realization inherently the result of a mystical experience?

Not necessarily. I think that most of us, one way or another, have had at least a fleeting sense that the apparent fragmentation of our world is an illusion but that, in truth, everything is one.

One last question. In The Book of Words, *you advise people to buy a cemetery plot—and to visit it. That struck me for some reason, and I wanted to ask, Why?*

If you go to your plot, and stand there, you're forced to confront the fact that you won't live forever. There are two ways to deal with that reality. It can be debilitating and depressing or you can say, "Yes, I'm going to die, *but I'm not dead yet.*" That's one of the great religious insights of all time. Going to your cemetery plot can be an important spiritual experience.

And the amazing thing about being a rabbi is that you go to the cemetery and the next day you're doing a wedding and a hospital visit and a baby naming and then it's back to the cemetery. Being a rabbi forces you to confront the important moments of life. It's like a brick in your face every single day.

NYPD BLUE

ACROSS FROM WHERE I USED TO TEACH IN NEW YORK CITY a film crew had taken over most of the sidewalk and part of the street. There were big halogen lamps, cameras on elevated platforms, a huge crowd, and, of course, police barricades. What is it about the media that is so exciting and makes us so hungry? We must get close to what is happening.

After working my way to the front, I saw a cordon of police officers encircling two other police officers. Even though the two police officers in the bright lights were in plainclothes, I recognized them at once. Everyone else did also. They were two of the stars from *NYPD Blue*, a popular, evening adult drama about police work in the big city, which, I must confess, from time to time, I have been known to watch. Here were a man and a woman whom I knew (or, at least, had allowed myself to be convinced that I knew) all about. I had watched some of the more pivotal scenes in their lives. I was privy to many of the details of their professional stories. My god, I'd been in their bedroom during some of their most intimate moments!

But something else struck me as odd. Here I stood ignoring *real-life* police officers (in Manhattan they're everywhere—except when you need one) who were protecting the acting police officers from the rest of us. The real ones were not interesting. And, as I thought about it more, I realized that the real ones were not as *real* as the acting ones.

Critics have observed that movies are occasionally able to capture a scene better than the one in real life. We find ourselves saying about some breathtaking view or powerful drama that it is "just like in the movies," when of course it precisely the other way around. Or is it?

Maybe we have a new dimension of reality here that, until the creation of mass media, never before existed. Maybe what we, in our generation, call reality has begun to shift from what actually happens to how many people have seen it. And, if enough people have seen something in the movies or on TV, then, even if it never really happened, it's real—even more real than what really happened.

I could hardly wait until the episode I saw being acted out on that Manhattan street got aired on television, because then it would really be real and I could brag that I saw it happening while it was only acting.

A real police officer interrupted my reverie. "Excuse me, sir, but you'll have to move back behind the barricade … "

RESURRECTION OF FLOWERS

I CAN STILL REMEMBER THE LITTLE WOODEN BOX. Back in those days, of course, there wasn't any airport security. I just parked my car and walked in. The customs inspector was already there. He had a crowbar.

"Rabbi Kushner?" he said.

I nodded.

"It's over here."

We were in the old Eastern Airlines freight hangar at Boston's Logan Airport. The little box was on a palette in the middle of the floor, as if in quarantine. There was nothing around it but the concrete floor in every direction. A few workmen, in the distance, were doing poor jobs of concealing their curiosity.

That little crate reminded me of the few times I have seen other small wooden boxes. The two kinds are fused in my consciousness—whenever I think of one, I think of the other. But these other boxes are terrible, truly awful. I wish I could forget them. Boxes like these are so small there can only be a single pallbearer. One man, forearms straight out, like a human forklift, carries the coffin alone. And I remember how dumb I felt reading the words from a rabbi's manual at the funerals of small children. The words taste like ashes.

So there I am, standing in a hangar at Logan Airport decades ago looking at a little box. I had heard on the rabbinic grapevine that scrolls of the Torah were stashed in warehouses by the Nazis, who had intended to establish a museum for an extinct race! After the war, seventeen hundred of them wound up in the Westminster

Synagogue in London. The rabbi there tells of how, less than a week after their arrival, a young scribe (or *sofaer*) looking to earn a few pounds repairing Torahs knocked on the door. He wound up with his own apartment adjoining the synagogue and a lifetime job.

So my former congregation had raised the money for shipping, and now here I was standing with this guy who had a crowbar in front of a little box. His job was to confirm that it indeed contained a handwritten scroll of the Five Books of Moses. Mine was to figure out a way not to cry when I remembered the other little boxes I'd seen and when I imagined the Jews from the village of Vlasim, Czechoslovakia, who were the rightful owners of this Torah.

The customs inspector carefully, reverently, pried open the lid. But inside, I saw only the blossoms of delicate flowers. There must have been hundreds and thousands of them. They filled the whole box. They spilled out onto the floor all around us. They covered the airport runways. The whole city was bathed in their fragrance. I could hear them laughing.

5

MYSTICISM

WHAT IS KABBALAH?

EVERY GENERATION HAS ITS OWN DEFINING RELIGIOUS MODEL—ethical monotheist, rationalist, humanist, social activist. And while it is always risky to try to see the forest through the trees, for our time, the religious ideal seems to be moving toward the mystical. This shift began innocently enough as the desire for more intimately personal modes of organized religion or, as they have come to be known, spirituality. But, over the past few decades, this yearning for the spiritual has led increasing numbers of seekers to resurrect long-thought-dead mystical traditions and especially Judaism's own Kabbalah. Suddenly, mysticism is in. Signs of the first stirrings of a new paradigm abound: the appearance of the first volumes of the Pritzker-Matt translation of the Zohar, academic and popular conferences and seminars, rabbinic education, publishing houses, mainstream liturgies, adult education courses—all responding to a widespread, grassroots yearning. It is hard to imagine now, but less than a generation ago, mysticism was not even taught at rabbinic seminaries, there were virtually no popular books on Kabbalah, and as the theologian Arthur Green has wisely noted, in Judaism, instead of conferring respect, the word "mystic" was one of derision and scorn. Little wonder then that the topic still strikes us as strange and new. Charlatans, mountebanks, and charismatics abound.

Let us begin our exploration of Jewish mysticism with some primary questions and definitions.

A mystic is anyone who has the gnawing suspicion that the apparent discord, brokenness, contradictions, and discontinuities that assault us every day might conceal a hidden unity. Just beneath the apparent surface, everything is joined to everything else. To a mystic, therefore, what we call reality is but the myriad refractions of that ultimate, underlying unity. It is a Oneness in which all things—even and especially the self-consciousness of the mystic—are intermittently dissolved, annihilated. Now, only the One remains, or in Yiddish: *Alz ist Gott*—everything is God!

Such a definition obviously casts a wide net. It includes many people who probably don't usually consider themselves mystics—indeed, it deliberately includes anyone who might accidentally catch only a fleeting glimmer of the underlying unity. For only a moment, a bit of light sparkles through. This window might be laughing with a child, looking at a flower, or sitting at the bedside of a sick friend. In the words of the Hasidic maxim, nothing is beneath being a footstool for the holy. This certainly is not to deny that in every generation, there are those who are blessed with great mystical experiences and the poetic skill to be able to capture them in words. But, for the rest of us, encounters with the One are only momentary, less dramatic. No epiphany is vouchsafed; the roof does not fly off; the Mormon Tabernacle Choir does not sing; light does not stream from our facial apertures. Such pyrotechnics are not a necessary precondition of being a mystic or for having a mystical experience. As long as the self is dissolved into the unity of all being, no matter how tame the affect, it is mystical. In other words, it might also be about you.

In order to better understand this melting or loss of self into the One, let us consider two models for understanding our relationship with God (or, if you prefer something less religious, then, the Source of All Being.)

The first model is classical, Western, vertical theism. It is the model with which most of us have been raised and that determines the syntax of most of our God-talk. God here can be represented by a big circle at the top and the individual by a tiny circle far below it. Obviously, in such a schema, God is *other* than creation. God is both vertically above and beyond it, presumably running it. He—and, since it's so inescapably hierarchical, God is naturally a "He"—may be actively and compassionately involved or dispassionately absent. God can be doing a good job of supervising creation or a lousy one. God gives us commandments, tells us to do things—Don't murder, Give charity, Be nice—and we offer our own supplications and prayers—Let me pass the exam, Please make Johnny well again, Stop war, and so forth. The key idea here is that God is outside, above and beyond the world; God is *other than* creation.

The second model initially has a more Eastern flavor, but we also find it in various forms throughout the history of religion in the West. According to this conception, God is still portrayed as a big circle. But the little circle, representing the individual, now lies *within* the big circle of God. Here God is literally all of being. God is simply all there is. *All reality is one and it is all God.* And therefore, the separateness, discreteness, boundaried-ness, and autonomy of anyone or anything must be illusory. Everything is only a manifestation of God—and God obviously doesn't have any parts. God is the ocean and we are the waves. In the words of the prophet Isaiah, "The fullness of the whole earth is the presence of God!" (Isaiah 6:3).

This way of thinking turns many of the notions of a God who is above and other than creation on their head. Prayer is no longer a conversation. God can no longer be blamed for what goes wrong. God cannot intervene in the workings of the world. (Mystics, as you can now easily understand, are not much comfort as grief counselors.) In such a mystical model, prayer now becomes an occasion for contemplation of and meditation on our presence within the Divine. Liturgy becomes a mantra. In such a model, what appears to be evil now only challenges us to try to comprehend how God could somehow be within it also. (Remember: A precondition for existence is the presence of the Divine within it, and if God's not in it, then it's not not-real, it's not even there!)

In such a system, you cannot have a relationship with a God of which you are already a dimension. You are simply made of it. You can contemplate how you are part of it, but you cannot have a conversation with it. Ultimately, even the border between your consciousness and the Divine becomes increasingly blurred. There is simply no God outside the system to whom you can complain, talk, or offer thanks. God is the One through whom everyone and everything is joined to everyone and everything.

Since this experience of the mystic-All is universal, every religion has its own mystical tradition, each with its own unique rituals and symbol sets. (Some scholars of religion go even as far as to maintain that mystical encounters are the touchstone for every organized religious tradition.) Beginning students of Judaism are often surprised to learn that it has several mystical traditions: *Merkava* (Chariot) and *Heykha-lot* (Heavenly Palace) mysticism of second-century Palestine; Abulafian meditation of thirteenth-century Spain; the intricate Lurianic cosmology of sixteenth-century Tsefat; Hasidic folk mysticism of eighteenth-century Eastern Europe; Abraham Isaac Kook's utopian mysticism of twentieth-century Israel; and, in the last generation, the extraordinary work of Martin Buber and Abraham Joshua Heschel. Nevertheless, when most people today speak of Jewish mysticism, they mean Kabbalah—a system that took shape in twelfth- and thirteenth-century Provence and Castile, reaching its apogee with the appearance of the Zohar at the beginning of the fourteenth century. The kabbalistic mystical tradition in Judaism is so rich, well-developed, influential, and widely known that, unless specified otherwise, Jewish mysticism and Kabbalah are, for all practical purposes, synonymous.

The great Israeli scholar Moshe Idel once suggested that Kabbalah can be characterized by three unique ideas: *Ayn Sof*, *sefirot*, and *mitzvot*, to which I would add Eros.

God—that is, the Oneness in which all being is dissolved and from which being continuously emerges—is called, in Hebrew, *Ayn Sof*, literally the One "without end." This is much more than simply the arithmetic concept of infinity. *Ayn Sof* is neither numeric nor mathematical. It means, instead, without boundary, without definition, without any characteristics whatsoever. Indeed, to say anything about it at all violates the essential notion of the term. *Ayn Sof* is the font, the source, the matrix, the substrate, the motherlode of being. It may also be being itself. It is to being what electricity is to the letters and words on a video computer monitor. And, as anyone who has not conscientiously backed up his or her work knows, turn off the power and the letters and words are as if they had never been. For kabbalists, therefore, creation is not some event that happened in the past but a continuous and ever-present process. When we express our gratitude for the world, it is because it has literally been created anew each day, each moment.

My youngest granddaughter at age nine months was just beginning to make syllables. *Beh, beh, mah mah, dah dah.* Soon they would become the rubrics of words and sentences and ideas. With language she will begin to name and then learn how to intellectually manipulate her world. And, like the rest of us, she will doubtless begin to think that, since she has names for all the parts of reality, reality indeed has all those parts. In this way, her world will become subdivided into myriad parts, each with its own name, geographic coordinates, descriptive characteristics, and if it is human, with its own agenda. But then, hopefully one day as a young woman, she will reencounter the Oneness of All Being in which all words and all the parts of her world will be (re)dissolved. And the only word she will be able to use to describe it will be "Nothing"—that is, no thing, the One without beginning or end, *Ayn Sof.*

A second characteristic of Kabbalah is the process through which this infinite One(ness) manifests itself and brings creation into being. Simply through being, by its very existence, there emerges from the One a series of concentric emanations or *sefirot,* literally, in Hebrew, "numbers." *Sefirot* are a metaphor for trying to comprehend how the One could possibly make this world of so many apparently discrete and discordant parts. The *sefirot* themselves are alternatively described as dimensions of the divine and the human psyche, the steps in the emanative process of creation, or because everything is made of God, the *sefirot* are also an image of the infrastructure of reality itself.

Kabbalists are quick to caution, however, that even though we speak of them as discrete entities, they are inseparable from the divine unity. Kabbalists see *sefirot* everywhere; creation is a manifestation of the *sefirot*. Every character, place, even color in the Hebrew Bible is an allusion to one of the *sefirot*. Indeed, the Bible itself can be read on a kabbalistic level as a description of the interactive workings of the *sefirot*. In the same way, every dysfunction in our universe is likewise understood as the result of a destabilization of the *sefirot*—which are also the divine psyche. Performance of religious deeds now becomes a kind of repair of and maintenance for the Divine. This brings us to a third aspect of Kabbalah.

Classical Kabbalah is predicated on the idea that human beings, through acts of goodness, worship, love, healing, and giving, or *mitzvot*, are able to influence the Divine. In the Aramaic maxim, *Al y'day itaruta dila-tata ba'ah itaruta d'l'ila,* "By means of awakening below comes awakening on High." Kabbalah, in other words, necessarily involves the performance of righteous deeds. The practitioner, as it were, becomes God's chiropractor. We can easily understand therefore why Kabbalah had such great appeal. It gave to the behavior of each individual Jew literally cosmic importance. Indeed, we suspect that one litmus test of a would-be mystical experience is whether or not it infuses its recipient with a heightened passion for righteous behavior.

Finally, to Idel's list, I would add Eros. While Rabbinic Judaism had a well-developed notion of the *Shekhina,* as the feminine, indwelling presence of God, Kabbalah developed an elaborate and often explicit theology of sexuality. God now had male and female sides, a Hebrew yin-yang, in which the feminine became an equal partner—all portrayed through sefirotic allusion and imagery. Erotic love becomes, if not a sacrament, then a religious act affecting worlds far beyond the two earthly lovers themselves. Righteousness restores a balance and harmony to the male and female dimensions of a One that has no dimensions.

One final caveat: Not everything called mysticism, of course, is mysticism. Because Kabbalah claims to offer knowledge of the inner workings of creation, we can understand how superstition and magic came to be associated with it in popular folk culture. Indeed, even today we carelessly assume that if something is otherworldly, paranormal, mysterious, awesome, magical, or just plain creepy, we should call it mystical. This includes ghosts, dybbuks, golems, weird dreams, bizarre coincidences, Bible codes, secret incantations as well as mostly everything in the general category of "Beam me up, Scotty." Anything claiming knowledge of how to manipulate ultimate reality becomes mystical. It was doubtless such associations with superstition that led nineteenth- and early twentieth-century rationalists to reject anything mystical and throw the baby out with the bathwater. Indeed, for most of the past century, references to the Jewish mystical tradition were effectively purged from the history books. We feel like amnesiacs.

So, let us begin, again.

READING MUSIC

To increase the likelihood that the milestone of my fifty-fifth birthday would be only a joyous event, my wonderful wife, the bride of my youth, after months of clandestine research, to my utter surprise and dumbfounded astonishment, presented me with a concert-grade, Buffet, B-flat clarinet. Now, this would just be the story of another extravagant and expensive gift were it not for one other fact: prior to that moment, I had never, in my entire life, even touched a clarinet! I wasn't even conscious I wanted one.

"How did you know?" I sputtered.

"I just listened," she replied. "For twenty years you've been muttering that someday you'd like to learn how to play the clarinet. I checked with the kids; they heard it too. Apparently you're the only one who didn't know."

Well, after taking lessons off and on for several years (I come right after an eleven-year-old Asian kid), I am a little disappointed that I still haven't had any feelers yet from major symphony orchestras. But, truth be told, I still can't read music very well. Reading music, it's becoming increasingly (and painfully) clear, will definitely take a few more months.

There are so many nuances: all those little Italian abbreviations; "Every Good Boy Does Fine"; dotted eighth notes; keys with six sharps or six flats; funny little squiggles and marks everywhere! And then, as if that weren't enough, there's keeping time. To help you count the rhythm, at the end of every measure, they put a little vertical bar line. I count: one, two, three, four, end of measure; one, two, three, four, end of measure.

My tutor says, "Why do you pause at the end of each measure?"

I say, "Because there's this little vertical line there."

She says, "You're not supposed to play *that*."

I say, "I'm not *playing* it."

She says, "Yes, you are. You're pausing at each one!"

I say, "But then how would anyone know it's the end of a measure?"

She sets down her clarinet and turns to face me. (This means I'm in big trouble and something important is about to come.) "The bar lines are not there!" she growls. "Yes, I know they're written in the sheet music. They're there to make it easier for you to count time. But the divisions are only arbitrary superimpositions. They are not *in the music*."

This reminded me of something I learned from Professor Daniel Matt, currently in the midst of a twenty-year-long project of translating the Zohar.

Just because we have words for all the parts of a tree, he once explained, does not mean that a tree really has all those parts. All our names are, likewise, only arbitrarily superimposed on what is, in truth, one great seamless reality.

The kabbalists explained it this way: There are two worlds. There is *Olam ha-Prayda*, "the World of Separation"—the one we inhabit most of the time, *this world*, with its infinite array of discrete and autonomous parts, each with its own name. And then there is the *Olam ha-Yihud*, "the World of Unity," a radical monism, wherein there are neither parts nor names, where everything is one. Or perhaps more accurately, everything is the One. (To ask: "Why, or how, does the One become many?" is effectively to ask how and why did God create the world. Why would God, the One, create this World of Separation?)

It will also come as no surprise that we will predictably understand our relationship with God depending on whichever of the two worlds we happen to inhabit at the moment. Most of the time the world is subdivided up into measures, each bordered by vertical bar lines, or parts, each distinguished by its own unique name and geographic coordinates. Our relationship with God here is likewise personal, one of two discrete, autonomous, and independent actors. And as in virtually all classical Western metaphors, God is *other* than the world—creating, designing, supervising, and hopefully running the place.

But the World of Separation lies within the bosom of the World of Unity. (They are still mutually exclusive but to realize that one resides within the other is itself already a form of monistic and mystical vision.) Here we have another way to understand how we relate to God. In this World of Unity there are no names, no parts, no separations, and therefore no relationships.

It is all one, the One, the One of All Being—you know: God. And, as music happens only when we are no longer aware of the discrete notes, measures, rhythms, in the same way, meaning comes only when we comprehend the unity which is the core of all being, when the World of Separation gives way to the World of Unity. And then, as in the imagination of the kabbalists, we will finally be able to pronounce all of scripture as one, long, uninterruptible Name of God.

But, alas, to learn how to make music, you must *first* subdivide the whole score into smaller pieces, each one separated from the other by a little vertical line.

BOSQUE DEL APACHE

"He said to him: You have not yet seen the wings of the bird in Eden / the Shekhina." (Zohar 3:71a–b)

WE READ IN EXODUS 25:20 OF THE ARK OF THE COVENANT. It is to be made of acacia wood overlaid with gold and carried by two long poles. And on top of this box containing the tablets of the law are to be placed two gold cherubim whose "wings are spread out above, shielding the cover [of the ark] with their wings."

These winged angels come up again in Ezekiel (1:24 and 10:14). The prophet has a psychedelic vision of God on a chariot that's borne by an eagle, a cherub, a lion, and a human being. Each creature had four wings. Ezekiel says, "[It was] like the noise of great waters, I heard the noise of their wings, like the voice of the Almighty...."

I am standing in the middle of the New Mexico desert several winters ago. It is thirty degrees and a half-hour before dawn. We are in the Bosque del Apache, "the Forest of the Apache," a bird sanctuary.

I am not a big-time naturalist, but my wife is an avid birder. And so, like spouses do, I tag along.

"For this one," teeth chattering, while sipping coffee from the thermos, I whisper, "I want extra points."

She smiles.

In the distance, the horizon is becoming visible now as a dark ribbon of deep red in the winter chill. And dawn comes. The whole sky explodes into bright orange.

And then, within the next fifteen minutes, we watch in awestruck silence, as *twenty-five thousand* snow geese, cranes, great blue herons, and God only knows who else, awake from their sleeping on the water and fly off for the next leg of their migration.

They are so close and there are so many of them, I can literally feel the flapping, wing-flung wind on my face. The park rangers call it "the flyaway." Last evening they warned: You're never the same after the flyaway. And I understand: somehow, simply being present to experience this event changes my perception of what it means to be a creature.

And here's the thing that chastens and humbles me: the birds do this all the time. Whether we're there to watch them or not, they land in the waters of the Bosque and come first light, they fly away into the dawn's early light, a sky full of wings and beaks and feathers on their way to somewhere else. And they do it year after year after year. Just like the great whales do it through the waters of the sea and mitochondria do it through the fluid within our cells. Great flowing streams of life, currents of protoplasm—flying, swimming, running, moving, flowing, praying—doing what they know how to do—doing the only thing they know to do—doing what they were "meant" to be doing, doing what they're "supposed" to do. While I, in my ignorance—obsessed with completing some writing assignment—am doing what I'm supposed to be doing, what I am meant to do. All these creatures, moving on their ways, going about their business, one orchestrated flow of life. My God, I can still feel the wind of their wings on my face.

Probably the holiest ritual moment in ancient Judaism was on the Day of Atonement, Yom Kippur, when the high priest entered the holy of holies in the Temple in Jerusalem. He only had one thing to do. He had rehearsed it for months. He had to pronounce one word: the ineffable Name of God. The Name made only of vowel letters. The Name made from the root letters of the Hebrew verb "to be." A Name that probably initially meant something like "the One who brings into being all that is."

And the room in which he would speak this Name was so sacred that if, God forbid, he should drop dead of a heart attack once inside, no one else would be able to go back in there to retrieve his corpse! Rabbi Isaac explained in the Zohar (3:102a) that they solved the problem by simply tying a rope around his leg.

Rabbi Judah further said that when the priest entered, even he closed his eyes—so as not to gaze where it was forbidden to gaze. But, as they sang their praises, he was able to hear *the sound of the cherubim's wings.*

I thought that was the end of the story until several years later when I was having breakfast at a hotel in Pittsburgh with three other rabbis. We were there for a convention. I don't remember how we got on the topic but Liza says, "I'll tell you about a time when I felt the wings of the *Shekhina.*" (The *Shekhina* is a Hebrew word for the feminine presence of God. The rabbis likened her to a bird, landing apparently from out of nowhere, easily frightened.) Liza always has neat things to say, but since I had just finished writing about the flapping of wings, I listened carefully.

"I'm at my obstetrician's for a routine appointment," she says. "This is already my fourth pregnancy, so the doctor and I have been friends for a long time. While she's hooking me up for the ultrasound, we just go on with our conversation. Somehow we had gotten to talking about birth order, and I asked my doctor if her husband was a first child."

"'Oh no,' she says. 'My husband's a twin.'"

"'A twin,' I say. 'My God, if I had twins, I'd need a new house, a new husband, a new life!'"

"The obstetrician turns on the ultrasound machine, and together we look in reverent silence at the image on the screen.

"'Here, do you see?' says the doctor, pointing to a tiny line. 'This is the spine.'"

"'And what's this?'" I ask, pointing to another line on the other side.

"She pauses for a moment. A smile forms on her lips. 'Why, that's the other one.'"

"I could feel the wind of the wings of the *Shekhina* flapping," whispered Liza. "It was as if God had come and gently fluttered open the next page of my life-book. The page had been written there all along; it was only waiting for me to see it."

PHYSICIAN OF TSEFAT

BECAUSE IT'S ON SUCH A STEEP MOUNTAIN, they have built a municipal elevator in the Galilean town of Tsefat (or Safed). You enter it from the back of the supermarket. There is a utility door, just behind the produce section. But there's no sign—someone has to tell you. And, let me tell you, this puppy is the ride of a lifetime. It traverses only six floors—but five centuries. On the top level, there's a modern Israeli street, complete with pizzeria, an ATM machine, and a one-hour photo shop. On the bottom, you have buildings from the sixteenth century where some of the greatest legal, kabbalistic, and spiritual minds in Jewish history studied, wrote, and prayed. What a congregation that must've been!

Two events had a powerful impact on Jewish life in the sixteenth century and especially on Tsefat. The first came in 1492 when Ferdinand and Isabella expelled the Jews from Spain. It was a cataclysm of staggering proportions: centuries of Spanish Jewish civilization were abolished—buildings looted, fortunes lost, families scattered, libraries vanished. And then, in 1516, less known, the Ottomans conquered the Mamluk Turks, replacing harsh Mamluk oppression with tolerance and freedom. The Jewish migrations resulting from these two events transformed Tsefat into the largest and most vibrant community in Palestine. Exile and redemption were in the air. (I suspect that, just as their preoccupation with redemption following exile can be traced to their expulsion from Spain, so our preoccupation with Jewish continuity can be traced to the incineration of European Jewry during the Holocaust.)

Among Tsefat's more accomplished residents were Jacob Berab, who set out to reinitiate rabbinic ordination by reestablishing an unbroken line back to Moses; Elijah de Vidas, author of *Reshit Hokhma* (The Beginning of Wisdom), one of the most influential ethical works in Judaism; Moses Cordovero, author of *Pardes Rimonim* (Orchard of Pomegranates) and one of the greatest kabbalists of all time; Eleazar Azikri, author of *Sefer Haredim* (Book of the Pious); and Hayim Vital, author of *Aytz Hayyim* (The Tree of Life). Shlomo Alkabetz, author of the Sabbath hymn *Lekha Dodi* (Come, My Beloved), was a member of the community, as was the preeminent legal authority Joseph Karo, author of the *Shulchan Arukh*, (The Set Table), the definitive code of Jewish law. (My teacher Eugene Borowitz once referred to sixteenth-century Tsefat as the Upper West Side of Manhattan.)

The synergy of such intellectual power gave birth to customs and innovations, many of which are still widely practiced even by very nonmystical, liberal Jews to this day: the custom of *Kabbalat Shabbat*, a service welcoming the Sabbath, including going out into the fields to welcome the Sabbath bride and facing the door for the final verse of *Lekha Dodi*; the custom of wearing white or new clothes on the Sabbath; and the custom of a *tikkun layl Shavuot*, an all-night study session on the holiday of Shavuot—all inventions of the kabbalists of Tsefat. (There were also many other, sometimes ascetic, sometimes erotic, sometimes psychic, and much, much more bizarre customs that, thankfully, no one practices anymore.)

To this mélange of Tsefat liturgists, kabbalists, halakhists, and poets, we now add Rabbi Isaac Luria, or, as he is known, ha-Elohi (the saintly) Rabbi Yitzhak—or by the acronym of his name, the Ari. (*Ari* is also Hebrew for "lion.") A seminal religious presence, Luria's bold and complex innovations in theosophy and cosmogony would forever alter the face of Kabbalah and subsequent Jewish history.

Isaac Luria was born in Jerusalem in 1534. His father died while Luria was a child, and his mother moved the family to live with her wealthy brother in Egypt. There, Luria began his esoteric studies, ultimately moving to a small island in the Nile. In 1570, he moved to Tsefat, already a center of Jewish mystical life. The documentary evidence on Luria is meager. And, to make matters more confusing, most of the many historical gaps about Luria's life have been filled in with pious legends elevated, over the centuries, to the status of historic truth. We do know that Luria took peripatetic walks with his students, that he communed with the souls of deceased teachers, and that he claimed he had visionary encounters with the souls he found residing in organic and inorganic matter. He wrote nothing of his system down, claiming it was inchoate, nor did he permit propagation of his teachings during his lifetime. He died during an epidemic on July 15, 1572, at the age of only thirty-eight, less than three years after coming to Tsefat.

In addition to Luria's own refusal to record his life and teaching, there are at least three other very good and interrelated reasons why so few people know about Lurianic practice. First, hardly any of the primary material has been translated into English. In 1942, for example, Gershom Scholem's first doctoral student, Isaiah Tishby, wrote a Hebrew essay on Lurianic Kabbalah, which "amazingly ... would remain the only serious and sustained study of Luria's teachings for the following forty-five years" (Lawrence Fine, *Physician of the Soul, Healer of the Cosmos: Isaac Luria and His Kabbalistic Fellowship* [Palo Alto, CA: Stanford University Press, 2003], 7). Second, the sources that do exist are at best intricate, at worst convoluted, opaque, self-contradictory, multiauthored, and often, simply off-the-wall. (You don't "get into" Lurianic Kabbalah; you struggle to make sense of it.) The third, and final, reason is that kabbalistic research has been primarily interested in Lurianic Kabbalah's theology but not in what Fine calls its "social, devotional, and experiential dimensions" (ibid., 8).

Fortunately, Dr. Lawrence Fine of Mount Holyoke College, a scholar of enormous competence and spiritual depth, has produced the definitive English text on Luria and his circle: *Physician of the Soul, Healer of the Cosmos: Isaac Luria and His Kabbalistic Fellowship*. This academic text (there are 895 footnotes) is clear, fascinating, well-argued, ambitious, and important—and also an excellent introduction to kabbalistic thought. Fine asks: Just who was this person Isaac Luria and these guys with whom he surrounded himself? What was the psychodynamic of their *hevra* (fellowship)? Did they have a larger plan, and if so, what was it?

One of the most startling realizations that emerges from Fine's masterful presentation is a vision of what I am tempted to call Kabbalah on steroids. Indeed, some of it is so foreign to our modern sensibilities that we can begin to comprehend why nineteenth-century German rationalist historians were so horrified at what they euphemistically called kabbalistic superstitions. It was much more than just superstition. Lurianic Kabbalah was a system of pious practice, personal ritual, meditation, and devotion designed to heal its practitioners, their community, world history, and the cosmos itself. Much, if not the majority, of their regimen will strike beginning students as bizarre.

Fine introduces us, for instance, to such customs as *yihudim* with the dead, that is, stretching yourself out on a grave, face down," as a way of communing with the deceased. The Lurianic kabbalists also practiced running permutations on the four letters of the tetragrammaton, God's most mysterious four-letter Name; involuntary vocal-automatism; ascetic practices ranging from month-long fasts to self-flagellation; and reading invisible Hebrew letters on the foreheads of strangers as a form of psychic diagnosis, as just a few examples. Luria "did not wait for the sinner to voluntarily seek him out, but was able to determine a person's sin merely by gazing upon the person's face" (ibid., 186).

"Luria found it natural," notes Fine, "to speak in a language of divine genitalia, seminal and vaginal fluids, lactating breasts, divine parents, children, and lovers" (ibid., 13). Luria was particularly fascinated by the Zoharic myth of how, on the seventh day of Pesach, a pregnant hind, travailing in labor, would be bitten by a snake as a sexual act. Fine, in a typically almost offhand observation, notes that "the flawed character of existence as a whole can be traced back to misuse of masculine sexuality" (ibid., 355).

In a similarly matter-of-fact way, Fine dares to wonder, for instance, "Was Isaac Luria's wife curious about why sexual relations were essentially limited to Friday nights, while non-kabbalistic wives could have sexual relations with their husbands on other nights of the week?" (ibid., 15). And surely one of Professor Fine's most penetrating observations is that Luria probably believed he was the reincarnation of Shimon bar Yohai, who was, in turn, a reincarnation Moses. (Each generation gets just one.) Rabbi Shimon bar Yohai is the purported author of the Zohar—who, it just so happened, was buried in Meron, only six miles down the road from Tsefat. Is that why Luria made the move from Egypt?

While Fine is primarily concerned with the psychodynamics of Luria and his disciples, their pietism, and their experience, he does provide us with an excellent synopsis of Luria's cosmogenic myth. For many readers this will be worth the price of admission alone. Luria's story of the creation is so important and still resonates so deeply within the Jewish psyche that Jews today who have never heard of Isaac Luria or Tsefat or even Kabbalah embrace it. It is, notes Fine, "without doubt the most elaborate such story in all of Jewish tradition" (ibid., 124).

Here, in brief, is Luria's creation myth: According to earlier Spanish Kabbalah, in the beginning there was only God—limitless, boundary-less, beyond definition, utterly unknowable. God was *Ayn Sof:* without end. Everything was One. And everything was filled with the limitless light of the presence of God. There was only one logical problem: There was no room for creation. So, according to Luria, God withdrew God's self, making a space so there could be room in which to make the world. This voluntary self-contraction he called *tsimtsum*. It is not unlike what any good parent or teacher must routinely do: get out of the way so that the child or student can have room in which to learn and grow.

The resulting vacuum, however, was not exactly empty. Apparently there remained a faint trace, a *reshimu*, of the Divine. As the late Dr. Alexander Altman once taught me, it was like the remnant aroma in an empty perfume bottle. Into this space, God sent a ray of light to illuminate, animate, organize, and make ten lights. These lights then arranged themselves into concentric circles and, simultaneously, the form of a cosmic, archetypical human form, or *Adam Kadmon* (not to be confused with *Adam ha-Rishon*, the first Adam of the Garden of Eden). This primordial form contained the whole world within itself, and his soul contained all souls yet to come. (When you meet a stranger to whom you are mysteriously drawn, you are meeting someone whose soul used to reside next to yours in the cosmic body of *Adam Kadmon!*)

But alas, God underestimated God's own creative power. The light was simply too powerful. And, in Luria's bold imagination, the result was a cataclysm of literally cosmic proportions. Luria called it *shevirat ha-kelim*, the shattering of the lower vessels. In this way, sparks, or *nitzotzot*, of divine light became scattered everywhere and trapped within the pieces of the broken vessels. These shards, or *kelipot*, are the chief source of evil and the basis of our present world: a heap of broken pottery, shards containing imprisoned sparks of divine light, bestowing vitality, and, above all, yearning to go free. As Fine writes:

> *Particles of divine light have* fallen *into the material world, utterly alienated and estranged from their sublime and transcendent origin. These sparks of light instinctively long to be liberated and reunited with the divine source from which they originally flowed.*
>
> (Ibid., 137)

But there is more to Luria's great creation myth. Divinity desires now to mend itself. The Hebrew word for mend, fix, or repair is *tikkun*. According to Luria, the sparks captive in the *kelipot* are unable to free themselves alone. That is why human beings—you and I—are here. Everything we do must be directed toward this sacred, ultimate goal. According to Luria, *Adam ha-Rishon*, the first Adam, was designed to have been *Adam ha-Achron*, the last person, the redeemer. Adam and Eve could have repaired the whole thing, returning the cosmos to eternal, divine light. But alas, that was in a galaxy long, long ago and far, far away. We find ourselves here, living amidst cosmic debris, exiled, conflicted, and broken. And this brings us to Luria's unwitting but vital contribution to contemporary religious action: *tikkun olam*—"repairing the world."

Fine (using a different transliteration of the Hebrew word *tikkun*) explains that, for Isaac Luria,

[167]

> *the most fundamental and ultimate goal of all human existence is* tiqqun. *The project of tiqqun, the liberation of divine light in all of its forms from its entrapment in the material sphere, its return to its source on high, and the ascent of all the worlds to their proper place within the structure of the cosmos, required the most elaborate and painstaking regimen of contemplative devotion.*
>
> (Ibid., 144)

Indeed, Fine explains, "God is no longer regarded as being in complete control of all history ... rather, God's own well-being is contingent upon human action[!]" (ibid., 58). You will note here, however, that Luria is not talking about politics or fixing what is wrong with society. (Indeed, as a theology of religious action, *tikkun olam* is probably not even dateable prior to forty years ago.) For Luria, the word *olam* in *tikkun olam* does not mean "world" but "being" or "eternity." And the goal, for him and his *hevra*, his little society of disciples, was nothing short of repairing the cosmos. Their strategy was conspicuously meditative, ritualistic, inward, elitist, and religiously Jewish. And the mechanism for the repair, therefore, is the proper performance of *mitzvot*, sacred religious deeds: studying Torah, fasting on Yom Kippur, giving charity, refraining from gossip, not eating shellfish, praying daily, not wearing clothing made from linen and wool, observing the Sabbath—yes, all 613 of the traditional commandments. They are the way for Jews, the only way. Each *mitzvah* liberates another trapped and exiled spark. Each *mitzvah* restores more of the cosmos to its intended pattern. Each *mitzvah* testifies to our partnership with (or participation within) the Divine.

Indeed, the principal flaw in much of contemporary, liberal political action is not the absence of passion but the absence of God. We are, many of us, so frightened we will sound evangelical, fundamentalist, zealous, or right wing that we have abandoned the spiritual dimension of our task. We are, to paraphrase my teacher Rabbi Arnold Jacob Wolf, passionate about our calling but seem to have forgotten who is calling.

And this brings us back to Professor Fine's real fascination.

Luria and the members of his fellowship believed themselves to be the protagonists at the center of a great cosmic drama.... It entailed bringing an end to exiled existence at every level of being and affecting the redemption of the whole cosmos.

(Ibid., 12)

For all their excesses and all the obstacles to understanding their plan, Luria and his fellowship offer us in the twenty-first century what may be the most potent metaphor for political action. And Lawrence Fine's *Physician of the Soul; Healer of the Cosmos: Isaac Luria and His Kabbalistic Fellowship* is your personal invitation to join in the great and sacred task.

SPELL-CHECKER

SOMETIMES A MOVIE CAN BE IMPORTANT FOR ITS INACCURACIES. Take *Bee Season*, for example. The story takes place in Oakland and ricochets off the foibles of the members of the Naumann family: Eliza, a grade school girl with a gift for spelling; Aaron, her older brother, who is a seeker; their mother, who, it turns out, is bonkers; and their father, who is a religion professor and failed kabbalist. It is a beautifully photographed but unsatisfying rendition of Myla Goldberg's beautifully written but unsatisfying novel of the same name. Despite its disappointments, however, *Bee Season* inadvertently offers some highly instructive insights into the state of religion and Kabbalah in America today. Permit me three examples.

Its most insidious mistake comes from Professor Saul Naumann, played by Richard Gere, when he tells his daughter Eliza that "a mystic can talk with God and have God listen." This should come as a big surprise to anyone who has ever offered a prayer, because it means that he or she is now a de facto mystic. (And you thought that communicating with God only made you religious!) Sorry, Professor, you get that one wrong on the exam. (Mysticism, unlike religion in general, is *not* about communicating with God; it is about dissolving yourself into the divine All and becoming one with God.) Far more fascinating, however, is the damning implication here that if the only way to commune with God is to be a mystic, then mysticism therefore must be the only bona fide form of religion. And all other nonmystical forms of religion are really just condemning their practitioners to spinning their (prayer) wheels. In other words: according to the movie's error, we realize that in America today, perhaps the only way to be truly religious is to be a mystic!

A second inadvertent but instructive error concerns Jewish kids becoming Hare Krishnas. Seeking love, we suspect, more than spirituality, Naumann's older son Aaron finally dons a saffron robe (although this defection does require a blonde knockout as bait). But given the absence of any expression of Judaism whatsoever in the Naumann home—no candles, no religious books, no blessings, no melodies, no prayer—it is at least encouraging that the kid has enough good sense to try to find something religious somewhere else. (In the novel, Saul Naumann is a cantor, which, we suspect, might have been an easier reach for Gere but also a box office albatross.) There's only one problem: Jewish kids don't become Hare Krishnas anymore. Thirty years ago it was different. Then, virtually everyone in the Jewish community knew of a kid who went off and became a Hare Krishna, joined an ashram, took up Zen Buddhism or something else Eastern or even more esoteric. The question the movie inadvertently raises is why does Aaron's heresy, even in Oakland, seem so dated? (Here in the Bay Area today, Buddhist meditation is in vogue as Judaism's primary competition, but so far, it does not seem to pose much of a threat nor to have had much of an impact.)

The instructive answer is that nowadays a young Jew on a spiritual search need look no farther than—of all places—the local synagogue! Today, Judaism's own mystical tradition, Kabbalah, is not only out of the closet, you can learn it in *People* magazine! Everyone, it seems, is eager to know and observe some recondite tradition. (Haven't you heard? Organized religion is boring, secular, and irrelevant.) And, while *Bee Season* tries to employ this new mystical paradigm, its Kabbalah seems tacked onto the plot but with little authentic substance.

This may be another inadvertent insight: Kabbalah is in. And why is it all the rage? For two reasons: Contemporary Judaism, now finally beginning to recover theologically from the Holocaust, has begun to re-search its own mystic heritage. And now that it's accessible again, Hollywood has found it.

To be sure, as throughout so much of Jewish history, charlatans, mountebanks, and quacks still abound. Yet, with even modest
persistence, anyone can learn a lot about real Kabbalah, and if you
are also willing to commit yourself to a traditional Jewish lifestyle,
you can even practice it, too.

Perhaps the movie's most egregious and revealing religious
error, however, concerns its (and the novel's) failure to understand
the meaning of language in Judaism and in Kabbalah. The way you
say "I create" in Aramaic (a cognate of Hebrew and the language of
both the Talmud and the Zohar) is *avara*. The way you say "I
speak" is *davara*. And the way you say "I create as I speak" is *avara
k'davara*—abracadabra. Words make reality. According to the
Hebrew Bible, that is how God commences creation: "God said,
'Let there be ... ' and there was...." But there's more.

Joseph Dan, the Israeli historian of Jewish mysticism, notes an
important difference between the Hebrew Bible and the New
Testament. Unlike Christianity's sacred text, which (with the
exception of six Aramaic words spoken by Jesus) is the story of
Jesus translated into Greek, the Hebrew Bible purports to be the
original and literal statements, words, and letters spoken by God.
To understand these word and letter rubrics and know how to
rearrange them in their intended order is to be able to perform
miracles, resurrect the dead, know the very secrets of creation.

For Judaism and Kabbalah, reality, therefore, is both *in* and *of*
Hebrew letters—*not* English ones. Don't get me wrong. English is
my mother tongue and a very beautiful language. But the letters of
our alphabet are only graphic signs for making sounds. In Hebrew,
on the other hand, letters are beings with existences independent
of ink and paper. Hebrew letters are the literal instruments of
divine creation. And to understand them is to understand the
secrets of being itself. It is hardly surprising, then, that kabbalists
devoted such sustained attention to the letters of the *l'shon kodesh*,
the holy language. But to jump from this and claim, as *Bee Season*
does, that the thirteenth-century Spanish kabbalist, Abraham
Abulafia's idiosyncratic exercises involving ecstatic alphabetic
meditations and permutations as recorded in Naumann's doctoral
dissertation could help someone learn how to ace English spelling

bees, much less proffer direct access to the Divine, is simply uninformed. Kabbalah is not about spelling and it is not about English. But here, too, there is an inadvertent insight. Does this error in the film perhaps betray a yearning to unearth something sacred in our otherwise secular society?

The eighteenth-century Hasidic master Rabbi Yaakov Yosef of Polnoye offered the following parable: Once some travelers got lost and decided to go to sleep until someone came along who knew the right way. Someone gave them bad directions and sent them to a place of wild beasts and robbers. Then someone else came along and showed them the right path. It's the same way with the letters of the words of sacred text. They have come to this world as travelers but have lost their way and fallen asleep. When someone comes along, however, and studies the Torah *with holy intent*, such a one leads the letters back to the right path so they can cleave to their root.

Now, to be sure, trying to return the letters to their supernal source, just as any loss of ego boundaries, can be psychologically destabilizing—especially for borderline personalities (you know who you are)—but for most of the rest of us it does seem worth the risk. I do not doubt that, over the ages, some mystical seekers have indeed slipped over the edge, and I have personally known a few people who have had bad, drug-induced trips, but I have never heard of anyone having a seizure from trying to get too close to God. (It should only be our worst problem.) But perhaps that's what the young heroine of *Bee Season* intuits when she symbolically renounces such intimacy with the Divine in a conspicuously nonmystical attempt to heal her dysfunctional family and this otherwise dysfunctional movie.

MIDRASH AS HYPERTEXT

JEWS DIDN'T INVENT TWO-POLED SCROLLS. They are simply an inevitable result of putting too much parchment on a single roller, or *megilla*. The second pole is (to borrow an image from the last generation's technology) a "take-up reel."

To my disappointment, I now understand that Jews didn't even invent that visual arcade of commentary and argument epitomized by a page of Talmud. It was a creation of gentile type-setters. What we Jews seem to have given the world (to the dismay of fundamentalists everywhere) was the mischievous notion of a revealed tradition perpetually in flux—beautifully symbolized by a Torah scroll or a page of Talmud.

But an even better metaphor for this comes from the way information is now routinely processed on the World Wide Web—you know, when the cursor changes from an arrow to a little pointing finger (*yad*?!) whispering, "Click me, please." Doing so takes us somewhere else—perhaps in the same document or perhaps halfway around the world. These "blue" or "underlined words" that "turn an arrow into a human hand" are called "hyper-text," words invisibly linked to some other noncontiguous text.

Indeed, the whole idea of midrash (and maybe all Jewish education) seems predicated on this idea that, ultimately, each word in scripture is connected to every other word—a mystical syntax in which every word is joined to every other word—a luminous organism of coherence, meaning, and unity: the body of God.

A KABBALAH LEXICON

A FEW YEARS AGO, AT SAN FRANCISCO'S JEWISH COMMUNITY CENTER, I had the great honor of conducting a public interview with Moshe Idel, arguably the world's leading scholar of Jewish mysticism. (His bibliography is longer than most of my books.) We all found him to be personable, mischievous, and brilliant.

Toward the end of the session, figuring it was the elephant in the closet, I asked him the "Madonna Question": "Is she a kabbalist?" The gist of his reply was that "I have a hard enough time figuring out the past, let alone the future. [And then, paraphrasing the Aramaic *pok khazi* (go and see), he added:] Let's just wait and see what the Jews are doing." Kabbalah, in other words, he chastened us, is an open system.

Sociologically, historically, and even theologically, its rubrics, its boundaries, and even its players remain continuously fluid. Gershom Scholem said one thing about it, and Moshe Idel (his student) came along with other texts and redrew the playing field. Consider this: the library of the Hebrew University contains microfiche of hundreds and perhaps thousands of kabbalistic fragments and manuscripts that have not yet been published or even studied!

What is Kabbalah? *People* magazine has one definition, the faculty of the Hebrew University another, the fund-raisers at the Kabbalah Centre yet another, New Age Aquarians still another. (And that's only *Jewish* Kabbalah, spelled with a "K" or sometimes a "Q" but never a "C.") If we add Cabbala, we get tarot, alchemy, and horoscopes, too! The toothpaste is, as they say, out of the tube. And, while I do intend to offer my own definitions of genuine mysticism and (at least) classical, theoretical Kabbalah, I also believe Jewish teachers ought to caution one another about succumbing to the gatekeeper syndrome. (Look where it got us with "Who is a Jew?") Instead of who gets to carry a membership card, we might more profitably focus our energies on whether the respective teachings and their outcomes bring souls closer to right acting and the Holy One.

That said, permit me to offer some working but, hopefully, still open definitions that I have found helpful.

Rabbi Abraham Joshua Heschel observed in *God in Search of Man: A Philosophy of Judaism* ([New York: Farrar, Straus and Giroux, 1955]), that "in modern society, anyone who refuses to accept the equation of reality with the physical world is considered a mystic" (p. 142). In other words, for a mystic, there's more to reality than meets the eye. Permit me a working definition: a mystic is someone who suspects that the apparent brokenness, contradictions, and discord of this everyday world conceal a hidden unity. Somehow—even though any fool can see that superficially it makes no sense—everything is connected. It's all one; or, as we Jews say, God is One.

Think about it: What's the alternative? That reality is only what you can see and that only a *few* things are mechanically connected? That everything else is just dumb luck, happenstance, chance, playing the lottery, rolls of the dice? Or, if you believe there's a God, that God is only involved in *some* things but not *every* thing? No, for a mystic, God is not only involved in everything, God *is* everything. And a mystical experience is when you get it and then, in retrospect, you realize you have been (and now are) present within the divine unity all along.

William James, in his classic *Varieties of Religious Experience*, identifies four characteristics of mystical experiences: (1) They're *transient*—they come and go on their *own* schedule. (2) The recipient is always *passive*—you can't have them on demand; instead, they *have* you. (3) They're *noetic*—the experience vouchsafes

health, wealth, and eternal life. (Yossi Klein Halevi, writing in the *New Republic*, a few years ago, suggested that this last one may have been what hooks movie stars.)

Full disclosure: about such *Kabbalah Ma-asit*, I must confess my own skepticism. It strikes me as odd, for example, that of all the people who claim to have been reincarnated over the centuries, for example, not one single one of them has ever told anyone of where they hid the money. I feel the same way about Bible codes and gematria. I once gave a lecture on Kabbalah in Minneapolis. During the Q & A, a young man said, "I came here on bus number 37. What does that mean?" The best answer I could think of was (and is): "It means you should go home on bus number 37."

Zalman Schachter-Shalomi used to tell the story about a guy who was born on May 5 (May is the fifth month) in 1955. He lived at 555 Fifth Street. He had five kids. His whole life had been in fives. His accountant had just told him his net worth was $555,555.55. And, on the same day, he saw in the paper that there was a horse named "Number Five" running in the fifth race. Convinced it was a sign, he put his entire life savings on "Number Five." And what do you think happened? He won! That's right, his horse came in fifth! The point of the story is that stuff like that is out there in the universe; we just don't understand all the rules, and attempts to manipulate them are not only foolhardy but perilous.

In a similar vein, my teacher Arnold Jacob Wolf was fond of pointing out that the Deuteronomic prohibition against talking to ghosts does not deny their existence. It just says don't to talk to them.

But alas, because Kabbalah claims to know something about the secret inner nature of reality and the principles that govern the universe, it easily lends itself to the yearnings of people who want a shortcut or a hot stock tip so they can pull off the theological equivalent of insider trading. And, where there is such a "market," quacks are everywhere. I am reminded here of the Holy Yehudi's (Yaakov Yitzhak ben Asher of Przysucha, d. 1814) dismissal of the alleged wonder-working rebbes of his own generation: "Miracles," he said, "phooey! Anybody can do miracles. But to be a Jew, this is very hard."

KABBALAH IYU-NIT / THEORETICAL KABBALAH

Theoretical Kabbalah, on the other hand, strikes me (with the possible exception of *sefirot*) as the core of an emerging American Jewish mystical revival. (Joseph Dan said that if you pray, you're religious, but if you believe it, you're a mystic.) *Kabbalah iyu-nit* began in Provence with the teachings of Rabbi Avraham ben David of Posquières, or the RaVaD, in the twelfth-century. They were continued with Yitzhak the Blind. From southern France, they spread west to Gerona and then throughout most of the Iberian Peninsula. They reached their apogee in the thirteenth century with the appearance of the Zohar. This classical Kabbalah is characterized by four astonishingly fecund new ideas: (1) God is now understood as the *Ayn Sof*; (2) God, every human psyche—indeed, all reality—can be envisioned symbolically, if you will, diagramed, as ten *sefirot* or dimensions of consciousness joined to one another through twenty-two channels; (3) God has both male and female dimensions, which exist dynamically in a state of erotic yearning; and (4) righteous human action (read: *mitzvot*) fulfills a *tsorech gevohah*, a need on High, a divine yearning. Kabbalah, in other words, is a supercharged way "to do Jewish"—Judaism on steroids. Let us look more closely at each of these ideas.

AYN SOF / THE ALL

In order to explain a God who is literally incomprehensible, kabbalists often resort to two Hebrew words. The first is *yesh*, "somethingness" or simply "isness." The other is *ayin*, "nothingness"—not zip, *gornicht*, or *bupkis* (which is Yiddish for small goat droppings), but the absence of any "thingness." And, if some "thing" is no "thing," then, logically, it has no boundaries. It is literally boundless. Therefore *ayin* is also without beginning, without end; it is another name for eternity.

Kabbalah invests these two words with cosmic, metaphysical significance. *Yesh* comes to refer to the created world, this one in which we spend most of our time. But *yesh* connotes much, much more than merely the material or the physical. It includes spatial, temporal, intellectual, even emotional reality also. The key notion here is that all the things of *yesh* have definitions, beginnings and ends, and, above all, boundaries. Living in the world of *yesh* is not bad—indeed, it's obviously inescapable and often beautiful. *Yesh* is only dangerous if you think that's all there is.

Ayin, on the other hand, connotes not the absence of being, but the absence of any boundaries. It is a no-thing, a nothing that encompasses and permeates all creation. *Ayin* is therefore the font of all being, the substrate of creation. That is why the kabbalists call God *Ayn Sof*. Not only can't you own *ayin*, you cannot alter it, change it, or affect it in any way whatsoever. You cannot point to it. You probably can't even accurately say as much about it as I've already said. We are all waves made of the ocean of *ayin*, manifestations of that great underlying Nothingness—the Oneness of All Being.

Dr. Daniel Matt, currently well into a twenty-year-long project of translating the Zohar into English, once explained that just because we have words for all the parts of a tree does not mean that a tree has all those parts. The words make it easier for us to organize, comprehend, and manipulate reality. They are, if you will, a taxonomy. All our words are only arbitrary human super-impositions on what is, in truth, the seamless unity of all being. And, for that reason, we must be careful not to allow ourselves to fall into the habit of thinking that just because we have words for "leaf," "twig," "branch," "trunk," and so forth, that therefore a tree really has all those parts.

The leaf does not know, for example, when it stops being a leaf and becomes a twig. Nor does the branch know when it is no longer a branch and now the trunk. And the trunk couldn't care less that it has stopped being a trunk and is now the roots. Indeed, the roots do not know when they stop being roots and become soil—nor the soil the moisture, nor the moisture the atmosphere, nor the atmosphere the sunlight. All our words are a human taxonomy of being. (Indeed, noting the gibberish of the seventy-two three-letter Names of God in Exodus 14:19–21, Joseph Dan has gone so far as to suggest that the goal of mysticism is the annihilation of language.)

Or, to put it another way: It is all one, *ayin*, the *Ayn Sof*, the One, the One of All Being, you know, God—in the Yiddish, "*Alz ist*

Gott!" (What did the Kabbalist say to the hot dog vendor? Make me *one* with everything.) For a mystic, meaning is the result of dissolving into the unity at the core of all being, when the *yesh* of this *Olam ha-Prayda*, "World of Separation," gives way to the *ayin* of the *Olam ha-Yihud*, "World of Unity," when we realize that we are present within the divine *ayin*, the great ocean Nothingness, the sea of Being.

SEFIROT / INFRASTRUCTURE

Of all kabbalistic images, *sefirot* are probably the most well-known, frequently portrayed, and least understood. (Liberal Jewish theologian Eugene Borowitz once told me that he thought the primary reason Kabbalah remained esoteric was because no one who understood *sefirot* had yet figured out a way to explain them to someone who didn't.) *Sefirot* claim to describe and envision the deep and hidden structure of reality, the emanations of God's creative process, the divine being, and, therefore also, the inner dynamic of our own psyches. *Sefirot* are an attempt to speak about the parts of the One who has no parts. You might say that they are to being what the words for all the parts of a tree are to a tree.

The *sefirot* are frequently portrayed as ten concentric circles or "spheres," but the English word *sphere* has no relation to the Hebrew word *sefira*, which only means "number." (It is interesting that because of this linguistic coincidence, most of us persist in thinking of them as globes anyway.) Like fractals, we find the sefirotic diagram everywhere, beneath the most sophisticated microscopes and beyond the most powerful telescopes.

Kabbalists teach that comprehending *sefirot* and their dynamic structure is the closest we can come to glimpsing the inner workings of God. But they are equally adamant that the entire sefirotic system is, in reality, one unified and indivisible divine organism.

In one classic metaphor, the *sefirot* are also a diagram of our own psyches. We each have tendencies toward being too strict or too lenient. And, at any given moment, these tendencies could be either in or out of balance. Or we each have different modes of knowing. In our culture, if you are a woman, you might have an *intuition*—an idea mysteriously *wombed* from within; if you are a man, you might have an *insight*—an idea gained by *piercing* the darkness with a spark of light. Of course, regardless of our gender, we all have both feminine and masculine—yin and yang, or, as the Zohar calls them, *botzina d'Qardinuta* and *Alma d'Atay*—sides to our personalities. The goal, obviously, is to get them in balance. You might be surprised, as I was, to discover that loving and permissive parenting winds up on the masculine side of the sefirotic tree, while strict and judgmental parenting is on the feminine side. (I once pointed this out to Daniel Matt, who said he figured that the author of the Zohar must've had one helluva mother.)

According to this sefirotic model of reality, what's wrong with us is also what's wrong with the world and is also, as it were, what's wrong with God. They are all manifestations of the same, underlying World of Unity. And the goal, therefore, would be somehow to re-balance these internal psychic forces, first in our selves, then in reality, and finally in God. Remember: all being is organically interconnected; everything depends on everything else; it's all one organism.

The sefirotic diagram is Kabbalah's metaphor for envisioning and restoring a balance between insight and intuition, between justice and mercy, between strength and softness, between male and female. And the goal of right religious action is the restoration of harmony—within ourselves, within our world, and, ultimately, also within God.

ZIVUG L'ILAH / HEAVENLY SEX

Moshe Idel points out in his important book *Kabbalah & Eros* that while Judaism is routinely considered monotheism, one of the most frequently repeated phrases in the traditional prayer book is *l'shaym Yihud Kudsha barikh hu ush-khin-tay* "for the sake of unifying the Holy One, Blessed be He with His feminine presence."

Whether kabbalists were sexual innocents or sex-crazed old men remains a topic of scholarly debate. But everyone agrees that Kabbalah brought Eros into the Divine. Before Kabbalah, the God of the Hebrew Bible (so preposterously masculine and prone to fits of anger) hadn't had any sex since before the creation of the world; after Kabbalah, Eros (in the form of a feminine side to the Divine) entered heaven. God may have no image, no family, no birth or death, but with Kabbalah, God now experiences—as it were—erotic yearning and consummation within God's self. Most commonly this union was between the *sefirot* of *Malkhut / Shekhina / Kenesset Yisroael* and *Tiferet* (or sometimes *Yesod*), but it also occurred between *Hesed* and *Gevurah* and between *Binah* and *Hokhma*. Furthermore these "couplings on High" are directly affected by human loving in our sublunar world. The mythic implications are endless and doubtlessly the reason for their widespread acceptance among the Jews.

TSORECH GEVOHAH / HEAVEN'S NEED

And this brings us to the fourth and last face of classical, theoretical Kabbalah: *tsorech gevohah*, "heaven's need." It is also, I believe, why ordinary Jews over the centuries have embraced Kabbalah with such enthusiasm. *Tsorech gevohah* is about why we do what we do, specifically about the performance of *mitzvot* and how they affect the highest orders of being.

"Go ahead," say the Jews, "persecute us, expel us, God forbid, pogrom us." It is of little concern because, by what we do, in what might appear to be even trivial or routine ritual acts—reciting blessings, refraining from eating shellfish, leaving the corners of our fields, observing Shabbos, clothing the naked, studying Torah—we literally restore and maintain the yin-yang balance of creation. You might say that through the performance of *mitzvot*, kabbalists imagine that we Jews are, as it were, God's chiropractors.

The Hasidic master Dov Baer of Mezritch once explained that "God's creation of the heavens and the earth was, indeed, wondrous: God made something from Nothing. But the deeds of the righteous, he says, are even greater. For, through everything they do, they take something and turn it back into Nothing" (*Magid Devarav L'Yaakov* 9).

It is important to point out here that we are not talking about generic good deeds. They are certainly important and everyone should do as many as he or she can, and indeed, many of them seem obviously good for the universe. But, for a kabbalist, they do not mystically restore the balance in higher worlds. That *only* happens through doing *mitzvot* (which is why you must be a serious Jew *before* you can be a classical kabbalist). *Mitzvot* affect worlds far beyond anything we can imagine; they open channels of otherwise calcified divine energy; they repair creation, even as they heal those who do them.

I do not pretend to know if or how apparently trivial religious acts affect times and places and worlds beyond our own, but I do know that for classical, theoretical Kabbalah it remains a continual and wondrous possibility. The goal (as I believe, for every variety of mysticism) is getting your ego out of the way (*bittul yesh*), which also turns out to be a prerequisite for a mystical experience. Indeed, perhaps that is the ultimate *kavana*: that through the performance of this sacred deed you are dissolved into the agency of the Holy One(ness) of All Being. And once you do that, you realize your presence within the *Ayn Sof* and begin to heal creation.

LITERALISM AND METAPHOR

One final observation: We must leave it to the historians of some future generation to explain why Kabbalah seems to have returned to Jewish life with such vigor at the dawn of the twenty-first century. Doubtless, they will speak of nineteenth-century German enlightened rationalism's horror at anything that even whispered the nonrational or superstitious. Historians may also mention the toll taken by the wholesale defection of two generations of young Jewish spiritual seekers to the mystical religions of the East. But it also seems increasingly possible that the reemergence of Kabbalah in our generation may also be understood as an unconscious, corrective response to the fundamentalist literalism so rampant in the religions of the West. From Islamic radicalism to Evangelical Christianity, the loudest religious voices, nowadays, shout that "what it says is what it is." The text (and life?) is as it appears and no further searching is necessary or appropriate.

[185]

To such a worldview Kabbalah responds: Everything is more than what it says. Things are never as they appear. There is more to reality than meets the eye. Meaning is concealed. And, for this reason, Kabbalah may be understood as the returning of metaphor to Judaism. Every text, every situation, being itself are metaphors for and refractions of *the* primary reality lying within, beneath, and above: God is One—which, I suppose, brings us back to the Heschel: "In modern society, anyone who refuses to accept the equation of *reality* with the *physical world* is considered a mystic." In the words of the Zohar (3:152a): "Rabbi Shimon said, 'Woe to those who claim that Torah comes only to tell stories of this world in ordinary language. If this were so, we could write an even better Torah!'"

6

HOLINESS

OPEN MY LIPS

IT SEEMS ODD THAT, AS A PRELUDE TO THE *AMIDAH* (a bouquet of prayers of praise, petition, and thanksgiving), which is the most intensely conversational script of the entire prayer book, someone thought to throw in Psalm 51:17: "God, open my lips so that my mouth may declare Your praise."

Wouldn't it make more sense to say something like, "Here I am, God, ready to begin our conversation," or "Permit me to introduce myself," or "I know we haven't always seen eye to eye on certain things"—something that would accentuate the dialogic nature of what will follow. In order for there to be a conversation, an intercession, there must be two discrete parties. It takes two to tango.

In much (but not all) of the Hebrew Bible and the prayer book, God and people are separate, distinct, discrete, autonomous, independent, and apart from one another. God says this, we say that. God does this, we do that. God's there, we're here. The energy of the whole thing comes precisely from our being separate from one another. So why begin our personal prayers with a denial of that mutual autonomy and free will?

The psalm says, "God, would you please open my mouth." Hey, who's working my mouth anyway, God or me? Who's praising God, me or God? What's going on here?

What's going on here is another spiritual paradigm, one in which God and people are not only *not* distinct from one another but are literally *within* one another. God is the ocean and we are the waves. In the words of the Hasidic maxim, "It's all God." My mouth is God's mouth. My praises are God's words. In the teaching of Rabbi Kalynomos Kalmish Shapira of Piesetzna (who perished in the Warsaw ghetto), "Not only does God hear our prayers, God prays them through us as well!"

The words of the *Amidah* that will follow may *sound* like they come from me, but in truth they come from a higher source. Prayer may ultimately be an exercise for helping us let go of our egos. They seem so hopelessly anchored to this world where one person is discrete from another and from God. We yearn, instead, to soar heavenward where there is a Holy One of All Being—where we realize that we have been an expression *of it* all along. "God, open my lips so that my mouth may declare Your praise."

SPIRITUAL GREED

WE ALL HAVE PEOPLE WHO ARE EVEN LESS-THAN-ACQUAINTANCES. They carry on their anonymous lives at the outermost edge of our circles of awareness. Beyond them are only faceless strangers. But they are part of our lives.

That is who this woman is for me, less-than-an-acquaintance. She works one of the counters at LaGuardia where I catch the shuttle home after teaching my weekly seminar for rabbinic students. Maybe every third or forth trip, I wind up in her line. A few years ago, I accidentally gave her the wrong credit card, the one that, instead of saying "Lawrence Kushner," said "Rabbi Lawrence Kushner."

"Oh," she said, with a deferent smile, involuntarily caressing the Jewish star on her necklace, "it's a pleasure to meet you, Rabbi." (Two Jews meeting in New York, big deal.) I forgot all about it. But she didn't.

Our subsequent, forty-five-second transactions have identical scripts but with one humorous twist. The shuttle between New York and Boston is hardly restful. Everyone waiting in any line seems to be in a big hurry, carries a cell phone, and thinks he is definitely more important than the person ahead of him in the queue. But now, when my turn comes to the head of the line of the World's Most Important People, I get treated like the pope.

"Oh, hello, Rabbi. How have you been?" For all I know, I am her rabbi.

I wound up in her line again last week. After our routine business, we wished each other a happy New Year, and I went over to select a few complimentary magazines before they called my flight. But this time, I realized that she had walked over to the giveaway rack too. I smiled. And then, as if she were completing a "drop" for the CIA, while pretending to the rest of the commuters in the departure lounge as if she were merely choosing a magazine, she leaned over and, without looking at me, whispered, "Rabbi, my husband's out of work."

I recognized the code at once. It was the emergency rabbi signal. "I understand," I nodded and gave her the secret countersign. "Do you know his Hebrew name?" (I knew she would.) "I will be glad to include him in my prayers." There were tears in her eyes as she spoke it. I might as well of said, "Don't worry about a thing, the old fixeroo is in."

But then she said something that surprised even me. It seemed at once both hopeful and greedy, pious and selfish, something maternal, primal, sacred. "And my two children, Rabbi, one is ill, and the other just doesn't seem to know what to do with his life. Would it be too much, could you perhaps, I know you're so busy, mention their names too—please?"

So many names to mention. So many holy requests. From people we hardly know, less-than-acquaintances. You don't have to be a rabbi to include someone else's names in your prayers. It couldn't hurt.

SILENT PRAYER

Rabbi Abbahu said in the name of Rabbi Yohanan: When God gave the Torah no bird twittered, no fowl flew, no ox lowed, none of the Ophanim stirred a wing, the Seraphim did not say "Holy, Holy," the sea did not roar, the creatures spoke not, the whole world was hushed into breathless silence and then the Voice went forth: I am the Lord your God. —Exodus Rabba 29:9

MY FAVORITE PART OF SAILING COMES ABOUT FIFTEEN MINUTES into the voyage, after we've loaded all our gear aboard, removed all the covers, freed all the neatly coiled lines, pumped the bilges, checked the safety equipment, opened the sea cocks, turned "on" the batteries, hoisted the "iron genoa" (started the engine), cast off the mooring line, negotiated our way through the maze of boats in the harbor, raised the main, unfurled the jib, trimmed the sails, set a course— then the moment comes.

I reach down to the throttle and pull it backward all the way, back past "idle" (there's a spring somewhere in there to keep you from doing it accidentally), and shut off the fuel to the diesel. It takes a second or two to take effect.

The engine obediently chugs and sputters to a stop. Now, except for the whisper of the wind in the sails and the gurgle of water rushing past the hull, there is only silence. There's nothing to say. Indeed, to say anything would damage the serenity of the moment.

We are better at making noise than enduring silence. But silence is better than noise. Attaining silence may just be the reason for the prayers.

The classical Reformers must have figured this out long ago when they made the "silent meditation" the culmination of the liturgy. And, for most of us, it was. After you did all your prayer work, there was silence. It lasted for several minutes. It taught, effectively, that the purpose of prayer was stillness, patience, passivity, listening. The meditation ended with the choir singing a stylized version of Psalm 19:15, "May the words of my mouth and the meditations of my heart be acceptable, in Thy sight O Lord, my Rock and my Redeemer. Amen."

A reasonable, short-term goal for all of us might be to create a five-minute morning ritual that could be performed at home each day—perhaps nothing more than holding a prayer book, or putting on a tallit or tefillin, closing one's eyes, reciting a favorite line from the liturgy, "shutting off the engine," and waiting in meditative silence for an answer.

English novelist George Eliot said:

> *If we had a keen vision and feeling for all ordinary human life, it would be like hearing the grass grow, the squirrel's heart beat, and we should die of that roar which lies on the other side of silence.*

> (Nathan Sheppard, ed.,
> *The Essays of George Eliot*
> [New York, NY: Funk & Wagnalls,
> 1883], 19)

A BLESSING FOR THE CZAR

A FEW MONTHS AGO I WAS INVITED TO PARTICIPATE IN A SYMPOSIUM at the Jewish Theological Seminary (where they train Conservative rabbis) in New York City on making Jewish education more spiritual. There were a half-dozen religious types and a half-dozen psychologists plus an audience. It was a fascinating and instructive event. For me, however, the epiphany didn't come until the rush-hour car trip back to Kennedy. I wound up sharing the ride with Dr. Todd Kashdan, assistant professor of psychology at George Mason University, who is completing what promises to be a big book on happiness. He has read all the research and done a whole lot of his own, too. And what do you think are the common denominators of happy people? (Before you read further, stop and try to guess for yourself.)

It turns out that there are three universal factors. The first two are commonsense easy: meaningful human relationships and health. (Duh.) But the third—the one, he said, that shows up as a spike on virtually every study of personal happiness ever done—is gratitude. People who are happy are all grateful. They've woven it into their everyday lives, ritualized it. But what are you supposed to do if you don't feel particularly grateful? That's where Judaism and its obsession with blessings, or *berakhot*, come in. For us Jews, life is one blessing after another. Each *berakha* reminds us that even when life is difficult or painful or, God forbid, terrible, it is still good.

I remember visiting a man in the hospital who was dying of cancer. While we talked and joked and wept, the nurse brought his

[195]

lunch. "Don't let your food get cold," I said, "you eat and I'll talk." He nodded, took a slice of bread from the tray, closed his eyes, and whispered, "*Barukh ata Adonai* … "

Every blessing gets us to say, "I am grateful to be alive for one more day." We have specific, ritualized phrases for blessing the Torah before we read it, our children at the Sabbath table, affixing a mezuzah to the door, washing our hands after using the toilet, breaking the bread we are about to eat, the moon, not being slaves, and the rooster's ability to distinguish between night and day. We bless dwarfs and trees in first blossom. We bless hearing good news and especially good wine later in the meal (with the identical blessing). We have a blessing for seeing a non-Jewish king or head of state (which I suppose would be "a proper blessing for the czar"). We bless hearing thunder, experiencing tornados, and yes, even earthquakes: … *sh'kokho ug-vurato maley olam,* "whose power and might fill the world."

According to tradition, in a normal day, a Jew should get off one hundred blessings. This is neither as rigorous nor compulsive, however, as it sounds. The weekday morning liturgy alone contains several dozen *berakhot.* Add to the liturgy the fulfillment of daily commandments (like washing your hands before a meal) and routine life functions (like waking up in the morning) and even ordinary Jews like you and me come off very grateful.

The Sephardim even have a Sabbath tradition—when the thirteen intermediate petitionary blessings are omitted from the four *Amidot* (*Shacharit, Musaf, Mincha,* and *Ma-ariv*), resulting in a major blessing loss. They boost their "daily blessing count" back up to one hundred by serving a Sabbath afternoon meal but without any bread (the blessing for which would cover all subsequent foods). Instead, the menu features all sorts of different foods, each of which (now, without the blessing over bread) requires its own unique *berakha.*

With each blessing we Jews extend the boundaries of the sacred and ritualize our gratitude for life—one hundred times a day. Everywhere we turn, everything we touch, everyone we see: *Barukh ata Adonai Elohaynu melekh ha-olam,* "Holy One of Blessing your Presence fills creation," Your presence fills me with gratitude.

BIKING WITH PELICANS

SINCE WE MOVED OUT TO SAN FRANCISCO, I've taken up road biking. Sure, I know, there are the hills, but unlike in Boston, you get to do it twelve months a year. My route is—I suppose you'd have to say—spectacular: it's all along the Marina and Crissy Field; I go by Alcatraz, Angel Island, Sausalito, the Marin Headlands and then up to the Golden Gate Bridge itself. And, because of the fog, every day it's a whole new and different panorama. Sometimes the view can be pretty dreary. That's the way it was not long ago. Even for San Francisco it was unusually damp and raw. The parking lots were empty and I had a few miles of overcast oceanfront all to myself. The cloud cover was a very low, gray, and opaque ceiling you could almost reach up and touch.

So here I was, just biking along, doing maybe twelve, thirteen miles an hour, minding my own business, when I glanced over my right shoulder toward the bay, and there, not more than twenty feet away from me, flying in a perfect "V" formation toward the bridge, were about three dozen pelicans—huge prehistoric creatures with their long, pouched beaks and enormous black wingspreads, doing about twelve, thirteen miles per hour.

They were so low that we were on the same eye level—if you will—the same plane, except, of course, I was on a bicycle on the land and they were in the air above the ocean. And then, as I looked at them, they turned their heads and they looked at me.

And then one of them spoke.

She said, "It's good to be alive."

"Yes, ma'am," I whispered, out of breath from trying to keep up with them.

"You and us, we're all just creatures, you know," said the big bird leading the formation.

But before I had a chance to agree, he only nodded and led the formation up into fog and out of sight.

But, you know, the pelicans, they're still out there. So are the seals and the microscopic creatures in our protoplasm, disease-carrying mosquitoes, hurricanes, children laughing in playgrounds, adult movie theaters, income taxes, the galaxy of Andromeda, this essay—one great organism of being.

THE ZEN
OF AIRLINE TICKETS

WE HAD TO FLY FROM BOSTON TO LOS ANGELES for a big family party. This, normally, would have been just an excuse for much happiness were it not for that fact that we couldn't leave until Sunday morning and that would run us afoul of what was then called the Saturday Night Stay-over Rule. The rule states, with chilling inflexibility, that the cost of any round-trip, transcontinental airfare that does not involve staying over a Saturday night will increase by the speed of light in centimeters squared. Thus a normal round-trip between Boston and LA including a Saturday night stay-over goes for around $400, but without a Saturday night, it can cost well over $1,000!

"Isn't there some way around it?" I implored my travel agent. And, sure enough, a few days ago she called with a clever solution.

"If you're willing to change planes and fly out of a small airport another forty-five minutes farther away," she offered, "the round-trip will cost you only $209!"

I was ecstatic. "That's wonderful; you're a genius," I told her. "Just let me check with the family and call you first thing tomorrow."

But when I called the next morning, she informed me that, to her dismay, the fares had gone up—literally overnight—to $450. "But what happened to my $209 fare?"

"I'm afraid that was yesterday," she replied, "but $450 is still very good."

"No, it's not, it's terrible," I said. "Where's my $209 fare?"

"You don't understand," she explained. "Right now, $450 is all you have. Sure, yesterday you had something even better, but right now, what you've got is what you got."

And then it dawned on me: some people have travel agents; me, I have a Zen monk. My insistence that I had something I never really had was making me miserable. Come to think of it, if I were to make a list of all the stocks I should have bought or sold ten years ago, I could make myself feel pretty lousy, too. But that was then and this is now.

And that's what it all comes down to: at any given moment, by logical necessity, you can only have what you have. That doesn't mean that you can't hope and work to have something else later, but liberation from suffering comes from accepting that right now "what you've got is what you got."

"Okay," I told her, "buy 'em at $450; just don't tell me if they go down again."

MEMORY AND REDEMPTION

Jonathan Cott is a prolific New York author, interviewer, and poet. He interviewed me for his book, On the Sea of Memory: A Journey from Forgetting to Remembering.

> *Remembrance is the secret of redemption.*
> *Forgetfulness leads to exile.*
> —*Baal Shem Tov*

JONATHAN COTT: *The Hebrew word* zakhor—*meaning "remember"—is an injunction and commandment. According to Yosef Yerushalmi, the verb* zakhar *appears 169 times in the Bible, usually referring to Israel or God as the subject ("Remember now the Creator in the days of thy youth"—Ecclesiastes). The Bible also proposes a reciprocal relationship such that if you remember God, God will remember you ("Go and assemble the elders of Israel and say to them: The Lord, the God of your fathers, the God of Abraham, Isaac, and Jacob has appeared to me and said: I have surely remembered you"). Conversely, in the Bible there is also the minatory fear that God may forget you ("The Lord has forsaken me; my God has forgotten me"—Isaiah ... an entreaty foreshadowing Jesus's stricken cry from the cross). And then there is God's own fear that He will be forgotten ("O Israel, never forget me"—Isaiah), suggesting the old rabbinic notion that God himself is in exile, that man and God are collaborators in each other's destiny, and that God requires man to redeem Him from exile. The act of memory is an imperative for this redemption.*

Why in the Jewish tradition is there such an intense need and desire to remember? Throughout history collective memories were important to fortify the identity of a persecuted and dispersed people. Today, however, there is a decline of Jewish collective memory, and there is an ambivalence with regard to the nostalgia for the past and sense of rejection of that past that many Jews feel today. As Hans Meyerhoff has written, "Previous generations knew much less about the past than we do, but perhaps felt a much greater sense of identity and continuity with it."

What are some of your immediate thoughts about the idea of remembering in the Jewish tradition?

LAWRENCE KUSHNER: Let me start with the siddur, the Jewish prayer book, in which at the end of the morning liturgy there's something called *Shesh Z'khirot,* which means "six things to remember." There are six things that we are commanded to remember in the Torah. And it is a very interesting list. The first one is to remember the going out from Egypt; the second is to remember the Sabbath day; the third is to remember standing at Sinai; the fourth is to remember the way our parents tried God in the wilderness or: "remember and never forget how you provoked the Lord your God in anger in the wilderness"; the fifth is to remember what God did to Miriam, the sister of Moses, on the journey out of Egypt—she was afflicted with leprosy apparently for bad-mouthing Moses, who had married a Cushite woman; and the sixth is to remember Amalek [a marauding Negev tribe and the paradigm enemy of Israel]. And this last one is the most fascinating from the point of view of memory because the commandment literally says: "You shall blot out the memory of Amalek from under heaven. Do not forget." It's a double whammy loop: "Remember it; forget it. Remember it; forget it." So there are six times when the word "remember" is used and they do comprise a fascinating list and the mind just begs to find the pattern.

What interests you about this list?

What fascinates me is that somebody would bother to put them in a prayer book. Remember Egypt, remember Shabbos—that's easy; remember Sinai—a piece of cake. But number four—remember how your parents were obnoxious in the wilderness—that's not considered to be high Judaism. Quoting it, it says: "Remember your parents' waywardness, your obstinacy"—that's the kind of thing we like to repress and forget. There are more terrible things to remember and that injunction is a very subtle thing to remember.

As for the injunction about Miriam, I don't know what that's doing there. Of all the things to remember that God did, I mean there are people who did worse things and to whom God did more dramatic things, so why that injunction? I just don't know. And the last commandment to remember Amalek is very important. It has to do with remembering what your enemies did to you.

What's fascinating about that is that it seems to be a violation of the commandment that says that you shouldn't remember the bad that people did to you because that would constitute bearing a grudge. According to the Talmud if you even remember that somebody hurt you, your job is to go to that person, tell him that he hurt your feelings, and if he apologizes, accept his apology and forget it. And if he doesn't, well, then it's his problem; it's not yours; you've got to get on with your life. So the injunction about Amalek poses an interesting problem: that we should remember our enemy so that we can blot out his name. It sort of hits you on both sides of the jaw at the same time.

What else do you think about concerning the Jewish sense of memory?

Judaism never portrays itself as young, it always portrays itself as an old man who remembers everything. To make the point, when was the last time you saw a picture or a painting of a young Jew? No such thing. It's always an old Jew whose face is wrinkled by what he remembers. Christianity has infants, but there are no pictures of Jewish infants. When you see pictures and photos in the tourist shops in Israel, it's generally those depicting old Jews. We reverence age and the wisdom that comes with it. It's interesting to remember philosopher Franz Rosenzweig's idea that the old man conducting the Passover Seder is indistinguishable from the four-year-old grandchild sitting across from him at the table.

Why do you think there's such a strong need to remember in the Jewish tradition?

I'm uncomfortable with making that a basic tenet of our teaching. Because it seems to me that any healthy religion is going to have memory as a central gesture. It feels a bit too chauvinistic for my comfort to claim that only we Jews remember things. Everybody remembers stuff. It's more instructive to ask what do Jews do with memory.

What do you think Judaism does with it?

Well, we reenact things. What happened was—and this is an insight of the great scholar of Jewish mysticism Gershom Scholem— that a lot of Jewish holidays and ceremonies were originally mythic, and by mythic I mean that they celebrated events that were eternally recurring and circular. In pagan religions, God dies and is reborn; and it happens every year at the same time. But Scholem points out that Judaism took these mythical celebrations that were originally agrarian (which is why they were circular and annual) and made them historical. Living in the bounty of the harvest at Sukkot, for example, became a memory of our wandering in the wilderness where we lived in huts. And on Passover the celebration of the first spring lamb and the first sheaf of barley that happened every year became a commemoration of our redemption from Egypt. And Shavuot, the festival of weeks, came to commemorate the receiving of the Torah.

Now the festivals celebrated historical events. And the important thing about historical events is that they are unrepeatable; history is linear, not circular. And therefore history is not repeatable; each day brings with it an obligation and urgency. In pagan religion there is an attitude of: Well, if we don't do it right this year, we'll do it right next year or the one after that. It's relaxed. But Judaism is more urgent because there will never be a tomorrow that's like today; what is available for us to do today will never be available again.

Dr. Daniel Matt, a translator of the Zohar [Book of Radiance], once shared with me an amazing responsum. A responsum is a formal reply to a legal question—Jews would write a letter to their rabbi, and the rabbi might forward the query to the ranking doyen of the generation, and the answer acquired the status of a legal precedent. Apparently, some sultan in celebration of his birthday announced that everyone who was in his jail would be permitted to be free for one day and the prisoner could pick which day. And some guy actually wrote his rabbi asking which day he should pick. Should he go free on Purim, which celebrates salvation from our enemies, or should he go free on Passover, which celebrates redemption from Egypt? Or should he do it on Hanukkah or Yom Kippur? And the rabbi writes back, effectively saying, "Schmuck, do it today!" I mean: Today is it; there is no tomorrow.

So Judaism as a religion of linear history and non-repeatable events remembers the past with an often bittersweet feeling because of what we could have done but didn't. The window of the past is forever closed. We have this same theme at the conclusion of Yom Kippur when we say that the gates are closing and that once the gate is closed it doesn't open again. Prayers that could have been offered, deeds that could have been done, words that could have been spoken—that day will be forever gone.

Yosef Yerushalmi writes that if Herodotus was the father of history, the fathers of meaning in history were the Jews, and for the Jews God seems to be known only insofar as He reveals Himself historically.

In *The Prophets* Abraham Joshua Heschel talks about the prophets bringing a new dimension to the idea of meaning in history. He says that God and Jews talk to one another through the non-repeatable events of history. So we have a sense of prophetic urgency and the importance of action. I would say that the expulsion from the Garden of Eden began history. Prior to that nobody had calendars or watches and after that everything is recorded and remembered.

You've written that "Leaving the garden is a metaphor for our forgetting that we are one with the universe. Holy awareness is the only way to return." What is the connection between the act of becoming aware and remembering?

Let me take half a step back. One of my colleagues, Rabbi Nehemia Polen, an Orthodox rabbi in Boston, says that because God has infinite awareness, God cannot remember anything or dream anything because, for God, there is no past or future. To enter that mode of mystical awareness is to swallow all time. Then Eden means an unimpeded, undifferentiated presence within the divine flowing, infinite consciousness. After that, history begins and you start remembering what you don't have anymore and yearn to go back. I suspect that the only way to go back is through *unio mystica*, the mystic moment, loss of the self's boundaries, dissolution into the divine timelessness. My novel, *Kabbalah: A Love Story*, begins with the following quotation: "Time is just God's way of making sure that everything doesn't happen all at once." That's by George Carlin.

The comedian?

Yes. I think it's brilliant.

So we leave the garden and our sense of primordial unity and then forget that we are one with the universe.

That's right. Because now, at this moment, I think you're different from me. I think you're in New York and I'm in San Francisco and that yesterday we spoke on the phone and are talking again now ... but this separateness, this otherness, from a mystical point of view is illusory. When we're back inside that divine presence we have no need for memory because there is no past, no history (and no future), only an eternal present.

In the Passover Haggadah it says that in every generation each person should regard him- or herself as if he or she personally had come forth from Egypt. I had a congregant who once took a geography course at the local high school and the teacher asked if anyone had been to Egypt. The congregant student raised her hand and replied, "Yes, every year for about an hour!"

In your book Honey from the Rock: An Introduction to Jewish Mysticism *you write: "Judaism focuses on the point where the two worlds [this world and the other world] meet: Sinai. And the inscrutable record of that encounter: Torah. We seem to gain our invitation to the holy world by virtue of our presence there at that awesome mountain. Because the Jew is a member of a community who was present when the other world flooded this one with meaning, we are able to return as often as we wish, simply by remembering."*

Rabbi Zalman Schachter-Shalomi says the Torah is a postcard we've written to ourselves to be read at some later time when we've forgotten what it was like at Sinai. The Torah is a mnemonic device; whenever I read it, Sinai comes alive again. It's like looking through the pages of a photo album: oh, I remember that summer when we lived at that house and we did this and that and it was so beautiful and now it all comes back to me. And, if that family album happens to record the most meaningful event in history, then it becomes that much more holy.

Steve Thomas in his book *The Last Navigator: A Young Man, an Ancient Mariner, and the Secret of the Sea* tries to find out how the ancient Polynesians were able to navigate the Pacific without instruments. He befriends a man named Piailug, who was the last navigator: "There was no powerful mathematical model that one could apply as in western navigation, nor were there primers and instruction books in case one forgot something. Piailug had only his senses and his memory. So critical was memory to navigation that it defined his notion of courage. Piailug said to me, 'To navigate, you must be brave and to be brave you must remember. If I am brave it is because I remember the words of my fathers.'"

There's another amazing story by the Hasidic rabbi Nahman of Breslov called "The Seven Beggars." The scene is a memory competition regarding the Garden of Eden. The contestants vie to see who has the earliest memory. One remembers, "When they cut the apple from the branch." Another remembers, "When the fruit first began to be formed." Still another remembers, "The taste before it enters the fruit." Finally, the blind beggar, who is telling the story, says, "I was yet a child, but I was there too, I remember all these events, I also remember nothing." And they answered, "This is indeed an older memory than all." How does one remember nothing?

... When the blind beggar says, "I remember nothing," what I think he's saying is, I remember the infinite, the eternal; I remember God; I remember the source from which all being comes. In other words, by the way you pick up a fork, by the way you hold a pen, by the way you hold your lover, by any deed that you do, you potentially can raise it and yourself to the order of *ayin*, to boundlessness. You effectively take something and turn it back into

Nothing! What makes all this so fascinating is that we're playing with this shift back and forth between a world in which time is essential and a world of timelessness in which memory is dissolved into an eternal present.

The philosopher Avishai Margalit in his book The Ethics of Memory *writes about how in the Jewish tradition one distinguishes between forgiveness and forgetting. And he quotes God's words from Jeremiah: "For I will forgive their wrongdoing and remember their sin no more," and Margalit says that while God forgets what he has forgiven, we do forgive but do not forget.*

I like it and I don't like it. Jews are stuck with this notion—and this goes back to the Amalek quote—that you've got to remember what people did to you or otherwise they can do it again. But you have to put that together with what I think is the need of a person who, for example, has been abused to forget everything because, if you go on remembering it, it goes on abusing you. Unfortunately you see that in a lot of Jews today. Personally I have turned down several VIP tours of the Holocaust Museum in Washington because I don't want to remember and I don't think I want the world to waste time remembering me as a victim either. I want to remember its horror only to make sure that such a thing never happens to me or to anyone else ever again. I wish I had a different obligation but you don't get to select your memories. If I was abused, I was abused. The trick is (perhaps as with the Amalek commandment) only to figure out a way to keep it in consciousness long enough that it doesn't happen again but then forget it. The best thing for someone who has been through something horrific is to get on with it. I mean, what good does it do you?

But what about George Santayana's famous remark that he who doesn't remember the past is condemned to repeat it?

And I can see that that is a wise thing. I guess I'm thinking that there are two kinds of forgetting. There's a kind of forgetting where something is totally gone and you have no recollection of it, and there's a kind of forgetting such that it's out of consciousness but there's an alarm that goes off whenever the conditions obtain that can lead it to happening again.

Let's say I walk down a dark alley and get mugged. Remembering I got mugged serves me no useful purpose. But I don't want to forget it entirely. I want to have some psychic mechanism so that the next time I'm walking down the street and want to cut through a dark alley, all of a sudden a bell starts ringing and says: No, no, remember. I'm not going down this alley. I'll take a different route. And then I forget it again.

Obviously, with the Holocaust, the Jews have learned a horrible lesson about what it means to be victimized by the full power of a technocratic state gone mad. But I would argue that we seem to have forgotten how to help other people who are suffering it now.

In my former congregation I helped form a group whose subtitle was "Jews Against Genocide" but the name of the group was "If Not Us, Who?" And that's how I would respond to a Holocaust memory. I'm not interested in looking at pictures of a gas chamber. I'm interested in looking at pictures of Rwanda or other places where genocidal things are occurring right now. I know about that in my gut, as a Jew, and that places a unique obligation on me—that's the part I don't want to forget.

In Hasidism, such a deliberate loss of self, dissolution of ego, is called *bittul yesh*, literally "nullifying being." The goal is simply letting go of one's ego. Indeed, this may be the *summum bonum* of all spirituality: to die into God. But to do that you must first get yourself out of the way so that there can be room for God. In the words of the Talmud (*Arakhin* 15b), "God says, 'My I and your I are not able to live in the same dwelling.'" (It always comes off sounding a bit like a line from an old Gary Cooper western where the sheriff says to the bad guy: Ain't room enough in this here town for your ego and Me. You pick!) Or, to turn a more contemporary phrase: It's your ego, stupid!

In the words of the Hasidic master Yehiel Mikhal of Zlotchov, we become "like a drop that has fallen into the great sea and ... is one with the waters of the sea and it is not possible to recognize it as a separate thing at all." Our aim, in other words, is to literally lose our selves in the divine All. Yes, that does sound a bit like death. (We recall again the core *Yontif* teaching.)

This brings us back to the verb *ma'avirin*, usually rendered as "avert." But that is not its only meaning. The root of *ayin vet resh* (*avar*) seems to be something like "to cross over, to get to the other side, to go beyond, to transcend." We speak of a transgression as an *averah*, a going over to the other side (of the Force)! The Jewish Book of the Dead, *Ma'avar Yabok*, takes its name from the "ford at the River Yabok," which Jacob, our father had to "cross over" in order to meet Esau and earn his destiny.

Maybe the verb *ma'avirin* doesn't mean "to avert," that is, "to annul" the terrible decree (of our death). Life experience and common sense tell us that is not an option. Maybe it means to go beyond our terror of death by beating it to the punch and giving our egos away, even though we're still alive! To be sure, our suffering and our demise won't go away. But, mysteriously, through renouncing our fantasies that we are gods, through renouncing our egos and their appetites, through making ourselves as (the divine) Nothing, we can be liberated from our terror. In the words of the *Adon Olam*, *b'yado afkid rukhi*—"into God's hands I commit my soul."

Dov Baer of Mezritch said that "the work of the pious is greater than the creation of the heavens and the earth (*Ketuvot* 5a).

For, while the creation of the heavens and the earth was making something from Nothing, the pious transform something back into Nothing. Through everything that they do, even with mundane acts ... they transform something into Nothing."

Indeed, despite the gruesome machinations of his death, Rabbi Amnon does seem "beyond" it all. Despite his torments, we envision the man going to his death, on *Yontif*, with a beatific and untroubled smile. The words of poet Stephen Mitchell speaking of Job also apply to Rav Amnon: "Life is ... the breath-thin surface of a bubble, and everything else, inside and outside, is pure radiance. Both suffering and joy come then like a brief reflection, and death like a pin" (*The Book of Job*, trans. Stephen Mitchell [San Francisco: North Point Press, 1987], xxviii).

Amnon's death testifies to his life teaching: through the self-lessness of *teshuva*, repentance (I return my self to its Source), *tefilla*, prayer (I pour out my self before God), and *tsedaka*, charity (I make myself the gift), we too can *ma'avirin*, transcend, the terror of our own death. Now, you get a roomful of people to all try to think that way for a day and you've got yourself a day that is, in the words of the prayer, "holiness full of awe and dread."

On his deathbed, Rabbi Simha Bunam of Przysucha said to his wife, "Why are you crying? My whole life was only that I might learn how to die."

THE BAND ON THE TITANIC

I AM FASCINATED BY THE BAND ON THE *TITANIC*. Their resolution to continue playing amidst the chaos has attained something like mythic status. I suspect that the phrase "and the band played on" probably now refers to the band on the *Titanic*. I am also puzzled that their continued music making while the great ship went down is often misunderstood as an act of futility: a string quartet playing Mozart or Schubert while the world falls apart. (One member of my former congregation once joked that the only difference between his aged mother's finances and the *Titanic* was that the *Titanic* had a band!) I am now convinced that the musicians' decision to continue playing, despite their obvious fate, was a gesture of mutual respect, dignity, and even piety. Everyone was going to die. The only operative question remaining now was how?

While I cannot corroborate this yet, I do have it from a reliable source that the violinist, or whomever it was who kept the band playing, in a strange but surely unmistakable gesture of respect, was apparently the only non-first-class passenger buried among the first-class passengers. Whether or not this is accurate, the line that director James Cameron gives him in the movie *Titanic* belongs in the Yom Kippur liturgy.

Remember the scene? All the lifeboats are either gone or full. The ship has begun to list. Deck chairs begin to slide. Passengers are running this way and that, screaming in terror, and the band members agree that it's time to stop playing. They start to put away their instruments, but then it dawns on, I think it was the violinist, that there is nowhere to go. In such a situation, the only thing to do is the only thing you know how to do. And, if you happen to be a musician, that means to go on making music as best you can. So the violist turns back to the ensemble and offers one of the greatest lines of all time. Through tears, picking up his instrument, with all humility, dignity, and piety, he says, "Gentlemen, it's been a privilege playing with you tonight."

It occurs to me that that may just be all any of us ever get to say: "It's been a privilege playing with you." Would that we too could speak those words *without* the threat of an imminent death. To live in such a way as to be able to honestly say that line to the "other members of the band" with whom we come in contact day after day.

We are all the musicians in a ship's band. The boat may not be sinking, but like it or not, we are *all* dying. This sobering Yom Kippur realization can make us run wild with terror, just like most of the people aboard the *Titanic*, or, as with the *klezmorim*, it can lend dignity, grace, and beauty to the music we play.

For truth be told, we are all doing the *very best* we can at what may finally be the only thing we know how to do. What a holy place to be! What an extraordinary orchestra! So much trust. We whisper to one another, "It's been a privilege playing with you."

Afterword

"OUR TOWN"

THIS HERE MEDITATION IS CALLED "OUR TOWN." It was inspired by a Pulitzer Prize-winning play by Thornton Wilder of the same name. Kids nowadays don't read it the way we did when I was in high school, but it's still a very fine drama. It is a short play about life and marriage and death in a small New Hampshire town called Grover's Corners, just over the Massachusetts line. It is narrated in part by a stage manager who also plays the role of the clergyman and gets to say a few wise things every now and then. He starts chatting with the audience before the house lights go down ...

The members of the cast are you, your families, and your friends. That's sort of how it goes in the Wilder play. Then, the date was 1901. But today, the date is today and the time is sometime in the evening of the tenth day of Tishri. And that would make it *Kol Nidre*.

Several summers ago, when the children were just children, Karen and I took them to Washington to visit the nation's capitol. We saw most of the official sights and the kids had a good time. One afternoon we finished a tour early and wound up across the street from the National Archives. We decided to see if we could find any record of the Kushner family's arrival in the United States. We had heard that, with a rough idea of when and where a family arrived, one might be able to locate the steamship manifest. This, in turn, often contained fascinating bits of genealogical and personal information.

First we had to translate our name into the soundex code. I had to make a few long-distance phone calls to my father to find out my aunts and uncles probable Yiddish names. Then I needed to call my eighty-two-year-old aunt Betty to see if she could remember the name of the boat. She thought it was the *Koray*. Soon we were all huddled over the machine that reads the microfilm, rolling through page after page of names and dates. Then we found a Moshka Kushner who arrived in New York in 1907. Could this have been Uncle Morris? We reasoned that if we could find someone else with the last name of Kushner who arrived on the same date, we might have located the boat.

I will make the story short. We were lucky. On September 23, 1907, at 10 a.m., a ship named the *Korea*, after sailing for twenty days from the Baltic port of Libau, arrived in New York with—we had to read through what seems like thousands of names—a mother and six children. The manifest says that they came from the town of Kalerka in the Gubernyia, or province, of Kiev. That is where the family says they came from. There were two entire pages of people from that shtetl; my God, the whole town must have have been on that boat.

I returned the next day; I was hooked. After a much longer search, we located one Yakob Kuszner. He arrived two years earlier on September 13, 1905, aboard the steamship *Georgia*, which had sailed from Trieste on the Adriatic Sea. His passage took twenty-seven days. He also had come from Kalerka. The manifest said he had ten dollars in his pocket and was going to a friend's home at 55 West 28th Street. His race was listed as Hebrew.

I looked at the neatly penned information and dared to wonder if they, in their wildest dreams, could have imagined that I would someday write about their journey. Will one of your progeny someday remember you and wonder if you could have imagined them?

From Washington we drove to Detroit. Like so many people nowadays whose families live far away, we would go back to our parents' home for a few weeks every summer. For us, Detroit is the "old country." I wonder if it is not meant to be that each year, at about the time I begin to think about what is in me to share with my congregation on *Yontif*, I am in the land of my birthplace. Sitting like a little boy in his parents' home.

I wander through the neighborhood where I grew up, which used to be a suburb and is now inner city. Black people and Lubavitcher Hasidim are everywhere. I wonder where the years have gone. And I wonder if my parents then wondered when they were my age where all the years had gone. And I wonder if my children will wonder the same thing.

It would be foolish to try to say something profound about any of this; it is the stuff of which life is made. But it also would be sacrilegious to ignore it. It is an abiding source of wonderment and mystery. I mention it now only in the hope that it will evoke for you your own memories, your own tears, your wonderment, your mystery, your family, your birth, your death.

When I was a kid there was a program on television called *The Naked City*. The camera would show an aerial view of Manhattan, play some weird music, and the narrator would say something like, "There are eight million stories in the naked city and tonight, we will tell you one of them." It was terrific. I had forgotten all about it until one Rosh Hashanah when, just as services were about to begin, I leaned over to the cantor, and said, "I may know at least one story about everyone in this room!"

It also occurs to me that I may know too much. I don't mean that you'll have to hire a Mafia hit-man to get rid of me. No, when I say that I may know too much, I mean it is a sacred burden to know so many stories. The happiness shatters into sadness which compassionately transforms itself again and again into joy. It gives rabbis an eerie slant on life. Are we happy now or are we sad? I keep getting the past and the future mixed up. There's too much to remember.

I suppose that's why I identify with the stage manager in Thornton Wilder's play. Maybe it is the rabbi's job to simply be present for all the great passages of life. I am supposed to remember what most folks don't have time to think about every day and every night. Hey, maybe that's why the Jews have designed this rabbi job, to see to it that at least one of us gets to the births and the deaths and the marriages and somehow tries to remember them, and to integrate them all and, then, to try and make some sense out of all the life-stuff.

I'll let you in on a trade secret: After you do enough weddings, you realize that every bride and groom are the same. Don't misunderstand me, of course each one is unique. But in a broader context, every bride and every groom are Adam and Eve. They are players in an eternal drama. They look at one another, their heart's desire, and realize that the other person is a stranger. They live together for forty or fifty years and realize that, for all of their love, the other person is still a mystery. The power of their love is that these feelings transcend them as individuals. That mystery smelts us down into one lump of humanity and makes literature and art possible. The greater the emotion, the more intensely personal and intimate the feeling, the more likely it is shared with all human beings.

I sit in a room filled with mourners who have just lost a member of their family. I try with every ounce of skill I have to hear their feelings so that I can be a fitting mouthpiece for them the following day at the funeral. But in truth, save for a fond memory here or a colorful personal quirk there, all the mourners say pretty much the same thing but in an infinite number of ways: He was our daddy, we loved him. She was our mother, we loved her. This one was our brother, that one was our sister, this one was my spouse, that one was our daughter, this one was our son. We loved him. We didn't say it enough.

The second act of *Our Town* opens after three years have elapsed. The stage manager muses, in a laconic New Hampshire drawl:

> *"Yes, the sun's come up over a thousand times. Summers and winters have cracked the mountains a little bit more and the rains have brought down some of the dirt. Some babies that weren't even born before have begun talking*

regular sentences already; and a number of people who thought they were right young and spry have noticed that they can't bound up a flight of stairs like they used to, without their heart fluttering a little. All that can happen in a thousand days. Nature's been pushing and contriving in other ways, too: a number of young people fell in love and got married...."

"You know how it is: You're twenty-one or twenty-two and you make some decisions; then whissh! you're seventy: You've been a lawyer for fifty years, and that white-haired lady at your side has eaten over fifty thousand meals with you." (Thornton Wilder, *Our Town* [New York: Harper & Row, 1985], 46, 60)

I remember how, once, I was showing the pre-school around the temple. I showed the children the library, the prayer hall, and the bima. I showed them the ark and told them that the next time we met, I would open it so that they could see what was inside. Their teacher later informed me that their curiosity had generated a lengthy discussion.

One kid thought it was empty. Another thought it was filled with precious things. Another rather unimaginative child thought it held the Torah. But one kid said, "You're all wrong. I'll tell you what's in there. When the rabbi-man opens that curtain next week, there will just be a big mirror!" Well, my friends, welcome to the "Big Mirror." We're all there—each one of our faces peering back out of the ark. The whole congregation of Israel:

Rich people and poor people. Wise and foolish. Beautiful and plain. From choppers of wood to drawers of water. People who just got married and ones who just got divorced. People who just got out of the hospital and people who are going in real soon. People who just got born and people who, God forbid, won't be here next year. People whose lives are finally coming together and people whose lives are falling apart.

We come together as a community to be aware of the great mystery of life and to remind ourselves about what is truly important in our lives—before we die.

In the last act of *Our Town*, a young mother, Emily Webb, dies during the birth of her second child. She sits in a symbolic graveyard, along with others from the town who have died. Being a recent arrival and sensing that she could return to the world, she asks the others in the cemetery if it is possible. They tell her it is. But they also warn her not to go. They say it will be too painful. But she refuses to understand. Her bonds to the living are still too strong.

She asks the stage manager why it will be painful and he patiently explains:

> *"You not only live it: but you watch yourself living it.... And as you watch it, you see the thing that they—down there—never know. You see the future. You know what's going to happen afterwards."* (Ibid., 91–2)

She understands but she is determined to find out for herself. She finally selects her twelfth birthday as the time to which she will return. It is in the morning of February 11, 1899. She finds herself at home amidst a loving family too busy living to realize that they are alive.

> *"Oh, Mama, just look at me one minute as though you really saw me. Mama, fourteen years have gone by. I'm dead. You're a grandmother, Mama. I married George Gibbs, Mama. Wally's dead, too. Mama, his appendix burst on a camping trip to North Conway. We felt just terrible about it—don't you remember? But, just for a moment now we're all together. Mama, just for a moment we're happy. Let's look at one another."* (Ibid., 99)

But, of course, her mother cannot hear, for she is back then, among the living. In the words of a friend who had felt herself very close to death, "I stopped looking at trees; I look at every leaf. I no longer heard music, I listen to every note. When I am with my children, I cherish every touch." In the play, it was the same for Emily Webb. She is overwhelmed with loving and sadness. Now she also has learned too late:

"I didn't realize. So all that was going on and we never noticed. Take me back—up the hill—to my grave. But first: Wait! One more look. Good-by, Good-by, world. Good-by, Grover's Corners ... Mama and Papa. Good-by to clocks ticking ... and Mama's sunflowers. And food and coffee. And new-ironed dresses and hot baths ... and sleeping and waking up. Oh, earth, you're too wonderful for anybody to realize you." (Ibid., 100)

We Jews have many ways of remembering such eternal truths. The words of Psalm 90 have always been a comfort to me:

Lord, you have been our dwelling place in all generations.
Before the mountains were brought forth ...
For a thousand years in Your sight
Are but as yesterday when it is past,
As a watch in the night ...
So teach us to number our days,
That we may get us a heart of wisdom." (1, 2, 4, 12)

One of the *mohel*s who has served the Jewish community of greater Boston for many decades always concludes the *kiddush* immediately following a *bris* (wherein a Jewish boy is given his name) with: "And may we all dance at the Bar Mitzvah!" The first time I heard it, I thought it powerful and poetic. But when I heard it again and again, after every *bris*, I thought it was just corny. Now when I hear it, I think it is even more powerful and poetic than when I first heard it.

There are only a half dozen or so great life truths and each one of them has but a handful of coherent ways to be told. And all we can do for the truly important moments in life is repeat them, and stand reverent in their mystery. I'll tell you one now: May we all dance at the wedding!

SOURCES

1. RABBI

WHO AM I?

From *Jewish Mysticism and the Spiritual Life: Classical Texts, Contemporary Reflections*, eds. Or Rose, Eitan Fishbane, and Lawrence Fine (Woodstock, VT: Jewish Lights Publishing, 2010).

WE'LL WAIT BACK HERE

Founders' Day address: Hebrew Union College–Jewish Institute of Religion, Los Angeles, CA, April 22, 2001. © 2001 Lawrence Kushner, used by permission of the author.

THE CALLING

From *Hineini in Our Lives: Learning How to Respond to Others through 14 Biblical Texts & Personal Stories*, by Norman J. Cohen (Woodstock, VT: Jewish Lights Publishing, 2003).

MY OTHER FATHER DIED

Eulogy for Rabbi Arnold Jacob Wolf, Congregation K A M Isaiah Israel, Chicago, IL, December 26, 2008. © 2008 Lawrence Kushner, used by permission of the author.

THE TENT PEG BUSINESS

In *New Traditions*, vol. 1, Boston, MA, Spring 1984. © 1984 Lawrence Kushner, used by permission of the author.

THE HUMAN PYRAMID

Keynote address, Union of American Hebrew Congregations Biennial Convention, Dallas, TX, 1997. © 1997 Lawrence Kushner, used by permission of the author.

THE RABBI BUSINESS

Sermon, Hebrew Union College–Jewish Institute of Religion, New York, NY, March 25, 2004. © 2004 Lawrence Kushner, used by permission of the author.

BEING SOMEBODY ELSE

© 1990 Lawrence Kushner, used by permission of the author.

THE LAST GIFT

© 2000 Lawrence Kushner, used by permission of the author.

2. JUDAISM

WHY I'M A JEW

In *Moment* Magazine, December 1992.

FILENE'S BASEMENT

© 1985 Lawrence Kushner, used by permission of the author.

INTERMARRIAGE

Based on "The Problem of Judaism in America," special supplement of *Conservative Judaism*, vol. 56, 2004. Reprinted with permission from The Rabbinical Assembly.

GETTING MORE JEWS

Originally published as "Who Needs Outreach?" in *Chronicle*, Purim issue, The Congregation Emanu-El of San Francisco, March, 2003.

CUSTOMS AS SACRED TEXT

From the foreword to *The Book of Customs*, by Scott-Martin Kosofsky (New York, NY: Harper Collins, 2004).

TWO JEWISH MOTHERS

In *Central Conference of American Rabbis Newsletter*, 1998. © 1998 Lawrence Kushner, used by permission of the author.

(RE)THINKING SHABBAT

In *Reform Judaism*, Spring 1984. © 1984 Lawrence Kushner, used by permission of the author.

KOSHER

Sermon for *Shabbat Shemini*, Hebrew Union College–Jewish Institute of Religion, New York, NY, 2001. © 2001 Lawrence Kushner, used by permission of the author.

THE LIFE OF TORAH

Based on the foreword to *Our Lives as Torah: Finding God in Our Own Stories*, by Carol Ochs (San Francisco, CA: Jossey-Bass, 2001).

3. FAMILY

VISITING YOUR CHILDREN

From a Rosh Hashanah sermon, Congregation Beth El, Sudbury, MA, 1998. © 1998 Lawrence Kushner, used by permission of the author.

UNDERSTANDING YOUR PARENTS

Baccalaureate sermon, *Erev Shabbat Bamidbar*, Amherst College, Amherst, MA, May 22, 2004. © 2004 Lawrence Kushner, used by permission of the author.

TELLING KIDS THE TRUTH

In *Jewish Education News* (Coalition for the Advancement of Jewish Education), Winter 2002.

BOOMPA

© 1997 Lawrence Kushner, used by permission of the author.

AND UNTO US A CHILD IS GIVEN

A Hanukkah story, commissioned by National Public Radio, 1998. © 1998 Lawrence Kushner, used by permission of the author.

TWO JEWISH MOTHERS

In *Central Conference of American Rabbis Newsletter*, 1998

BABUSHKA

In *Chronicle*, The Congregation Emanu-El of San Francisco, September, 2007.

TURKEY SHOOT

Commentary on National Public Radio's *All Things Considered*, Thanksgiving, 1996. © 1996 Lawrence Kushner, used by permission of the author.

GENERATIONS

© 1996 Lawrence Kushner, used by permission of the author.

4. WORLD

WHAT ISRAEL MEANS TO ME

In *What Israel Means to Me*, ed. Alan Dershowitz (Hoboken, NJ: John Wiley & Sons, 2006).

MY LUNCH WITH JESUS

In *Jesus Through Jewish Eyes*, ed. Beatrice Bruteau (Maryknoll, NY: Orbis Books, 2001).

CARDBOARD SUKKAH

Sermon, Congregation Beth El, Sudbury, MA, Sukkot, October 13, 1995.

BILL NOVAK'S QUESTIONS

Kerem: Creative Explorations in Judaism Magazine, vol. 6, 1999. © 1999 Lawrence Kushner, used by permission of the author.

NYPD BLUE

Commentary on National Public Radio's *All Things Considered*, November, 1996. © 1996 Lawrence Kushner, used by permission of the author.

RESURRECTION OF FLOWERS

From the bulletin of Congregation Beth El, Sudbury, MA, 2000, and in *Chronicle*, The Congregation Emanu-El at San Francisco, October, 2007.

5. MYSTICISM

WHAT IS KABBALAH?

Introduction to *The Beliefnet Guide to Kabbalah*, by Arthur Goldwag (New York, NY: Three Leaves Press/Random House, 2005).

READING MUSIC

© 1984 Lawrence Kushner, used by permission of the author.

BOSQUE DEL APACHE

© 1984 Lawrence Kushner, used by permission of the author.

PHYSICIAN OF TSEFAT

Review of *Physician of the Soul; Healer of the Cosmos: Isaac Luria and His Kabbalistic Fellowship*, by Lawrence Fine, *Tikkun: A Bi-Monthly Interfaith Critique of Politics, Culture & Society*, May/June, 2004.

SPELL-CHECKER

Review of the movie *Bee Season* (movie), *Beliefnet*. www.beliefnet.com.

MIDRASH AS HYPERTEXT

Reprinted with premission from *Sh'ma: A Journal of Jewish Responsibility*, October, 1997.

A KABBALAH LEXICON

Adapted from *CCAR Journal: The Reform Jewish Quarterly*, Fall 2007, Copyright © 2007 Central Conference of American Rabbis; and is under the copyright protection of the Central Conference of American Rabbis and reprinted for use by permission of the CCAR. All rights reserved.

6. HOLINESS

OPEN MY LIPS

Union of American Hebrew Congregations, Meditation Kalla, Prescott, AZ, 1996. © 1996 Lawrence Kushner, used by permission of the author.

SPIRITUAL GREED

Commentary on National Public Radio's *All Things Considered*, 1996. © 1996 Lawrence Kushner, used by permission of the author.

SILENT PRAYER

Union of American Hebrew Congregations, Meditation Kalla, Prescott, Arizona, 1998. © 1998 Lawrence Kushner, used by permission of the author.

A BLESSING FOR THE CZAR

In *Chronicle*, The Congregation Emanu-El of San Francisco, January, 2008.

BIKING WITH PELICANS

In *Chronicle*, The Congregation Emanu-El of San Francisco, February, 2006.

THE ZEN OF AIRLINE TICKETS

Commentary on National Public Radio's *All Things Considered*, 1998; and as "Zen, Airline Tix & the Market" in *Chronicle*, The Congregation Emanu-El of San Francisco, November, 2008. © 1998 Lawrence Kushner, used by permission of the author.

MEMORY AND REDEMPTION

"Remembering in the Jewish Tradition," in *On the Sea of Memory: A Journey from Forgetting to Remembering*, by Jonathan Cott (New York: Random House, 2005).

DEATH WITHOUT DYING

"Death without Dying," in *Who by Fire, Who by Water*—Un'taneh Tokef, ed. Lawrence A. Hoffman (Woodstock, VT: Jewish Lights Publishing, 2010).

THE BAND ON THE TITANIC

From a *Kol Nidre* sermon, Congregation Beth El, Sudbury, MA, 1998. © 1998 Lawrence Kushner, used by permission of the author.

AFTERWORD: "OUR TOWN"

A *Kol Nidre* sermon, Congregation Beth El, Sudbury, MA, 1986. © 1986 Lawrence Kushner, used by permission of the author.

Bar/Bat Mitzvah

The JGirl's Guide: The Young Jewish Woman's Handbook for Coming of Age
By Penina Adelman, Ali Feldman and Shulamit Reinharz This inspirational, interactive
guidebook helps pre-teen Jewish girls address the many issues surrounding coming
of age. 6 x 9, 240 pp, Quality PB, 978-1-58023-215-9 **$14.99** *For ages 11 & up*
Also Available: **The JGirl's Teacher's and Parent's Guide**
8½ x 11, 56 pp, PB, 978-1-58023-225-8 **$8.99**

Bar/Bat Mitzvah Basics, 2nd Edition: A Practical Family Guide to Coming of Age
Together *Edited by Helen Leneman; Foreword by Rabbi Jeffrey K. Salkin*
6 x 9, 240 pp, Quality PB, 978-1-58023-151-0 **$18.95**

The Bar/Bat Mitzvah Memory Book, 2nd Edition: An Album for Treasuring the
Spiritual Celebration *By Rabbi Jeffrey K. Salkin and Nina Salkin*
8 x 10, 48 pp, 2-color text, Deluxe HC, ribbon marker, 978-1-58023-263-0 **$19.99**

For Kids—Putting God on Your Guest List, 2nd Edition: How to Claim the
Spiritual Meaning of Your Bar or Bat Mitzvah *By Rabbi Jeffrey K. Salkin*
6 x 9, 144 pp, Quality PB, 978-1-58023-308-8 **$15.99** *For ages 11–13*

Putting God on the Guest List, 3rd Edition: How to Reclaim the Spiritual
Meaning of Your Child's Bar or Bat Mitzvah *By Rabbi Jeffrey K. Salkin*
6 x 9, 224 pp, Quality PB, 978-1-58023-222-7 **$16.99**; HC, 978-1-58023-260-9 **$24.99**
Also Available: **Putting God on the Guest List Teacher's Guide**
8½ x 11, 48 pp, PB, 978-1-58023-226-5 **$8.99**

Tough Questions Jews Ask: A Young Adult's Guide to Building a Jewish Life
By Rabbi Edward Feinstein 6 x 9, 160 pp, Quality PB, 978-1-58023-139-8 **$14.99** *For ages 11 & up*
Also Available: **Tough Questions Jews Ask Teacher's Guide**
8½ x 11, 72 pp, PB, 978-1-58023-187-9

Bible Study/Midrash

The Modern Men's Torah Commentary: New Insights from Jewish
Men on the 54 Weekly Torah Portions *Edited by Rabbi Jeffrey K. Salkin*
A major contribution to modern biblical commentary. Addresses the most important concerns of modern men by opening them up to the messages of Torah.
6 x 9, 368 pp, HC, 978-1-58023-395-8 **$24.99**

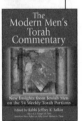

The Genesis of Leadership: What the Bible Teaches Us about Vision, Values and
Leading Change *By Rabbi Nathan Laufer; Foreword by Senator Joseph I. Lieberman*
6 x 9, 288 pp, Quality PB, 978-1-58023-352-1 **$18.99**

Hineini in Our Lives: Learning How to Respond to Others through 14 Biblical Texts and
Personal Stories *By Rabbi Norman J. Cohen, PhD* 6 x 9, 240 pp, Quality PB, 978-1-58023-274-6 **$16.99**

A Man's Responsibility: A Jewish Guide to Being a Son, a Partner in Marriage,
a Father and a Community Leader *By Rabbi Joseph B. Meszler*
6 x 9, 192 pp, Quality PB, 978-1-58023-435-1 **$16.99**

Moses and the Journey to Leadership: Timeless Lessons of Effective Management from
the Bible and Today's Leaders *By Rabbi Norman J. Cohen, PhD*
6 x 9, 240 pp, Quality PB, 978-1-58023-351-4 **$18.99**; HC, 978-1-58023-227-2 **$21.99**

Righteous Gentiles in the Hebrew Bible: Ancient Role Models for Sacred
Relationships *By Rabbi Jeffrey K. Salkin; Foreword by Rabbi Harold M. Schulweis;
Preface by Phyllis Tickle* 6 x 9, 192 pp, Quality PB, 978-1-58023-364-4 **$18.99**

The Triumph of Eve & Other Subversive Bible Tales *By Matt Biers-Ariel* 5½ x 8½, 192 pp,
Quality PB, 978-1-59473-176-1 **$14.99** *(A book from SkyLight Paths, Jewish Lights' sister imprint)*

The Wisdom of Judaism: An Introduction to the Values of the Talmud
By Rabbi Dov Peretz Elkins 6 x 9, 192 pp, Quality PB, 978-1-58023-327-9 **$16.99**
Also Available: **The Wisdom of Judaism Teacher's Guide**
8½ x 11, 18 pp, PB, 978-1-58023-350-7 **$8.99**

Or phone, fax, mail or e-mail to: **JEWISH LIGHTS** Publishing
Sunset Farm Offices, Route 4 • P.O. Box 237 • Woodstock, Vermont 05091
Tel: (802) 457-4000 • Fax: (802) 457-4004 • www.jewishlights.com
Credit card orders: (800) 962-4544 (8:30AM–5:30PM ET Monday–Friday)
Generous discounts on quantity orders. SATISFACTION GUARANTEED. Prices subject to change.

Congregation Resources

Empowered Judaism: What Independent Minyanim Can Teach Us about Building Vibrant Jewish Communities
By Rabbi Elie Kaunfer; Foreword by Prof. Jonathan D. Sarna
Examines the independent minyan movement and the lessons these grassroots communities can provide. 6 x 9, 224 pp, Quality PB, 978-1-58023-412-2 **$18.99**

Spiritual Boredom: Rediscovering the Wonder of Judaism *By Dr. Erica Brown*
Breaks through the surface of spiritual boredom to find the reservoir of meaning within. 6 x 9, 208 pp, HC, 978-1-58023-405-4 **$21.99**

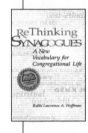

Building a Successful Volunteer Culture
Finding Meaning in Service in the Jewish Community
By Rabbi Charles Simon; Foreword by Shelley Lindauer; Preface by Dr. Ron Wolfson
Shows you how to develop and maintain the volunteers who are essential to the vitality of your organization and community. 6 x 9, 192 pp, Quality PB, 978-1-58023-408-5 **$16.99**

The Case for Jewish Peoplehood: Can We Be One?
By Dr. Erica Brown and Dr. Misha Galperin; Foreword by Rabbi Joseph Telushkin
6 x 9, 224 pp, HC, 978-1-58023-401-6 **$21.99**

Inspired Jewish Leadership: Practical Approaches to Building Strong Communities
By Dr. Erica Brown 6 x 9, 256 pp, HC, 978-1-58023-361-3 **$24.99**

Jewish Pastoral Care, 2nd Edition: A Practical Handbook from Traditional & Contemporary Sources *Edited by Rabbi Dayle A. Friedman, MSW, MAJCS, BCC*
6 x 9, 528 pp, Quality PB, 978-1-58023-427-6 **$30.00**; HC, 978-1-58023-221-0 **$40.00**

Rethinking Synagogues: A New Vocabulary for Congregational Life
By Rabbi Lawrence A. Hoffman, PhD 6 x 9, 240 pp, Quality PB, 978-1-58023-248-7 **$19.99**

The Spirituality of Welcoming: How to Transform Your Congregation into a Sacred Community *By Dr. Ron Wolfson* 6 x 9, 224 pp, Quality PB, 978-1-58023-244-9 **$19.99**

Children's Books

What You Will See Inside a Synagogue
By Rabbi Lawrence A. Hoffman, PhD, and Dr. Ron Wolfson; Full-color photos by Bill Aron
A colorful, fun-to-read introduction that explains the ways and whys of Jewish worship and religious life. 8½ x 10½, 32 pp, Full-color photos, Quality PB, 978-1-59473-256-0 **$8.99**
For ages 6 & up (A book from SkyLight Paths, Jewish Lights' sister imprint)

Because Nothing Looks Like God
By Lawrence Kushner and Karen Kushner Introduces children to the possibilities of spiritual life. 11 x 8½, 32 pp, Full-color illus., HC, 978-1-58023-092-6 **$17.99** *For ages 4 & up*
Board Book Companions to *Because Nothing Looks Like God*
5 x 5, 24 pp, Full-color illus., SkyLight Paths Board Books *For ages 0–4*
How Does God Make Things Happen? 978-1-893361-24-9 **$7.95**
What Does God Look Like? 978-1-893361-23-2 **$7.99**
Where Is God? 978-1-893361-17-1 **$7.99**

The Book of Miracles: A Young Person's Guide to Jewish Spiritual Awareness
Written and illus. by Lawrence Kushner
6 x 9, 96 pp, 2-color illus., HC, 978-1-879045-78-1 **$16.95** *For ages 9 & up*

In God's Hands *By Lawrence Kushner and Gary Schmidt* 9 x 12, 32 pp, Full-color illus., HC, 978-1-58023-224-1 **$16.99**

In Our Image: God's First Creatures *By Nancy Sohn Swartz*
9 x 12, 32 pp, Full-color illus., HC, 978-1-879045-99-6 **$16.95** *For ages 4 & up*

Also Available as a Board Book: **How Did the Animals Help God?**
5 x 5, 24 pp, Full-color illus., Board Book, 978-1-59473-044-3 **$7.99** *For ages 0–4*
(A book from SkyLight Paths, Jewish Lights' sister imprint)

The Kids' Fun Book of Jewish Time
By Emily Sper 9 x 7½, 24 pp, Full-color illus., HC, 978-1-58023-311-8 **$16.99**

What Makes Someone a Jew? *By Lauren Seidman*
Reflects the changing face of American Judaism.
10 x 8½, 32 pp, Full-color photos, Quality PB, 978-1-58023-321-7 **$8.99** *For ages 3–6*

Children's Books by Sandy Eisenberg Sasso

Adam & Eve's First Sunset: God's New Day
Explores fear and hope, faith and gratitude in ways that will delight kids and adults—inspiring us to bless each of God's days and nights.
9 x 12, 32 pp, Full-color illus., HC, 978-1-58023-177-0 **$17.95** *For ages 4 & up*

Also Available as a Board Book: **Adam and Eve's New Day**
5 x 5, 24 pp, Full-color illus., Board Book, 978-1-59473-205-8 **$7.99** *For ages 0–4*
(A book from SkyLight Paths, Jewish Lights' sister imprint)

But God Remembered: Stories of Women from Creation to the Promised Land   Four different stories of women—Lilith, Serach, Bityah and the Daughters of Z—teach us important values through their faith and actions.
9 x 12, 32 pp, Full-color illus., Quality PB, 978-1-58023-372-9 **$8.99** *For ages 8 & up*

Cain & Abel: Finding the Fruits of Peace
Shows children that we have the power to deal with anger in positive ways. Provides questions for kids and adults to explore together.
9 x 12, 32 pp, Full-color illus., HC, 978-1-58023-123-7 **$16.95** *For ages 5 & up*

For Heaven's Sake
Heaven is often found where you least expect it.
9 x 12, 32 pp, Full-color illus., HC, 978-1-58023-054-4 **$16.95** For ages 4 & up

God in Between
If you wanted to find God, where would you look? This magical, mythical tale teaches that God can be found where we are: within all of us and the relationships between us.   9 x 12, 32 pp, Full-color illus., HC, 978-1-879045-86-6 **$16.95** *For ages 4 & up*

God Said Amen
An inspiring story about hearing the answers to our prayers.
9 x 12, 32 pp, Full-color illus., HC, 978-1-58023-080-3 **$16.95** For ages 4 & up

God's Paintbrush: Special 10th Anniversary Edition
Wonderfully interactive, invites children of all faiths and backgrounds to encounter God through moments in their own lives. Provides questions adult and child can explore together. 11 x 8½, 32 pp, Full-color illus., HC, 978-1-58023-195-4 **$17.95** *For ages 4 & up*

Also Available as a Board Book: **I Am God's Paintbrush**
5 x 5, 24 pp, Full-color illus., Board Book, 978-1-59473-265-2 **$7.99** *For ages 0–4*
(A book from SkyLight Paths, Jewish Lights' sister imprint)

Also Available: **God's Paintbrush Teacher's Guide**
8½ x 11, 32 pp, PB, 978-1-879045-57-6 **$8.95**

God's Paintbrush Celebration Kit
A Spiritual Activity Kit for Teachers and Students of All Faiths, All Backgrounds
9½ x 12, 40 Full-color Activity Sheets & Teacher Folder w/ complete instructions
HC, 978-1-58023-050-6 **$21.95**
8-Student Activity Sheet Pack (40 sheets/5 sessions), 978-1-58023-058-2 **$19.95**

In God's Name
Like an ancient myth in its poetic text and vibrant illustrations, this award-winning modern fable about the search for God's name celebrates the diversity and, at the same time, the unity of all people.
9 x 12, 32 pp, Full-color illus., HC, 978-1-879045-26-2 **$16.99** *For ages 4 & up*

Also Available as a Board Book: **What Is God's Name?**
5 x 5, 24 pp, Full-color illus., Board Book, 978-1-893361-10-2 **$7.99** *For ages 0–4*
(A book from SkyLight Paths, Jewish Lights' sister imprint)

Also Available in Spanish: **El nombre de Dios**
9 x 12, 32 pp, Full-color illus., HC, 978-1-893361-63-8 **$16.95**

Noah's Wife: The Story of Naamah
When God tells Noah to bring the animals of the world onto the ark, God also calls on Naamah, Noah's wife, to save each plant on Earth. Based on an ancient text.
9 x 12, 32 pp, Full-color illus., HC, 978-1-58023-134-3 **$16.95** *For ages 4 & up*

Also Available as a Board Book: **Naamah, Noah's Wife**
5 x 5, 24 pp, Full-color illus., Board Book, 978-1-893361-56-0 **$7.95** *For ages 0–4*
(A book from SkyLight Paths, Jewish Lights' sister imprint)

Theology/Philosophy/The Way Into... Series

The Way Into... series offers an accessible and highly usable "guided tour" of the Jewish faith, people, history and beliefs—in total, an introduction to Judaism that will enable you to understand and interact with the sacred texts of the Jewish tradition. Each volume is written by a leading contemporary scholar and teacher, and explores one key aspect of Judaism. The Way Into... series enables all readers to achieve a real sense of Jewish cultural literacy through guided study.

The Way Into Encountering God in Judaism
By Rabbi Neil Gillman, PhD
For everyone who wants to understand how Jews have encountered God throughout history and today.
6 x 9, 240 pp, Quality PB, 978-1-58023-199-2 **$18.99**; HC, 978-1-58023-025-4 **$21.95**
Also Available: **The Jewish Approach to God:** A Brief Introduction for Christians
By Rabbi Neil Gillman, PhD
5½ x 8½, 192 pp, Quality PB, 978-1-58023-190-9 **$16.95**

The Way Into Jewish Mystical Tradition
By Rabbi Lawrence Kushner
Allows readers to interact directly with the sacred mystical texts of the Jewish tradition. An accessible introduction to the concepts of Jewish mysticism, their religious and spiritual significance, and how they relate to life today.
6 x 9, 224 pp, Quality PB, 978-1-58023-200-5 **$18.99**; HC, 978-1-58023-029-2 **$21.95**

The Way Into Jewish Prayer
By Rabbi Lawrence A. Hoffman, PhD
Opens the door to 3,000 years of Jewish prayer, making anyone feel at home in the Jewish way of communicating with God.
6 x 9, 208 pp, Quality PB, 978-1-58023-201-2 **$18.99**
Also Available: **The Way Into Jewish Prayer Teacher's Guide**
By Rabbi Jennifer Ossakow Goldsmith
8½ x 11, 42 pp, PB, 978-1-58023-345-3 **$8.99**
Download a free copy at www.jewishlights.com.

The Way Into Judaism and the Environment
By Jeremy Benstein, PhD
Explores the ways in which Judaism contributes to contemporary social-environmental issues, the extent to which Judaism is part of the problem and how it can be part of the solution.
6 x 9, 288 pp, Quality PB, 978-1-58023-368-2 **$18.99**; HC, 978-1-58023-268-5 **$24.99**

The Way Into Tikkun Olam (Repairing the World)
By Rabbi Elliot N. Dorff, PhD
An accessible introduction to the Jewish concept of the individual's responsibility to care for others and repair the world.
6 x 9, 304 pp, Quality PB, 978-1-58023-328-6 **$18.99**; 320 pp, HC, 978-1-58023-269-2 **$24.99**

The Way Into Torah
By Rabbi Norman J. Cohen, PhD
Helps guide you in the exploration of the origins and development of Torah, explains why it should be studied and how to do it.
6 x 9, 176 pp, Quality PB, 978-1-58023-198-5 **$16.99**

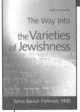

The Way Into the Varieties of Jewishness
By Sylvia Barack Fishman, PhD
Explores the religious and historical understanding of what it has meant to be Jewish from ancient times to the present controversy over "Who is a Jew?"
6 x 9, 288 pp, Quality PB, 978-1-58023-367-5 **$18.99**; HC, 978-1-58023-030-8 **$24.99**

Theology/Philosophy

Jewish Theology in Our Time: A New Generation Explores the
Foundations and Future of Jewish Belief *Edited by Rabbi Elliot J. Cosgrove, PhD*
A powerful and challenging examination of what Jews can believe—by a new generation's most dynamic and innovative thinkers.
6 x 9, 272 pp, HC, 978-1-58023-413-9 **$24.99**

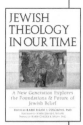

Maimonides, Spinoza and Us: Toward an Intellectually Vibrant Judaism
By Rabbi Marc D. Angel, PhD A challenging look at two great Jewish philosophers
and what their thinking means to our understanding of God, truth, revelation
and reason. 6 x 9, 224 pp, HC, 978-1-58023-411-5 **$24.99**

The Death of Death: Resurrection and Immortality in Jewish Thought
By Rabbi Neil Gillman, PhD 6 x 9, 336 pp, Quality PB, 978-1-58023-081-0 **$18.95**

Doing Jewish Theology: God, Torah & Israel in Modern Judaism *By Rabbi Neil Gillman, PhD*
6 x 9, 304 pp, Quality PB, 978-1-58023-439-9 **$18.99**; HC, 978-1-58023-322-4 **$24.99**

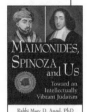

Ethics of the Sages: Pirke Avot—Annotated & Explained
Translation & Annotation by Rabbi Rami Shapiro 5½ x 8¼, 192 pp, Quality PB, 978-1-59473-207-2 **$16.99***

Hasidic Tales: Annotated & Explained *Translation & Annotation by Rabbi Rami Shapiro*
5½ x 8½, 240 pp, Quality PB, 978-1-893361-86-7 **$16.95***

A Heart of Many Rooms: Celebrating the Many Voices within Judaism
By Dr. David Hartman 6 x 9, 352 pp, Quality PB, 978-1-58023-156-5 **$19.95**

The Hebrew Prophets: Selections Annotated & Explained
Translation & Annotation by Rabbi Rami Shapiro; Foreword by Rabbi Zalman M. Schachter-Shalomi
5½ x 8½, 224 pp, Quality PB, 978-1-59473-037-5 **$16.99***

A Jewish Understanding of the New Testament *By Rabbi Samuel Sandmel;*
Preface by Rabbi David Sandmel 5½ x 8½, 368 pp, Quality PB, 978-1-59473-048-1 **$19.99***

Jews and Judaism in the 21st Century: Human Responsibility, the Presence of God and
the Future of the Covenant *Edited by Rabbi Edward Feinstein; Foreword by Paula E. Hyman*
6 x 9, 192 pp, Quality PB, 978-1-58023-374-3 **$19.99**; HC, 978-1-58023-315-6 **$24.99**

A Living Covenant: The Innovative Spirit in Traditional Judaism
By Dr. David Hartman 6 x 9, 368 pp, Quality PB, 978-1-58023-011-7 **$25.00**

Love and Terror in the God Encounter: The Theological Legacy of Rabbi Joseph B.
Soloveitchik *By Dr. David Hartman* 6 x 9, 240 pp, Quality PB, 978-1-58023-176-3 **$19.95**

The Personhood of God: Biblical Theology, Human Faith and the Divine Image
By Dr. Yochanan Muffs; Foreword by Dr. David Hartman
6 x 9, 240 pp, Quality PB, 978-1-58023-338-5 **$18.99**; HC, 978-1-58023-265-4 **$24.99**

A Touch of the Sacred: A Theologian's Informal Guide to Jewish Belief
By Dr. Eugene B. Borowitz and Frances W. Schwartz
6 x 9, 256 pp, Quality PB, 978-1-58023-416-0 **$16.99**; HC, 978-1-58023-337-8 **$21.99**

Traces of God: Seeing God in Torah, History and Everyday Life *By Rabbi Neil Gillman, PhD*
6 x 9, 240 pp, Quality PB, 978-1-58023-369-9 **$16.99**

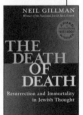

We Jews and Jesus: Exploring Theological Differences for Mutual Understanding *By Rabbi
Samuel Sandmel; Preface by Rabbi David Sandmel* 6 x 9, 192 pp, Quality PB, 978-1-59473-208-9 **$16.99***

Your Word Is Fire: The Hasidic Masters on Contemplative Prayer
Edited and translated by Rabbi Arthur Green, PhD, and Barry W. Holtz
6 x 9, 160 pp, Quality PB, 978-1-879045-25-5 **$15.95**

I Am Jewish
Personal Reflections Inspired by the Last Words of Daniel Pearl
Almost 150 Jews—both famous and not—from all walks of life, from all around
the world, write about many aspects of their Judaism.
Edited by Judea and Ruth Pearl 6 x 9, 304 pp, Deluxe PB w/ flaps, 978-1-58023-259-3 **$18.99**
Download a free copy of the *I Am Jewish Teacher's Guide* at www.jewishlights.com.

Hannah Senesh: Her Life and Diary, The First Complete Edition
By Hannah Senesh; Foreword by Marge Piercy; Preface by Eitan Senesh; Afterword by Roberta Grossman
6 x 9, 368 pp, b/w photos, Quality PB, 978-1-58023-342-2 **$19.99**

*A book from SkyLight Paths, Jewish Lights' sister imprint

Life Cycle
Marriage/Parenting/Family/Aging

The New Jewish Baby Album: Creating and Celebrating the Beginning of a Spiritual Life—A Jewish Lights Companion
By the Editors at Jewish Lights; Foreword by Anita Diamant; Preface by Rabbi Sandy Eisenberg Sasso
A spiritual keepsake that will be treasured for generations. More than just a memory book, *shows you how—and why it's important*—to create a Jewish home and a Jewish life. 8 x 10, 64 pp, Deluxe Padded HC, Full-color illus., 978-1-58023-138-1 **$19.95**

The Jewish Pregnancy Book: A Resource for the Soul, Body & Mind during Pregnancy, Birth & the First Three Months *By Sandy Falk, MD, and Rabbi Daniel Judson, with Steven A. Rapp* Medical information, prayers and rituals for each stage of pregnancy. 7 x 10, 208 pp, b/w photos, Quality PB, 978-1-58023-178-7 **$16.95**

Celebrating Your New Jewish Daughter: Creating Jewish Ways to Welcome Baby Girls into the Covenant—New and Traditional Ceremonies *By Debra Nussbaum Cohen; Foreword by Rabbi Sandy Eisenberg Sasso* 6 x 9, 272 pp, Quality PB, 978-1-58023-090-2 **$18.95**

The New Jewish Baby Book, 2nd Edition: Names, Ceremonies & Customs—A Guide for Today's Families *By Anita Diamant* 6 x 9, 336 pp, Quality PB, 978-1-58023-251-7 **$19.99**

Parenting as a Spiritual Journey: Deepening Ordinary and Extraordinary Events into Sacred Occasions *By Rabbi Nancy Fuchs-Kreimer, PhD*
6 x 9, 224 pp, Quality PB, 978-1-58023-016-2 **$16.95**

Parenting Jewish Teens: A Guide for the Perplexed
By Joanne Doades Explores the questions and issues that shape the world in which today's Jewish teenagers live and offers constructive advice to parents.
6 x 9, 176 pp, Quality PB, 978-1-58023-305-7 **$16.99**

Judaism for Two: A Spiritual Guide for Strengthening and Celebrating Your Loving Relationship *By Rabbi Nancy Fuchs-Kreimer, PhD, and Rabbi Nancy H. Wiener, DMin; Foreword by Rabbi Elliot N. Dorff*
Addresses the ways Jewish teachings can enhance and strengthen committed relationships. 6 x 9, 224 pp, Quality PB, 978-1-58023-254-8 **$16.99**

The Creative Jewish Wedding Book, 2nd Edition: A Hands-On Guide to New & Old Traditions, Ceremonies & Celebrations *By Gabrielle Kaplan-Mayer*
9 x 9, 288 pp, b/w photos, Quality PB, 978-1-58023-398-9 **$19.99**

Divorce Is a Mitzvah: A Practical Guide to Finding Wholeness and Holiness When Your Marriage Dies *By Rabbi Perry Netter; Afterword by Rabbi Laura Geller*
6 x 9, 224 pp, Quality PB, 978-1-58023-172-5 **$16.95**

Embracing the Covenant: Converts to Judaism Talk About Why & How
By Rabbi Allan Berkowitz and Patti Moskovitz 6 x 9, 192 pp, Quality PB, 978-1-879045-50-7 **$16.95**

The Guide to Jewish Interfaith Family Life: An InterfaithFamily.com Handbook
Edited by Ronnie Friedland and Edmund Case
6 x 9, 384 pp, Quality PB, 978-1-58023-153-4 **$18.95**

A Heart of Wisdom: Making the Jewish Journey from Midlife through the Elder Years
Edited by Susan Berrin; Foreword by Rabbi Harold Kushner
6 x 9, 384 pp, Quality PB, 978-1-58023-051-3 **$18.95**

Introducing My Faith and My Community: The Jewish Outreach Institute Guide for the Christian in a Jewish Interfaith Relationship
By Rabbi Kerry M. Olitzky 6 x 9, 176 pp, Quality PB, 978-1-58023-192-3 **$16.95**

Making a Successful Jewish Interfaith Marriage: The Jewish Outreach Institute Guide to Opportunities, Challenges and Resources *By Rabbi Kerry M. Olitzky with Joan Peterson Littman*
6 x 9, 176 pp, Quality PB, 978-1-58023-170-1 **$16.95**

A Man's Responsibility: A Jewish Guide to Being a Son, a Partner in Marriage, a Father and a Community Leader *By Rabbi Joseph B. Meszler*
6 x 9, 192 pp, Quality PB, 978-1-58023-435-1 **$16.99**

So That Your Values Live On: Ethical Wills and How to Prepare Them
Edited by Rabbi Jack Riemer and Rabbi Nathaniel Stampfer
6 x 9, 272 pp, Quality PB, 978-1-879045-34-7 **$18.99**

Holidays/Holy Days

Who by Fire, Who by Water—Un'taneh Tokef
Edited by Rabbi Lawrence A. Hoffman, PhD
Examines the prayer's theology, authorship and poetry through a set of lively essays, all written in accessible language.
6 x 9, 272 pp, HC, 978-1-58023-424-5 **$24.99**

Rosh Hashanah Readings: Inspiration, Information and Contemplation
Yom Kippur Readings: Inspiration, Information and Contemplation
Edited by Rabbi Dov Peretz Elkins; Section Introductions from Arthur Green's These Are the Words
An extraordinary collection of readings, prayers and insights that will enable you to enter into the spirit of the High Holy Days in a personal and powerful way, permitting the meaning of the Jewish New Year to enter the heart.
Rosh Hashanah: 6 x 9, 400 pp, Quality PB, 978-1-58023-437-5 **$19.99**
Yom Kippur: 6 x 9, 368 pp, Quality PB, 978-1-58023-438-2 **$19.99**

Jewish Holidays: A Brief Introduction for Christians
By Rabbi Kerry M. Olitzky and Rabbi Daniel Judson
5½ x 8½, 176 pp, Quality PB, 978-1-58023-302-6 **$16.99**

Reclaiming Judaism as a Spiritual Practice: Holy Days and Shabbat
By Rabbi Goldie Milgram 7 x 9, 272 pp, Quality PB, 978-1-58023-205-0 **$19.99**

7th Heaven: Celebrating Shabbat with Rebbe Nachman of Breslov
By Moshe Mykoff with the Breslov Research Institute
5⅛ x 8¼, 224 pp, Deluxe PB w/ flaps, 978-1-58023-175-6 **$18.95**

Shabbat, 2nd Edition: The Family Guide to Preparing for and Celebrating
the Sabbath *By Dr. Ron Wolfson*
7 x 9, 320 pp, Illus., Quality PB, 978-1-58023-164-0 **$19.99**

Hanukkah, 2nd Edition: The Family Guide to Spiritual Celebration
By Dr. Ron Wolfson 7 x 9, 240 pp, Illus., Quality PB, 978-1-58023-122-0 **$18.95**

The Jewish Family Fun Book, 2nd Edition: Holiday Projects, Everyday Activities,
and Travel Ideas with Jewish Themes *By Danielle Dardashti and Roni Sarig; Illus. by Avi Katz*
6 x 9, 304 pp, 70+ b/w illus. & diagrams, Quality PB, 978-1-58023-333-0 **$18.99**

The Jewish Lights Book of Fun Classroom Activities: Simple and Seasonal
Projects for Teachers and Students *By Danielle Dardashti and Roni Sarig*
6 x 9, 240 pp, Quality PB, 978-1-58023-206-7 **$19.99**

Passover

My People's Passover Haggadah
Traditional Texts, Modern Commentaries
Edited by Rabbi Lawrence A. Hoffman, PhD, and David Arnow, PhD
A diverse and exciting collection of commentaries on the traditional Passover Haggadah—in two volumes!
Vol. 1: 7 x 10, 304 pp, HC, 978-1-58023-354-5 **$24.99**
Vol. 2: 7 x 10, 320 pp, HC, 978-1-58023-346-0 **$24.99**

Leading the Passover Journey: The Seder's Meaning Revealed,
the Haggadah's Story Retold *By Rabbi Nathan Laufer*
Uncovers the hidden meaning of the Seder's rituals and customs.
6 x 9, 224 pp, Quality PB, 978-1-58023-399-6 **$18.99**; HC, 978-1-58023-211-1 **$24.99**

The Women's Passover Companion: Women's Reflections on the Festival of Freedom
Edited by Rabbi Sharon Cohen Anisfeld, Tara Mohr and Catherine Spector; Foreword by Paula E. Hyman
6 x 9, 352 pp, Quality PB, 978-1-58023-231-9 **$19.99**; HC, 978-1-58023-128-2 **$24.95**

The Women's Seder Sourcebook: Rituals & Readings for Use at the Passover Seder
Edited by Rabbi Sharon Cohen Anisfeld, Tara Mohr and Catherine Spector
6 x 9, 384 pp, Quality PB, 978-1-58023-232-6 **$19.99**

Creating Lively Passover Seders: A Sourcebook of Engaging Tales, Texts & Activities
By David Arnow, PhD 7 x 9, 416 pp, Quality PB, 978-1-58023-184-8 **$24.99**

Passover, 2nd Edition: The Family Guide to Spiritual Celebration
By Dr. Ron Wolfson with Joel Lurie Grishaver 7 x 9, 416 pp, Quality PB, 978-1-58023-174-9 **$19.95**

Ecology/Environment

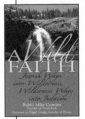

A Wild Faith: Jewish Ways into Wilderness, Wilderness Ways into Judaism
By Rabbi Mike Comins; Foreword by Nigel Savage 6 x 9, 240 pp, Quality PB, 978-1-58023-316-3 **$16.99**

Ecology & the Jewish Spirit: Where Nature & the Sacred Meet
Edited by Ellen Bernstein 6 x 9, 288 pp, Quality PB, 978-1-58023-082-7 **$18.99**

Torah of the Earth: Exploring 4,000 Years of Ecology in Jewish Thought
Vol. 1: Biblical Israel & Rabbinic Judaism; Vol. 2: Zionism & Eco-Judaism
Edited by Rabbi Arthur Waskow Vol. 1: 6 x 9, 272 pp, Quality PB, 978-1-58023-086-5 **$19.95**
Vol. 2: 6 x 9, 336 pp, Quality PB, 978-1-58023-087-2 **$19.95**

The Way Into Judaism and the Environment *By Jeremy Benstein, PhD*
6 x 9, 288 pp, Quality PB, 978-1-58023-368-2 **$18.99**; HC, 978-1-58023-268-5 **$24.99**

Graphic Novels/History

The Adventures of Rabbi Harvey: A Graphic Novel of Jewish Wisdom and Wit in the
Wild West *By Steve Sheinkin* 6 x 9, 144 pp, Full-color illus., Quality PB, 978-1-58023-310-1 **$16.99**

Rabbi Harvey Rides Again: A Graphic Novel of Jewish Folktales Let Loose in the
Wild West *By Steve Sheinkin* 6 x 9, 144 pp, Full-color illus., Quality PB, 978-1-58023-347-7 **$16.99**

Rabbi Harvey vs. the Wisdom Kid: A Graphic Novel of Dueling
Jewish Folktales in the Wild West *By Steve Sheinkin*
Rabbi Harvey's first book-length adventure—and toughest challenge.
6 x 9, 144 pp, Full-color illus., Quality PB, 978-1-58023-422-1 **$16.99**

The Story of the Jews: A 4,000-Year Adventure—A Graphic History Book
By Stan Mack 6 x 9, 288 pp, Illus., Quality PB, 978-1-58023-155-8 **$16.99**

Grief/Healing

Facing Illness, Finding God: How Judaism Can Help You and Caregivers
Cope When Body or Spirit Fails *By Rabbi Joseph B. Meszler*
Will help you find spiritual strength for healing amid the fear, pain and chaos of
illness. 6 x 9, 208 pp, Quality PB, 978-1-58023-423-8 **$16.99**

Midrash & Medicine: Healing Body and Soul in the Jewish Interpretive
Tradition *Edited by Rabbi William Cutter, PhD*
Explores how midrash can help you see beyond the physical aspects of healing to
tune in to your spiritual source. 6 x 9, 240 pp (est), HC, 978-1-58023-428-3 **$24.99**

Healing from Despair: Choosing Wholeness in a Broken World
By Rabbi Elie Kaplan Spitz with Erica Shapiro Taylor; Foreword by Abraham J. Twerski, MD
5½ x 8½, 208 pp, Quality PB, 978-1-58023-436-8 **$16.99**

Healing and the Jewish Imagination: Spiritual and Practical Perspectives on
Judaism and Health *Edited by Rabbi William Cutter, PhD*
6 x 9, 240 pp, Quality PB, 978-1-58023-373-6 **$19.99**; HC, 978-1-58023-314-9 **$24.99**

Grief in Our Seasons: A Mourner's Kaddish Companion *By Rabbi Kerry M. Olitzky*
4½ x 6¼, 448 pp, Quality PB, 978-1-879045-55-2 **$15.95**

Healing of Soul, Healing of Body: Spiritual Leaders Unfold the Strength & Solace
in Psalms *Edited by Rabbi Simkha Y. Weintraub, CSW*
6 x 9, 128 pp, 2-color illus. text, Quality PB, 978-1-879045-31-6 **$16.99**

Mourning & Mitzvah, 2nd Edition: A Guided Journal for Walking the Mourner's
Path through Grief to Healing *By Anne Brener, LCSW*
7½ x 9, 304 pp, Quality PB, 978-1-58023-113-8 **$19.99**

Tears of Sorrow, Seeds of Hope, 2nd Edition: A Jewish Spiritual Companion for
Infertility and Pregnancy Loss *By Rabbi Nina Beth Cardin*
6 x 9, 208 pp, Quality PB, 978-1-58023-233-3 **$18.99**

A Time to Mourn, a Time to Comfort, 2nd Edition: A Guide to Jewish
Bereavement *By Dr. Ron Wolfson; Preface by Rabbi David J. Wolpe*
7 x 9, 384 pp, Quality PB, 978-1-58023-253-1 **$19.99**

When a Grandparent Dies: A Kid's Own Remembering Workbook for Dealing
with Shiva and the Year Beyond *By Nechama Liss-Levinson, PhD*
8 x 10, 48 pp, 2-color text, HC, 978-1-879045-44-6 **$15.95** *For ages 7–13*

Social Justice

There Shall Be No Needy
Pursuing Social Justice through Jewish Law and Tradition
By Rabbi Jill Jacobs; Foreword by Rabbi Elliot N. Dorff, PhD; Preface by Simon Greer
Confronts the most pressing issues of twenty-first-century America from a deeply Jewish perspective.
6 x 9, 288 pp, Quality PB, 978-1-58023-425-2 **$16.99**; HC, 978-1-58023-394-1 **$21.99**
Also Available: **There Shall Be No Needy Teacher's Guide**
8½ x 11, 56 pp, PB, 978-1-58023-429-0 **$8.99**

Conscience: The Duty to Obey and the Duty to Disobey
By Rabbi Harold M. Schulweis
This clarion call to rethink our moral and political behavior examines the idea of conscience and the role conscience plays in our relationships to government, law, ethics, religion, human nature, God—and to each other.
6 x 9, 160 pp, Quality PB, 978-1-58023-419-1 **$16.99**; HC, 978-1-58023-375-0 **$19.99**

Judaism and Justice: The Jewish Passion to Repair the World
By Rabbi Sidney Schwarz; Foreword by Ruth Messinger
Explores the relationship between Judaism, social justice and the Jewish identity of American Jews.
6 x 9, 352 pp, Quality PB, 978-1-58023-353-8 **$19.99**; HC, 978-1-58023-312-5 **$24.99**

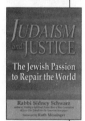

Spiritual Activism: A Jewish Guide to Leadership and Repairing the World
By Rabbi Avraham Weiss; Foreword by Alan M. Dershowitz
6 x 9, 224 pp, Quality PB, 978-1-58023-418-4 **$16.99**; HC, 978-1-58023-355-2 **$24.99**

Righteous Indignation: A Jewish Call for Justice   Edited by Rabbi Or N. Rose,
Jo Ellen Green Kaiser and Margie Klein; Foreword by Rabbi David Ellenson, PhD
Leading progressive Jewish activists explore meaningful intellectual and spiritual foundations for their social justice work.
6 x 9, 384 pp, Quality PB, 978-1-58023-414-6 **$19.99**; HC, 978-1-58023-336-1 **$24.99**

Spirituality/Women's Interest

New Jewish Feminism: Probing the Past, Forging the Future
Edited by Rabbi Elyse Goldstein; Foreword by Anita Diamant
Looks at the growth and accomplishments of Jewish feminism and what they mean for Jewish women today and tomorrow.
6 x 9, 480 pp, HC, 978-1-58023-359-0 **$24.99**

The Divine Feminine in Biblical Wisdom Literature
Selections Annotated & Explained
Translation & Annotation by Rabbi Rami Shapiro
5½ x 8½, 240 pp, Quality PB, 978-1-59473-109-9 **$16.99**
(A book from SkyLight Paths, Jewish Lights' sister imprint)

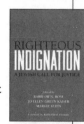

The Quotable Jewish Woman: Wisdom, Inspiration & Humor from the Mind & Heart
Edited by Elaine Bernstein Partnow   6 x 9, 496 pp, Quality PB, 978-1-58023-236-4 **$19.99**

The Women's Haftarah Commentary: New Insights from Women
Rabbis on the 54 Weekly Haftarah Portions, the 5 Megillot & Special Shabbatot
Edited by Rabbi Elyse Goldstein   Illuminates the historical significance of female portrayals in the Haftarah and the Five Megillot.
6 x 9, 560 pp, Quality PB, 978-1-58023-371-2 **$19.99**

The Women's Torah Commentary: New Insights from Women
Rabbis on the 54 Weekly Torah Portions
Edited by Rabbi Elyse Goldstein
Over fifty women rabbis offer inspiring insights on the Torah, in a week-by-week format.
6 x 9, 496 pp, Quality PB, 978-1-58023-370-5 **$19.99**; HC, 978-1-58023-076-6 **$34.95**

See Passover for *The Women's Passover Companion: Women's Reflections on the Festival of Freedom* and *The Women's Seder Sourcebook: Rituals & Readings for Use at the Passover Seder.*

Meditation

Jewish Meditation Practices for Everyday Life
Awakening Your Heart, Connecting with God
By Rabbi Jeff Roth
Offers a fresh take on meditation that draws on life experience and living life with greater clarity as opposed to the traditional method of rigorous study.
6 x 9, 224 pp, Quality PB, 978-1-58023-397-2 **$18.99**

The Handbook of Jewish Meditation Practices
A Guide for Enriching the Sabbath and Other Days of Your Life
By Rabbi David A. Cooper Easy-to-learn meditation techniques.
6 x 9, 208 pp, Quality PB, 978-1-58023-102-2 **$16.95**

Discovering Jewish Meditation: Instruction & Guidance for Learning an Ancient Spiritual Practice *By Nan Fink Gefen, PhD* 6 x 9, 208 pp, Quality PB, 978-1-58023-067-4 **$16.95**

Meditation from the Heart of Judaism: Today's Teachers Share Their Practices, Techniques, and Faith *Edited by Avram Davis*
6 x 9, 256 pp, Quality PB, 978-1-58023-049-0 **$16.95**

Ritual/Sacred Practices

The Jewish Dream Book: The Key to Opening the Inner Meaning of
Your Dreams *By Vanessa L. Ochs, PhD, with Elizabeth Ochs; Illus. by Kristina Swarner*
Instructions for how modern people can perform ancient Jewish dream practices and dream interpretations drawn from the Jewish wisdom tradition.
8 x 8, 128 pp, Full-color illus., Deluxe PB w/ flaps, 978-1-58023-132-9 **$16.95**

God in Your Body: Kabbalah, Mindfulness and Embodied Spiritual Practice
By Jay Michaelson
The first comprehensive treatment of the body in Jewish spiritual practice and an essential guide to the sacred.
6 x 9, 272 pp, Quality PB, 978-1-58023-304-0 **$18.99**

The Book of Jewish Sacred Practices: CLAL's Guide to Everyday &
Holiday Rituals & Blessings *Edited by Rabbi Irwin Kula and Vanessa L. Ochs, PhD*
6 x 9, 368 pp, Quality PB, 978-1-58023-152-7 **$18.95**

Jewish Ritual: A Brief Introduction for Christians
By Rabbi Kerry M. Olitzky and Rabbi Daniel Judson
5½ x 8½, 144 pp, Quality PB, 978-1-58023-210-4 **$14.99**

The Rituals & Practices of a Jewish Life: A Handbook for Personal Spiritual
Renewal *Edited by Rabbi Kerry M. Olitzky and Rabbi Daniel Judson*
6 x 9, 272 pp, Illus., Quality PB, 978-1-58023-169-5 **$18.95**

The Sacred Art of Lovingkindness: Preparing to Practice
By Rabbi Rami Shapiro 5½ x 8½, 176 pp, Quality PB, 978-1-59473-151-8 **$16.99**
(A book from SkyLight Paths, Jewish Lights' sister imprint)

Science Fiction/Mystery & Detective Fiction

Criminal Kabbalah: An Intriguing Anthology of Jewish Mystery &
Detective Fiction *Edited by Lawrence W. Raphael; Foreword by Laurie R. King*
All-new stories from twelve of today's masters of mystery and detective fiction—sure to delight mystery buffs of all faith traditions.
6 x 9, 256 pp, Quality PB, 978-1-58023-109-1 **$16.95**

Mystery Midrash: An Anthology of Jewish Mystery & Detective Fiction
Edited by Lawrence W. Raphael; Preface by Joel Siegel
6 x 9, 304 pp, Quality PB, 978-1-58023-055-1 **$16.95**

Wandering Stars: An Anthology of Jewish Fantasy & Science Fiction
Edited by Jack Dann; Introduction by Isaac Asimov
6 x 9, 272 pp, Quality PB, 978-1-58023-005-6 **$18.99**

More Wandering Stars: An Anthology of Outstanding Stories of Jewish Fantasy and Science Fiction *Edited by Jack Dann; Introduction by Isaac Asimov*
6 x 9, 192 pp, Quality PB, 978-1-58023-063-6 **$16.95**

Inspiration

The Seven Questions You're Asked in Heaven: Reviewing and Renewing Your Life on Earth *By Dr. Ron Wolfson*
An intriguing and entertaining resource for living a life that matters.
6 x 9, 176 pp, Quality PB, 978-1-58023-407-8 **$16.99**

Happiness and the Human Spirit: The Spirituality of Becoming the Best You Can Be *By Rabbi Abraham J. Twerski, MD*
Shows you that true happiness is attainable once you stop looking outside yourself for the source. 6 x 9, 176 pp, Quality PB, 978-1-58023-404-7 **$16.99**; HC, 978-1-58023-343-9 **$19.99**

A Formula for Proper Living: Practical Lessons from Life and Torah
By Rabbi Abraham J. Twerski, MD
Gives you practical lessons for life that you can put to day-to-day use in dealing with yourself and others. 6 x 9, 144 pp, HC, 978-1-58023-402-3 **$19.99**

The Bridge to Forgiveness: Stories and Prayers for Finding God and Restoring Wholeness *By Rabbi Karyn D. Kedar* 6 x 9, 176 pp, HC, 978-1-58023-324-8 **$19.99**

The Empty Chair: Finding Hope and Joy—Timeless Wisdom from a Hasidic Master, Rebbe Nachman of Breslov *Adapted by Moshe Mykoff and the Breslov Research Institute*
4 x 6, 128 pp, Deluxe PB w/ flaps, 978-1-879045-67-5 **$9.99**

The Gentle Weapon: Prayers for Everyday and Not-So-Everyday Moments— Timeless Wisdom from the Teachings of the Hasidic Master, Rebbe Nachman of Breslov *Adapted by Moshe Mykoff and S. C. Mizrahi, together with the Breslov Research Institute*
4 x 6, 144 pp, Deluxe PB w/ flaps, 978-1-58023-022-3 **$9.99**

God Whispers: Stories of the Soul, Lessons of the Heart *By Rabbi Karyn D. Kedar*
6 x 9, 176 pp, Quality PB, 978-1-58023-088-9 **$15.95**

God's To-Do List: 103 Ways to Be an Angel and Do God's Work on Earth
By Dr. Ron Wolfson 6 x 9, 144 pp, Quality PB, 978-1-58023-301-9 **$16.99**

Jewish Stories from Heaven and Earth: Inspiring Tales to Nourish the Heart and Soul *Edited by Rabbi Dov Peretz Elkins* 6 x 9, 304 pp, Quality PB, 978-1-58023-363-7 **$16.99**

Life's Daily Blessings: Inspiring Reflections on Gratitude and Joy for Every Day, Based on Jewish Wisdom *By Rabbi Kerry M. Olitzky* 4½ x 6¼, 368 pp, Quality PB, 978-1-58023-396-5 **$16.99**

Restful Reflections: Nighttime Inspiration to Calm the Soul, Based on Jewish Wisdom
By Rabbi Kerry M. Olitzky and Rabbi Lori Forman 4½ x 6¼, 448 pp, Quality PB, 978-1-58023-091-9 **$15.95**

Sacred Intentions: Daily Inspiration to Strengthen the Spirit, Based on Jewish Wisdom
By Rabbi Kerry M. Olitzky and Rabbi Lori Forman 4½ x 6¼, 448 pp, Quality PB, 978-1-58023-061-2 **$15.95**

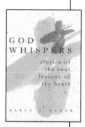

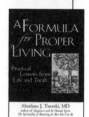

Kabbalah/Mysticism

Ehyeh: A Kabbalah for Tomorrow
By Rabbi Arthur Green, PhD 6 x 9, 224 pp, Quality PB, 978-1-58023-213-5 **$16.99**

The Flame of the Heart: Prayers of a Chasidic Mystic
By Reb Noson of Breslov; Translated and adapted by David Sears, with the Breslov Research Institute
5 x 7¼, 160 pp, Quality PB, 978-1-58023-246-3 **$15.99**

The Gift of Kabbalah: Discovering the Secrets of Heaven, Renewing Your Life on Earth
By Tamar Frankiel, PhD 6 x 9, 256 pp, Quality PB, 978-1-58023-141-1 **$16.95**

Kabbalah: A Brief Introduction for Christians
By Tamar Frankiel, PhD 5½ x 8½, 208 pp, Quality PB, 978-1-58023-303-3 **$16.99**

The Lost Princess & Other Kabbalistic Tales of Rebbe Nachman of Breslov
The Seven Beggars & Other Kabbalistic Tales of Rebbe Nachman of Breslov
Translated by Rabbi Aryeh Kaplan; Preface by Rabbi Chaim Kramer
Lost Princess: 6 x 9, 400 pp, Quality PB, 978-1-58023-217-3 **$18.99**
Seven Beggars: 6 x 9, 192 pp, Quality PB, 978-1-58023-250-0 **$16.99**

Seek My Face: A Jewish Mystical Theology *By Rabbi Arthur Green, PhD*
6 x 9, 304 pp, Quality PB, 978-1-58023-130-5 **$19.95**

Zohar: Annotated & Explained *Translation & Annotation by Dr. Daniel C. Matt; Foreword by Andrew Harvey* 5½ x 8½, 176 pp, .Quality PB, 978-1-893361-51-5 **$15.99**
(A book from SkyLight Paths, Jewish Lights' sister imprint)

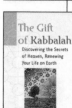

See also *The Way Into Jewish Mystical Tradition* in The Way Into... Series.

Spirituality

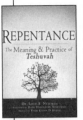

Repentance: The Meaning and Practice of *Teshuvah*
By Dr. Louis E. Newman; Foreword by Rabbi Harold M. Schulweis; Preface by Rabbi Karyn D. Kedar
Examines both the practical and philosophical dimensions of *teshuvah*, Judaism's core religious-moral teaching on repentance, and its value for us—Jews and non-Jews alike—today. 6 x 9, 256 pp, HC, 978-1-58023-426-9 **$24.99**

Tanya, the Masterpiece of Hasidic Wisdom
Selections Annotated & Explained
Translation & Annotation by Rabbi Rami Shapiro; Foreword by Rabbi Zalman M. Schachter-Shalomi
Brings the genius of *Tanya*, one of the most powerful books of Jewish wisdom, to anyone seeking to deepen their understanding of the soul.
5½ x 8½, 240 pp, Quality PB, 978-1-59473-275-1 **$16.99**
(A book from SkyLight Paths, Jewish Lights' sister imprint)

Aleph-Bet Yoga: Embodying the Hebrew Letters for Physical and Spiritual Well-Being
By Steven A. Rapp; Foreword by Tamar Frankiel, PhD, and Judy Greenfeld; Preface by Hart Lazer
7 x 10, 128 pp, b/w photos, Quality PB, Lay-flat binding, 978-1-58023-162-6 **$16.95**

A Book of Life: Embracing Judaism as a Spiritual Practice
By Rabbi Michael Strassfeld 6 x 9, 544 pp, Quality PB, 978-1-58023-247-0 **$19.99**

Bringing the Psalms to Life: How to Understand and Use the Book of Psalms
By Rabbi Daniel F. Polish, PhD 6 x 9, 208 pp, Quality PB, 978-1-58023-157-2 **$16.95**

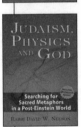

Does the Soul Survive? A Jewish Journey to Belief in Afterlife, Past Lives & Living with Purpose *By Rabbi Elie Kaplan Spitz; Foreword by Brian L. Weiss, MD*
6 x 9, 288 pp, Quality PB, 978-1-58023-165-7 **$16.99**

First Steps to a New Jewish Spirit: Reb Zalman's Guide to Recapturing the Intimacy & Ecstasy in Your Relationship with God *By Rabbi Zalman M. Schachter-Shalomi with Donald Gropman* 6 x 9, 144 pp, Quality PB, 978-1-58023-182-4 **$16.95**

Foundations of Sephardic Spirituality: The Inner Life of Jews of the Ottoman Empire
By Rabbi Marc D. Angel, PhD 6 x 9, 224 pp, Quality PB, 978-1-58023-341-5 **$18.99**

God & the Big Bang: Discovering Harmony between Science & Spirituality
By Dr. Daniel C. Matt 6 x 9, 216 pp, Quality PB, 978-1-879045-89-7 **$16.99**

God in Our Relationships: Spirituality between People from the Teachings of Martin Buber *By Rabbi Dennis S. Ross* 5½ x 8½, 160 pp, Quality PB, 978-1-58023-147-3 **$16.95**

The Jewish Lights Spirituality Handbook: A Guide to Understanding, Exploring & Living a Spiritual Life *Edited by Stuart M. Matlins*
What exactly is "Jewish" about spirituality? How do I make it a part of my life? Fifty of today's foremost spiritual leaders share their ideas and experience with us.
6 x 9, 456 pp, Quality PB, 978-1-58023-093-3 **$19.99**

Judaism, Physics and God: Searching for Sacred Metaphors in a Post-Einstein World
By Rabbi David W. Nelson 6 x 9, 352 pp, Quality PB, inc. reader's discussion guide,
978-1-58023-306-4 **$18.99**; HC, 352 pp, 978-1-58023-252-4 **$24.99**

Meaning and Mitzvah: Daily Practices for Reclaiming Judaism through Prayer, God, Torah, Hebrew, Mitzvot and Peoplehood *By Rabbi Goldie Milgram*
7 x 9, 336 pp, Quality PB, 978-1-58023-256-2 **$16.99**

Minding the Temple of the Soul: Balancing Body, Mind, and Spirit through Traditional Jewish Prayer, Movement, and Meditation *By Tamar Frankiel, PhD, and Judy Greenfeld*
7 x 10, 184 pp, Illus., Quality PB, 978-1-879045-64-4 **$16.95**

One God Clapping: The Spiritual Path of a Zen Rabbi *By Rabbi Alan Lew with Sherril Jaffe*
5½ x 8½, 336 pp, Quality PB, 978-1-58023-115-2 **$16.95**

The Soul of the Story: Meetings with Remarkable People
By Rabbi David Zeller 6 x 9, 288 pp, HC, 978-1-58023-272-2 **$21.99**

There Is No Messiah ... and You're It: The Stunning Transformation of Judaism's Most Provocative Idea *By Rabbi Robert N. Levine, DD*
6 x 9, 192 pp, Quality PB, 978-1-58023-255-5 **$16.99**

These Are the Words: A Vocabulary of Jewish Spiritual Life
By Rabbi Arthur Green, PhD 6 x 9, 304 pp, Quality PB, 978-1-58023-107-7 **$18.95**

Spirituality/Prayer

Making Prayer Real: Leading Jewish Spiritual Voices on Why Prayer Is Difficult and What to Do about It *By Rabbi Mike Comins*
A new and different response to the challenges of Jewish prayer, with "best prayer practices" from Jewish spiritual leaders of all denominations.
6 x 9, 320 pp, Quality PB, 978-1-58023-417-7 **$18.99**

Witnesses to the One: The Spiritual History of the *Sh'ma*
By Rabbi Joseph B. Meszler; Foreword by Rabbi Elyse Goldstein
6 x 9, 176 pp, Quality PB, 978-1-58023-400-9 **$16.99**; HC, 978-1-58023-309-5 **$19.99**

My People's Prayer Book Series: Traditional Prayers, Modern Commentaries *Edited by Rabbi Lawrence A. Hoffman, PhD*
Provides diverse and exciting commentary to the traditional liturgy. Will help you find new wisdom in Jewish prayer, and bring liturgy into your life. Each book includes Hebrew text, modern translations and commentaries from all perspectives of the Jewish world.

Vol. 1—The *Sh'ma* and Its Blessings
  7 x 10, 168 pp, HC, 978-1-879045-79-8 **$24.99**
Vol. 2—The *Amidah* 7 x 10, 240 pp, HC, 978-1-879045-80-4 **$24.95**
Vol. 3—*P'sukei D'zimrah* (Morning Psalms)
  7 x 10, 240 pp, HC, 978-1-879045-81-1 **$24.95**
Vol. 4—*Seder K'riat Hatorah* (The Torah Service)
  7 x 10, 264 pp, HC, 978-1-879045-82-8 **$23.95**
Vol. 5—*Birkhot Hashachar* (Morning Blessings)
  7 x 10, 240 pp, HC, 978-1-879045-83-5 **$24.95**
Vol. 6—*Tachanun* and Concluding Prayers
  7 x 10, 240 pp, HC, 978-1-879045-84-2 **$24.95**
Vol. 7—Shabbat at Home 7 x 10, 240 pp, HC, 978-1-879045-85-9 **$24.95**
Vol. 8—*Kabbalat Shabbat* (Welcoming Shabbat in the Synagogue)
  7 x 10, 240 pp, HC, 978-1-58023-121-3 **$24.99**
Vol. 9—Welcoming the Night: *Minchah* and *Ma'ariv* (Afternoon and
  Evening Prayer) 7 x 10, 272 pp, HC, 978-1-58023-262-3 **$24.99**
Vol. 10—Shabbat Morning: *Shacharit* and *Musaf* (Morning and
  Additional Services) 7 x 10, 240 pp, HC, 978-1-58023-240-1 **$24.99**

Spirituality/Lawrence Kushner

The Book of Letters: A Mystical Hebrew Alphabet
Popular HC Edition, 6 x 9, 80 pp, 2-color text, 978-1-879045-00-2 **$24.95**
Collector's Limited Edition, 9 x 12, 80 pp, gold-foil-embossed pages, w/ limited-edition silkscreened print, 978-1-879045-04-0 **$349.00**

The Book of Miracles: A Young Person's Guide to Jewish Spiritual Awareness
6 x 9, 96 pp, 2-color illus., HC, 978-1-879045-78-1 **$16.95** *For ages 9–13*

The Book of Words: Talking Spiritual Life, Living Spiritual Talk
6 x 9, 160 pp, Quality PB, 978-1-58023-020-9 **$16.95**

Eyes Remade for Wonder: A Lawrence Kushner Reader *Introduction by Thomas Moore*
6 x 9, 240 pp, Quality PB, 978-1-58023-042-1 **$18.95**

Filling Words with Light: Hasidic and Mystical Reflections on Jewish Prayer
By Rabbi Lawrence Kushner and Rabbi Nehemia Polen
5½ x 8½, 176 pp, Quality PB, 978-1-58023-238-8 **$16.99**; HC, 978-1-58023-216-6 **$21.99**

God Was in This Place & I, i Did Not Know: Finding Self, Spirituality and Ultimate Meaning 6 x 9, 192 pp, Quality PB, 978-1-879045-33-0 **$16.95**

Honey from the Rock: An Introduction to Jewish Mysticism
6 x 9, 176 pp, Quality PB, 978-1-58023-073-5 **$16.95**

Invisible Lines of Connection: Sacred Stories of the Ordinary
5½ x 8½, 160 pp, Quality PB, 978-1-879045-98-9 **$15.95**

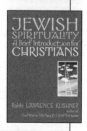

Jewish Spirituality: A Brief Introduction for Christians
5½ x 8½, 112 pp, Quality PB, 978-1-58023-150-3 **$12.95**

The River of Light: Jewish Mystical Awareness
6 x 9, 192 pp, Quality PB, 978-1-58023-096-4 **$16.95**

The Way Into Jewish Mystical Tradition
6 x 9, 224 pp, Quality PB, 978-1-58023-200-5 **$18.99**; HC, 978-1-58023-029-2 **$21.95**

About Jewish Lights

People of all faiths and backgrounds yearn for books that attract, engage, educate, and spiritually inspire.

Our principal goal is to stimulate thought and help all people learn about who the Jewish People are, where they come from, and what the future can be made to hold. While people of our diverse Jewish heritage are the primary audience, our books speak to people in the Christian world as well and will broaden their understanding of Judaism and the roots of their own faith.

We bring to you authors who are at the forefront of spiritual thought and experience. While each has something different to say, they all say it in a voice that you can hear.

Our books are designed to welcome you and then to engage, stimulate, and inspire. We judge our success not only by whether or not our books are beautiful and commercially successful, but by whether or not they make a difference in your life.

For your information and convenience, at the back of this book we have provided a list of other Jewish Lights books you might find interesting and useful. They cover all the categories of your life:

Bar/Bat Mitzvah	Life Cycle
Bible Study / Midrash	Meditation
Children's Books	Men's Interest
Congregation Resources	Parenting
Current Events / History	Prayer / Ritual / Sacred Practice
Ecology / Environment	Social Justice
Fiction: Mystery, Science Fiction	Spirituality
Grief / Healing	Theology / Philosophy
Holidays / Holy Days	Travel
Inspiration	Twelve Steps
Kabbalah / Mysticism / Enneagram	Women's Interest

Stuart M. Matlins, Publisher

Or phone, fax, mail or e-mail to: **JEWISH LIGHTS Publishing**
Sunset Farm Offices, Route 4 • P.O. Box 237 • Woodstock, Vermont 05091
Tel: (802) 457-4000 • Fax: (802) 457-4004 • www.jewishlights.com
Credit card orders: **(800) 962-4544** (8:30AM–5:30PM ET Monday–Friday)
Generous discounts on quantity orders. SATISFACTION GUARANTEED. Prices subject to change.

For more information about each book, visit our website at www.jewishlights.com